New Dimensions for Academic Library Service

Edited, with an Introduction
by
E. J. JOSEY

The Scarecrow Press, Inc.
Metuchen, N.J.   1975

Royalties from this book are being donated to the
Roy Wilkins Scholarship Fund

Library of Congress Cataloging in Publication Data

Josey, E   J   1924-
New dimensions for academic library service.

Includes index.
1. Libraries, University and college. 2. Library
cooperation.
Z675.U5J74   027.773   74-30062
ISBN 0-8108-0786-6

Dedicated

with

Love and Admiration

to

Sister Maddalena Marie Payne

who has dedicated her life

to

Young People and Libraries

CONTENTS

INTRODUCTION

When most of the colleges and universities were established in the United States, by and large, the collegiate model was fairly self-contained and served only the affluent and upper classes of society. The classical and honors studies reflected the wishes of the dominant white society whose students were unusually serious even if they were not all scholars. After graduate education became the focal point at many of the prestigious institutions of higher education, American universities took on the character of the German universities, with emphasis on research and scholarship, and less and less attention was given to the education of undergraduates. Those universities that were not emulating the German universities were aping Oxford, Cambridge, and the Sorbonne.

Following World War II and the advent of the G. I. Bill of Rights, a large number of students (including me) enrolled in institutions of higher education and, for all intents and purposes, it appeared as though higher education in America had become egalitarian and served all of American youth who wanted admission into the social and economic middle class. While the former World War II G. I.'s were admitted with great fanfare, most of America's colleges and universities failed to recognize differences in cognitive styles, past experiences, and accumulated knowledge. These institutions continued to portray themselves as a homogeneous community of scholars cloistered away from the problems of the real world.

Then came the 1960's with a massive infusion of Federal funds along with growing enrollments and a booming construction program. With the infusion of public funds and, concomitantly, the passage of the civil rights legislation, a new breed of student appeared on the predominantly white campuses of the Nation--blacks, Chicanos, poor whites, Puerto Ricans, and American Indians; the campuses suddenly erupted, and there were demands for accountability from America's citadels of learning, not only from the newcomers but also from the affluent and well-to-do white students. In short, the

1960's seemed to have brought a permanent state of siege on campus and a permanent state of debate that created a real challenge to long-cherished notions about academe.

Separate and not a part of the white academic procession were black institutions of higher education. Allen B. Ballard of The City University of New York, in his book, The Education of Black Folk, indicates that "some two hundred institutions of higher learning for blacks were created in the three decades after the Civil War.... They were almost totally bereft of either federal or state support and relied primarily on the largesse of churches and philanthropy." Over the years many of these institutions perished for lack of adequate funding, but the 112 predominantly black colleges which exist today have educated most of the black leaders of America. Just as the predominantly white institutions were affected by winds of change, so were black institutions of higher education.

In recent years there has been criticism about the importance and relevance of undergraduate and graduate education. This criticism has led to experimentation and innovation. The Carnegie Commission, in its report, Less Time, More Options: Education Beyond the High School, has called for a 3-year bachelor's degree, and many colleges and universities have instituted 3-year programs. Many institutions have established University-Without-Walls Programs that seem to break the lockstep in collegiate education. A variety of nontraditional study programs are developing on the Nation's campuses. The Board of Regents in New York State has established the Regents External Degree Program, and degrees are now being given by The University of the State of New York, the State Education Department. The State University of New York has established Empire State College, a nontraditional approach to a collegiate education. The development of these new learning modes has brought about a revolution in higher education in the United States.

The foregoing thumbnail sketch of higher education in America sets the stage for a discussion of academic libraries. What is the role of the academic library in higher education? By and large, the function of the academic library is to support the academic goals of colleges and universities. Viewed historically, library programs in colleges and universities have been rather passive, i.e., primarily, the storage and retrieval of books to support the curriculum. The establishment of collections and services has largely been dictated by the development of curricular and research programs. In this regard college and university libraries are a real reflection of the institutions they serve.

While the foregoing premise--that academic library programs are patterned after curricular decisions have been made by the parent institution--is indisputable, college and university librarians for many years have been urging their academic administrators to give them a larger role to play in the deliberations of curriculum committees and in the academic senate, where educational policy decisions are made which have serious implications for college and university library development. Because of their indefatigable determination to make the resources and services of the academic library contribute more effectively to the instructional programs of their colleges and universities, academic librarians have now become active participants in educational policy decision matters. No longer are academic librarians "handmaidens" to the faculty; they are now a part of the faculty, thereby making certain that the library truly undergirds the instructional and research programs of academic institutions in America.

With the academic library playing a more positive role in the education of young people, the Carnegie Commission on Higher Education admonition that, "in both undergraduate and graduate education, experimentation and flexibility are needed to provide for new options and alternatives" can very easily be accomplished, because of new programs that academic librarians have fashioned. Since the commission defines "nontraditional study as an attitude, rather than a system, that places emphasis on the student, that encourages diversity of individual effort, competence, and performance, and that deemphasizes time and space," no other agency on the American campus in this last quarter of the 20th century is more suited than the library to provide the proper educational setting for students and scholars to engage in nontraditional study to accomplish the goals as defined by the commission. Librarians have been saying loudly and clearly for a long time that study and research in libraries are equated with greater opportunity for lifelong learning. The academic library's stewardship, support, and thrust for the dissemination of all types of information to sustain study, teaching, and research has indeed brought about a blurring of educational territories, to the extent that librarians and educators unashamedly and immodestly speak in reverential terms about the library becoming the college and/or university or, in the words of Louis Shores, the Library-College. With the new breed of academic librarian, who insists that he or she become an equal partner in the educational process, and with libraries developing into learning resources centers stocked with media in a variety of formats, the academic library of the future will produce a college graduate who has learned how to learn; and because of this knowledge of libraries and library tools, the graduate can go on learning throughout his or her life, always capable of acquiring a new skill and avoiding obsolescence.

New Dimensions for Academic Library Service is a compilation of 25 essays that were especially written for this book to focus on a variety of initiatives undertaken by librarians, information scientists, and educators. The wide range of activities in our Nation's colleges and universities has produced demands on academic libraries. At the same time, funding for libraries has diminished. Nevertheless, librarians have been ingenious and have given a quick response to these changes through new organizational patterns, making use of new technologies and participating cooperatively in library networks.

The volume is divided into four parts and an epilogue. Part One focuses on the academic library as a vital component of higher education. The first essay, written by an academic administrator, sets the tone for the book. Charles Churchwell discusses forces which have provoked change in higher education and have affected decision-making, and which in turn have had a profound impact on academic library service. After his assertion that higher education is facing a "new depression," he dramatically calls attention to what invariably happens to library programs:

> it is having an erosive impact on the academic library's program; presidents, provosts, and vice presidents for academic affairs are faced with making hard decisions. Unfortunately, their decisions are often guided by considerations other than sound academic programs and needs, and the library program is the first to suffer.

The other four essays in Part One provide an analysis and description of change in four different types of academic libraries. Eldred R. Smith analyzes change affecting university libraries and warns that "in the future, university libraries may well be judged in qualitative terms" rather than in quantitative terms, as has been the case historically. In his essay, "The College Library Responds to Change," H. Vail Deale believes that the college library of the next

xii

century will not be primarily what 20th century academicians and librarians conceive. He theorizes that "it will be an evolutionary concept that breaks down barriers between student/teacher, librarian/faculty, and such arbitrary compartmentalization as: classrooms, faculty offices, library building...." In her assessment of the impact of change on the community college library, Louise Giles indicates that the "abundant utilization of media greatly affects the campus physical facilities...." Reflecting on the work of the community college librarian, it is her belief that "greater involvement with the newer media has made an undisputed impact on the work of the community college librarian...." The last essay in this section deals with the changing role of the undergraduate library in universities. James Davis, after having described recent developments affecting undergraduate libraries in universities, makes a strong case for separate undergraduate libraries in large universities and declares that "undergraduate libraries represent to their constituencies a haven...." It is, he declares, "the one egalitarian library service on the campus." All of the authors in this section agree that the "new depression" and the financial bind afflicting all segments of higher education are forcing a reexamination of, and changes in, academic library programs.

Part Two pertains to new approaches in solving academic library problems. Evert Volkersz, in his thesis on the need for change from hierarchical to collegial relationships in academic libraries, shows through illustrations that "the focus of collegial activity is a reorientation toward the needs of library users, toward people." Mohammed M. Aman calls for computer applications in academic library operations and postulates that "a library will also be able to combine technological elements such as computer storage, microreduction, and remote transmission ... which would hopefully place in the hands of every reader the text he wants instantly and at the least cost." Richard C. Quick addresses himself to the problems inherent in the coordination of collection building by academic libraries. He concludes that until there is an enabling technology generally applicable, e.g., facsimile transmission, "it would appear that the greatest benefit for the greatest number of students and faculty will derive from intimate collecting and sharing arrangements at the neighborhood and limited regional level." R. Dean Galloway and Zoia Horn advocate alternative ways to meet user needs. In an attempt to discover user needs they suggest that "probably the most useful technique for discovering user needs is to have library staff members involved in student and faculty activities." Suggesting many nontraditional

xiii

methods to meet different kinds of users' needs, they also propose that "if there is a need for a 'hot line' where students can call to get information on community services, the library should provide it."

In recent years, there have been heated debates over the need to take a new look at organizing materials in academic libraries, and especially over racism in the Library of Congress subject headings. Joan K. Marshall declares, "in establishing subject headings for peoples the terminology of the people concerned should be used." A large number of black colleges and universities are confronted by problems that severely limit their educational services. The "new depression" and inflation which torment higher education have also hurt these institutions severely. Their plight is far more tragic; of the $4 billion of Federal money appropriated annually for higher education, only $220 million is allocated to black colleges. The final essay in this part is related to the problems affecting black college libraries. Casper LeRoy Jordan's essay affirms Allen B. Ballard's thesis that "there has never been a national commitment to educational opportunity for black folk." After his cataloging of the multiplicity of difficulties and problems confronting black college libraries, one of his most penetrating statements is: "long before black was fashionable these institutions, without any extra money and with overworked staffs, kept the heritage of a people long despised. The account of this stewardship should go down in the annals of American librarianship as equal to any movement in the discipline."

Unscrambling critical academic library issues is the subject of Part Three of this volume. The first of the seven essays in this section is by Robert P. Haro, who appeals for creative library service for the new learners in higher education. Students from disadvantaged backgrounds are one of the groups defined by Haro as new learners in academia, and he sees a pivotal role for the librarian: "the role of the librarian, whether as interpreter, media specialist, or study skills counselor, provides the human interface between new learners and some of the complicated media forms and associated technology necessary for these students to survive the initial college experience." Dorothy Byron Simon's plea is for a more human approach to instruction in the use of academic libraries, and she puts forward the idea that "teaching the use of the library demands that the instructor be on the same wavelength as the class." Ann Knight Randall speaks valiantly for the user-oriented approach to reference services and makes it clear that "the general reference librarian is

xiv

involved in the basic, 'on-line' interface between the user and his or her information."

One of the critical issues of our time is education for academic librarianship. Ivan L. Kaldor and Miles M. Jackson provide a historical survey of library education and suggest a comprehensive plan for educating the academic librarian; they insist that "the library school could play an important role in the recruitment and professional education of college and university librarians." R. Patrick Mallory writes about making academic library facilities more functional. Rather than concerning himself with a treatise discussing library facilities in an abstract manner, he seizes upon the theme of "facilitating the flow of people, communications, and materials," and demonstrates creative functionality of academic library facilities. No academic library can remain afloat in academia and demand its share of institutional funds unless it gives some attention to cost effectiveness and management planning. Jerome Yavarkovsky tackles management planning to achieve academic library goals. He feels that "the emphasis in planning is on decision, commitment, and action directed toward the purpose of the enterprise rather than its problems." Large university libraries spend millions of dollars and are "big business," and academic library administrators will probably all agree with him that "planning be comprehensive and pervasive, encompassing all the activities of the library, rather than focusing on isolated activities or incremental changes in activity." In the essay which closes this section of the book, Harry Robinson, Jr. claims that "the employment of multimedia systems has become necessary to accommodate the changing student bodies and to meet their diverse needs and interests."

Patterns of library information systems, networks, and consortia providing information and library services to academic library users have been interwoven into a fabric that has a motif of networking, and are the concerns of Part Four. This is a recognition that no single academic library in the world today is self-sufficient and must of necessity engage in continuing cooperative endeavors. In addition to networks, attention is given to the role of nonacademic libraries in their support of post-secondary education.

The point of departure is Nina T. Cohen's graphic discussion of the 3R's system and the academic library community in New York State. After a discussion of the historical development of the 3R's systems and a description of typical programs of the systems, she discusses directions for the future. One of her warning signs is "networks must be perceived as developing, changing, [and] dynamic," and joint decisions, she says, will not cripple individual library programs. Frederick G. Kilgour provides a conceptual clarification and an analytical description of the Ohio College Library Center as a user-oriented library system. This library network has captured the imagination of the library world, with 200 institutions from Maine to Texas receiving on-line services. Commenting on the center, Kilgour states: "Various libraries that are making efficient use of the on-line shared cataloging system have demonstrated that it can be cost beneficial." The New England Library Information Network (NELINET) has been serving academic libraries in the New England region since 1967. Ronald F. Miller and David M. Wax discuss the programs of NELINET and NASIC (Northeast Academic Science Information Center) and the academic library user. While NELINET will provide a range of services, NASIC will "apply the concept of brokering computer-based information services on a multistate basis through promotion and marketing of services...." The Cooperative College Library Center is located in Atlanta, Georgia, and provides cooperative technical processing for 27 black academic libraries in the South. Hillis D. Davis gives the history and development of the center and indicates that the Cooperative College Library Center was established expressly "... to increase the purchasing power of the dollar through quantity purchasing." Both NELINET and CCLC have contracts with OCLC for on-line services. Davis expresses his satisfaction with the tie-in with OCLC, stating that "it is quite apparent to me that the Ohio College Library Center offers the best solution to most library problems."

It is virtually impossible for academic libraries to serve all of the students engaged in a variety of nontraditional post-secondary educational programs. Vivian D. Hewitt presents interesting vignettes of public library and special library programs that provide a significant service to this important sector of higher education. Of the public library she writes, "independent study is now evolving in many forms and formats. The forms that challenge the public library to this new role are those that rely on exemption examination...." She is also equally convincing about the role of the special library. The final essay by Robert S. Taylor is perceptive and in a sense challenges academic librarians on many engaging levels. In his patterns toward a user-centered academic library, he describes several possible routes that libraries may follow. In one case he suggests, "the user becomes the center of the institution--not the packages, not the systems, but the individuals in the community that is served. In this case the academic library will become a true switching center, a community center in which the dynamic process of negotiating and connecting users to people, materials, and media is the heart of the enterprise." The volume closes with an epilogue which tries, in a futuristic sense, to describe the academic library in the year 2000.

The essays that follow explore some of the new dimensions of academic library service that are now present and some of the academic library policy options that are, as of this writing, still available to us in the continuing effort to make the academic library the real heart of the university and/or college.

E. J. Josey

Albany, New York
March 1974

PART I

THE LIBRARY: A VITAL COMPONENT
IN HIGHER EDUCATION

THE LIBRARY IN ACADEMIA:
An Associate Provost's View

Charles D. Churchwell

This essay does not contain simply a catalog and description of new methods of delivering information to academic library users; indeed, only about a third of it is devoted to "new dimensions" in delivering information. The remainder is concerned with the identification of forces which helped to produce the new dimensions, and a discussion of the problems and opportunities these forces and services are producing for academic libraries and librarians.

It is important to identify and understand the forces which produce changes in academic library services because variations in their direction and intensity will determine whether or not there will be a curtailment or further expansion and improvement of academic library services during the next decade.

As a primary supporter of academic programs, the library is not free to set its own goals and immediate objectives; it must wait for the colleges and universities it serves to establish their goals, objectives, and educational policies. But the establishment of these, even by a single institution, is a task more often discussed than accomplished. The reasons for this are many and complex, but since "the academic library feels all the social forces of the educational, research, and service pressures acting on the private or state-supported institutions of which it is a part, " the chances of understanding the emergence of new patterns of academic library services, and managing their directions, will be enhanced by an identification of the major elements which interact and influence decision-making and educational policy in the field of higher education.

Although the enrollment in colleges and universities began to decline or stabilize near the end of the 1960's, the impact of enrollment had been a significant influence in the

decision-making process in academic institutions for almost
a decade, because the rapidity and magnitudes of the increases
affected every segment of the institution's programs. Between 1960 and 1970, the student population increased by more
than 133 per cent, a very sharp rise from almost 3.5 million
to more than eight million students. Among other factors,
this large and rapid increase in the student population, especially the undergraduates, gave impetus to the efforts in
large universities to decentralize library services according
to the pattern which Harvard started in 1949, with the establishment of its undergraduate library. While not now a
new dimension of academic service, this method of making
specially selected library materials easily available to large
numbers of undergraduate students was adopted by many leading universities in the country, so that by 1970, Michigan,
Cornell, UCLA, Stanford, Illinois, Berkeley, Texas, and
South Carolina had established excellent undergraduate library
services and facilities. To cope further with large numbers
of students, the idea of residence hall libraries was also
given renewed attention, since so many students lived long
distances from the nearest library and because there was a
growing desire to make the library a meaningful educational
force in the academic life of students. [1]

    Providing academic library services on the up-side of
student enrollment created problems and opportunities that
may be quite unlike those which will be created by a stabi-
lizing and declining enrollment during the next decade. [2] But
in both cases, enrollments will be seen as having a significant impact on decision-making in colleges and universities.

    Accompanying the rapid growth of the student popula-
tion was a concomitant increase in the teaching and research
faculties of colleges and universities; it has been estimated
that these groups increased by more than 151 per cent between 1950 and 1968, [3] and their large-scale demands for
rapid access to informational sources contributed to the expansion of such activities as selected dissemination of information to some faculty members.

    Increased Federal funding to higher education during
the 1960's was another force which greatly influenced decisions within academic institutions; the unprecedented expansion
of higher education during the 1960's was certainly due in
part to this factor. Decisions to expand academic programs,
research and research institutes, equipment and equipment
facilities, library buildings and library resources, scholarships

and student loan programs, and the teaching and research
faculties, all were encouraged by the liberal provision of
Federal funds and a growing concern about societal needs.
Grants for the construction of facilities alone reached a peak
of $518 million in 1966, and, for all activities combined,
more than $3 billion. It is impossible accurately to estimate
the impact of such financial support programs, but there is
no question of its importance to the continuance of growth
and quality within all areas of higher education, including university library services.   Like the student enrollment, however, Federal support to higher education began to decline in
1968, first in specific areas and, near the end of the decade,
in all areas; this is especially true in terms of real dollar
value.   According to a recently released report by the National Science Foundation,

> federal obligations to colleges and universities to-
> taled $4.1 billion in 1972, an increase of $643 mil-
> lion, or 18 per cent, over the 1971 total. This
> ... was the largest single-year gain since 1965-
> 66, when a one-year jump of $704 million was re-
> ported. Adjusted for inflation, however, the five-
> year increase in 'support' to colleges and univer-
> sities drops 0.4 per cent.... And a further analy-
> sis of the report indicated that the gains were
> largely 'paper' increases without effect on the fis-
> cal 1972 level of funding. [4]

Here again, the significant point is that during the era of substantial Federal support, impetus was given to an expansion
of library services which very likely would not have occurred
on such a massive scale without such outside help. And, as
will be seen later, important as such services are, their
continuance may be in serious jeopardy because they may not
be able to survive without a revitalization of the forces that
brought them into existence.

A fourth factor affecting decision-making in higher education, the impact of which is felt in the library as well as
other parts of the institution, is open access to post-secondary education.   Until relatively recently those attending post-
secondary institutions shared enough common goals and values
to be considered a homogeneous group of students, and their
college-university curricular and extra-curricular activities
were planned to meet their individual and group needs.   Not
only were more young people in college than at any other time
in history, but "they [were] of many more levels of academic

ability and academic preparation than in earlier times, from
many more cultural backgrounds, and with more 'diverse
career goals.' "[5] The principle of equal opportunity for all
persons, though far from realization, still holds sway in
many institutions within society, and it has logically led to
open admissions as practiced by The City University of New
York. [6] Hence today's student population is very heterogene-
ous. And they differ not only in their value systems and
life styles, but in their reading tastes and study habits as
well. The full impact of the "new students" on the organization and services of the university library remains to be felt,
but it is already clear that a more liberal acquisition policy
is developing.

A fifth and final force which is having an impact on
decision-making in higher education and which also affects
patterns of college and university library service is the surge
of interest being focused on the non-traditional student[7] and
the external degree. [8] Despite the many criticisms of it, the
academic degree is still the port-of-entry to most professions.
It is now widely known and accepted that

> the central function of higher education in America
> has always been vocational. Harvard was founded
> to train clergymen; and as the society has become
> more a mass, open society, its dependence on the
> university system for vocational training and place-
> ment has ... become greater and more complex. [9]

And, it might be added, more restrictive, because

> employers want evidence of skills acquired and of
> ability to accept training and discipline that goes
> with it. Employment officers, also, minimize the
> personal risks they encounter by making reference
> to prior certification rather than relying only on
> their own judgment. [10]

But

> degrees are more available to the young than to the
> middle-aged and the old; to men ... than to women;
> and to members of the higher than the lower income
> groups. The American dream promises greater
> equality than this, and American reality demands
> that age be served as well as youth, that women be
> served equally with men, and that the poor be served
> as well as the rich. [11]

Hence, improvement of opportunity in higher education so
that credentials may be obtained by non-traditional means,
that is by not having to attend college or university in residence full-time, is the thrust of the external degree programs. The development of such programs will not reduce the
demands for academic library services; on the contrary, it is
very likely to increase the needs not only for more information
but more in-depth reference and reader services. Of course,
the library has always been a haven for those seeking additional
education; the point here is that even greater service is going to
be required of libraries because of decisions made in other segments of society which are likely to evolve in a form of higher
education that will operate for many years. [12]

While there were, and still are, other factors which
affect decision-making in higher education, the five discussed
above have had considerable influence in shaping decisions
and educational policy that directly affect academic libraries
and the services they render. Some of these services have
already been briefly mentioned; it remains to sketch in more
detail some of the types of academic library services that
are of different dimensions. The objective here is not to
present a full catalog of new types of services, but to present representative programs to show both what is being done
on a limited scale and what can be done to affect radically
and on a large scale all academic library services.

Common to all new dimensions of academic library
services is an acceleration of the use of technology. An excellent example of this is the widespread use of the teletypewriter which has taken place during the last ten years.
While there are still many academic libraries without it,
the teletypewriter has become a standard way of sharing resources and providing users with rapid interlibrary loan and
reference services. Through the Inter-University Library
Council's Reference and Interlibrary Loan Services (RAILS)
in Ohio[13] a user is often able to receive material the same
day it is requested, and 24-hour service is quite common.
Similar services to academic library users are well established among academic, public, and private libraries in New
York, [14, 15] Texas, and many other states. Indeed, "the
TWX network is spread across the nation and is well established as the main method of network interface. The TWX
has the benefit of high-speed transmission at a reasonable
cost with hard copy in multiple units at the receiving or
sending stations."[16] The teletypewriter is also used in networks between academic libraries to receive reference ques-

tions and transmit answers to questions which cannot be
answered within a particular member library.   One library
within the system is chosen as the major resource center,
and the members pay for both the services provided and the
equipment, supplies, and personnel needed to give them. [17]
This easy access to information beyond the boundaries of a
particular campus has created among students and teachers,
especially those engaged in research, a greater appreciation
of the service role of the academic library.   However, since
the loan aspect of this important dimension of library service relies heavily on the ability to copy journal articles, its
continuation and further expansion will depend greatly on the
final form of the revised copyright legislation.

The computer is another example of the use of technological improvements to disseminate information to academic library users.   Unlike the TWX network systems, it
is relatively expensive although very versatile.   While it has
its detractors, [18] enough has been accomplished with the computer to justify the conclusion that, with careful planning,
it can be used effectively to provide easy and rapid access
to pertinent library information.   A few examples may illustrate this point.

Cooperation and the sharing of resources were operative among small liberal arts colleges for many years before
the advent of the computer, but its emergence has brought
improvements in the quality and quantity of cooperative endeavors.   By linking the computer with many of the old-line
methods of sharing scarce resources, small colleges are now
offering their students the benefits of large academic libraries.   By using book catalogs, a telephone hot-line, and
courier service, students at six colleges in Kansas

> have access to 300, 000 volumes and 2, 800 period-
> icals.   If ordered early in the day, a desired
> book can be in the hands of a student at any one
> of the colleges that same day.   Before central
> listing, only about 50, 000 volumes were available
> on any of the campuses. [19]

The Associated Colleges of Central Kansas (ACCK), a group
of liberal arts, four-year, church-related coeducational colleges, provides each of the member institutions with this
service by renting "time on an insurance company computer
at McPherson, Kan. , " to make lists of all books purchased
since 1971.   Each library receives copies of the monthly

master list and weekly supplements which list books by author, title, location, and status. If the desired material is not in the library of the college the student is attending, "the librarian is informed of the student's needs and he phones the proper library, " and the material is delivered by the courier who makes daily rounds to the six campuses. No one of the colleges in ACCK could afford such computer services, but together they are not only able to pay for it, but are also able to provide their students with a greater variety of reading materials since duplication has been reduced to a minimum.

Somewhat in contrast to the sharing of books and periodicals are the services of the Generic Library at Evergreen State College, Olympia, Washington.[20] In this library the computer's role is simply as one of the several learning and information aids available to students. This is a library geared to providing information to students in any form or format in which it may appear. Like most new ventures this one is still having to work out details of operation, but its intention--to provide college students with information regardless of the form it appears in and the equipment needed to use it--is well worth watching. The book, traditional librarians need to be reminded, is not the only means available to transmit information.

From the Evergreen College library one need only move to the Library of Ohio State University to get a fuller view of the new dimensions of services and to speculate about future possibilities for both the small and large academic library. The Ohio State University circulation system, described as "the world's first large-scale, computerized, on-line, remote library circulation system, " has been in operation for almost three years.[21] More than 50, 000 persons use the system; all of them

> have identification numbers, and each book has its own call number. All the would-be borrower has to do ... is telephone the library, when a clerk will type out the borrower's number, the book title and author and get a reply on the display screen, showing what copies of the volume are available, in what libraries, and how long ... the book may be kept out. Then the book is taken from the shelves and held at a desk for pickup. Books brought directly from shelves to the circulation desk are recorded then and there, and

charged out without the borrower having to fill out
a charge slip.   Later, if need be, the computer
will print an overdue notice and record the book's
final return; or it will arrange for renewal. [22]

This is undoubtedly the most complicated and sophisticated
circulation system in operation to date.   The system will
handle "more than 2,400,000 books, 400,000 music scores,
677,000 microfilm units and 150,000 maps.   And it takes in
23 libraries." The system also has the capacity for other
modules to be incorporated which will lead to better serial
and bibliographic access and control.   The use of the computer to introduce selective dissemination of information to
a single library user was a major innovation in the 1960's;
it enabled libraries to begin to provide personalized library
services to a limited academic audience.   The Ohio State
University Library system makes a total collection available
to a very large audience very quickly.   It is also important
to note that the system has demonstrated the feasibility of
one of the proposed services which will be provided by the
Ohio College Library Center, which is the last example to
be cited in this essay.

A recent excellent report on library networks states
that "cooperative computer centers are a new phenomenon
in library systems"; whatever one says about their effectiveness, therefore, is necessarily incomplete.   Still, there are
enough available data about the activities of the Ohio College
Library Center (OCLC) to support the conclusion that the
project "parallels and is as important to librarianship as
the space program is to science."[23]   A great deal of money
has already been spent, "but the advances made and the side
benefits are invaluable."   OCLC is not only serving as a
prototype for other networks; it is also providing services
to other networks and groups of libraries in the Midwest,
Northeast, and Southeast through its on-line cataloging system which has been in operation for almost two years.   The
on-line cataloging system is the first of a three-phased program which was planned when OCLC was created in 1967.
In discussing the potential use of computers for the improvement of access to informational resources, there has been
and still is much "blue-skying," but the simple fact is that
"OCLC is an operational unit--it works."   Hendricks has
summarized the case very well:

Anyone who can hunt and peck on a typewriter can
interrogate the data base.   The Library of Con-

gress staff has had a series of MARC users meetings around the nation describing the potential uses
of the MARC record, itself an expensive development.   OCLC, however, is the first effort wherein
these tapes were utilized in a depth approaching
their full potential.   The analogy with the space
program is not farfetched because the OCLC represents, for many librarians trained in a former
period, the first meaningful demonstration of the
power of a bibliographic machine.   The librarian
can operate the device and see for himself the
present and potential uses it possesses. [24]

The next two phases of the systems to be developed are the
serials and circulation control modules.   However, the location of and access to information in other libraries are already being accomplished to a limited degree by the acquisition, reference, and interlibrary loan librarians.   Before
expensive research items are ordered, the acquisitions librarians, by using the CRT (Cathode Ray Tube), can determine within seconds which other libraries in the systems
already have the item.   (It should be noted that only one
member library of OCLC has put its entire shelflist holdings
into the data base; others are working on procedures for
doing the same.)   The reference and interlibrary loan librarians can also determine in seconds the exact location of
recently purchased and cataloged materials, and all at relatively low cost, considering the other, and primary, use of
the terminals.   After the system is completed, access to
shared materials will be available faster than at any time
in the past.

    The objectives of OCLC--to make the resources of
an entire region readily available to users through an on-
line union catalog, to reduce the rate of rising costs of library services to students, and to get information to users
quickly when and where they need it--are being accomplished
to a limited extent. [25]   This limited accomplishment, however,
provides better overall service to the academic user than
has been available hitherto.   This accomplishment is perhaps
the most important new dimension to date in academic libraries.   But the success of OCLC, and other such systems,
should not obscure the difficulties still to be overcome, especially the financial ones.

    Relatively speaking, the Ohio College Library Center
is an expensive operation, but academic libraries as present-

ly operated are even more expensive, and all indications are
that their costs, like those of all other units of colleges and
universities, will continue to increase.

That all of higher education is facing a "new depression" is a well documented fact[26] and it is having an erosive
impact on the academic library's program; presidents, pro-
vosts, and vice presidents for academic affairs are faced
with making hard decisions. Unfortunately, their decisions
are often guided by considerations other than sound academic
programs and needs, and the library program is among the
first to begin to suffer.

Despite the absence or reduction of the forces which
gave impetus to the process of converting single-purpose
colleges to multipurpose universities, college and university
presidents, especially those of state-supported institutions,
are still motivated by the idea that status and prestige can
come only by emulating a Harvard or a Berkeley, "or at
least a University of Michigan or any one of a number of
major state universities."[27] The chief academic officers
are also encouraged by the research-oriented members of
their faculties to ignore the fact that great institutions and
research libraries are not created overnight, and that the
services required from these libraries can not be provided
without substantial cost. As they strive to determine the
objectives and goals of academic institutions, and indirectly
those of the libraries, members of the academic community
should pay heed to the words of John W. Gardner:

> In the intellectual field ... there are many kinds
> of excellence. There is the kind of intellectual
> activity that leads to a new theory, and the kind
> that leads to a new machine. There is the mind
> that finds its most effective expression in teaching
> and the mind that is most at home in research.
> There is the mind that works best in quantitative
> terms, and the mind that luxuriates in poetic
> imagery.[28]

The attempt to gain status and prestige in all areas of intellectual activity is an impossible dream for most colleges
and universities, and librarians need to urge this point with
greater force during the decision-making process in colleges
and universities. Moreover, faced with chief academic officers who think in terms of the "instant university and library," librarians should remind them that "a visitor once

asked A. Lawrence Lowell, then president of Harvard, what
it took to make a great university; his answer: 300 years. "
This may not be the quick route to winning friends for the
library, but it will remind the decision-makers within academic institutions that changing the name of the institution
from college to university, without at the same time providing massive sums of money and time, will not necessarily
result in the respect which academic institutions should seek
for all the programs they undertake.

Academic library administrators are aware, of course,
that it is becoming more difficult to obtain adequate fundings
for the library and its programs, but they must become
more sensitive to the pressures being brought by those,
sometimes external to the university, who are questioning the
value of the academic environment to the intellectual development of students.   Commenting on one extensive study of the
academic environment, one author stated:

> Our findings seem to have several implications for
> planning.   They suggest that it may be wise to re-
> examine traditional notions about institutional ex-
> cellence, particularly as it relates to the intellec-
> tual development of students.   The pursuit of
> brighter students, more money, better libraries
> and physical plants, more Ph. D.'s on the faculty,
> and other traditional indices of quality will not
> necessarily produce a better environment for
> learning. [29]

When presidents urge that more funds be provided for the
"traditional indices of quality, " they are likely to be confronted with such findings; and because of the absence of
research data in support of the "traditional indices of quality, " they find themselves ill-equipped to refute such conclusions.   Presidents and other academic officers need to
become aware "that if they continue to pursue 'excellence'
as it has been traditionally defined, some justification other
than an improved intellectual climate must be found. "[30]
Librarians, too, like the chief academic officers, must find
"valid grounds" for claiming more support for the academic
library.

New dimensions in academic library services were
greatly encouraged by the rapid growth of higher education
during the 1960's; the reduction or disappearance of the
forces which gave impetus to that growth have left higher

education in a precarious position, and the quality of their
programs, including the library, is seriously threatened.
To improve the situation, realistic objectives and goals and
rational reasons for their support must be developed. This
is a task not only for the chief academic officers of the colleges and universities, but for the chief librarians and their
staffs as well.

References

1.   Wilson, Logan. "Library Roles in Higher Education."
     In Thomas R. Buckman, Yukikisa Suzuki, and Warren
     M. Tsuneishi, eds. University and Research Li-
     braries in Japan and the United States. Chicago,
     American Library Association, 1972, pp. 14-19.
2.   Boutwell, W. K. "Formula Budgeting on the Down
     Side." In George Kaludis, ed. Strategies for Budget-
     ing (No. 2 Summer). San Francisco, Jossey-Bass
     Inc., Publishers, 1973, pp. 41-50.
3.   Booz, Allen & Hamilton, Inc. Problems in University
     Library Management. Washington, D. C., Associa-
     tion of Research Libraries, 1970, p. 13.
4.   National Science Foundation. "Highlights," Science Re-
     sources Studies, August 1, 1973, p. 1.
5.   The Carnegie Commission of Higher Education. Less
     Time, More Options: Education Beyond The High
     School. New York, McGraw-Hill Book Company,
     1971, p. 7.
6.   Healy, Timothy S. "The Case for Open Admissions.
     New Problems--New Hopes," Change, Summer 1973,
     pp. 24-29.
7.   Ray, Robert F. The C.I.C. Study of the Non-Tradi-
     tional Student (Report No. 1). Iowa, Division of Ex-
     tension and University Services, The University of
     Iowa, 1973, p. VII.
8.   Houle, Cyril O. The External Degree. San Francisco,
     Jossey-Bass Inc., Publishers, 1973, pp. 1-17.
9.   Friedenberg, Edgar Z. "The University Community in
     an Open Society," Daedalus, Winter 1970, p. 56.
10. The Carnegie Commission on Higher Education. Less
     Time, More Options, p. 10.
11. Ibid.
12. Houle, op. cit., pp. 170-80.
13. Schmidt, James and Shaffer, Kay. "A Cooperative In-
     terlibrary Loan Service for the State-Assisted Univer-
     sity Libraries in Ohio," College & Research Li-

braries, May 1971, pp. 197-204.
14. Josey, E. J. "The College Library in New York's 3R's
     System, " College & Research Libraries, January 1969,
     pp. 32-38.
15. Publishers Weekly, 198:11, November 1970.
16. Hendricks, Donald D. A Report on Library Networks
     (University of Illinois Graduate School of Library
     Science Occasional Papers, No. 108). Urbana, Ill.,
     University of Illinois Press, 1973, p. 9.
17. Schmidt and Shaffer, op. cit., pp. 197-202.
18. Mason, Ellsworth. "The Great Gas Bubble Prick't; or,
     Computers Revealed--by a Gentleman of Quality, "
     College & Research Libraries, 32:183-96, May 1971.
19. Blankenship, Ted. "Computerized Library Serves Six
     Colleges, " College Management, October 1973, p. 12.
20. "Not Just a Library, A Generic Library, " College and
     University Business, October 1973, p. 35.
21. Publishers Weekly, 198:9, December 1970.
22. Ibid.
23. Hendricks, op. cit., p. 18.
24. Ibid., p. 19.
25. Landis, Carolyn. "Networks and Disciplines, " Educom,
     7:5, 1972.
26. Cheit, Earl F. The New Depression in Higher Educa-
     tion--Two Years Later (A Technical Report Sponsored
     by The Carnegie Commission on Higher Education).
     New York, McGraw-Hill Book Company, 1973.
27. Dunham, Alden. Colleges of the Forgotten Americans:
     A Profile of State Colleges and Regional Universities
     (Second of a Series of Profiles Sponsored by The
     Carnegie Commission on Higher Education). New
     York, McGraw-Hill Book Company, 1969, p. 155.
28. Gardner, John W. Excellence: Can We Be Equal and
     Excellent Too? New York, Harper & Brothers Pub-
     lishers, 1961, pp. 127-28.
29. Astin, Alexander W. "What Goes Into Academic Plan-
     ning, " College and University Business, August 1969,
     p. 32.
30. Ibid.

CHANGES IN HIGHER EDUCATION
AND THE UNIVERSITY LIBRARY

Eldred R. Smith

As American university libraries move into the mid-1970's, they find themselves confronted with a major challenge and a major opportunity. The challenge derives from what has been described as "the new depression in higher education,"[1] and it confronts the university library with the need to maintain and even expand operations, services, and collections in the face of rising costs and relatively declining resources. The opportunity is presented by developments in higher education and the increased complexity of published information, which are making the university library a more central and critically important participant within the university and its educational and research mission. How each university library responds to this challenge and seizes this opportunity will have a decisive importance for its success in the years ahead.

During the past two decades, university libraries have experienced a period of unparalleled growth and expansion.[2] This growth was, of course, a part of the expansion of higher education during this period, when it was recognized as a top national priority and was supported by massive allocations of public and private financing. Within the last few years, this situation has changed dramatically. The priority that was extended to higher education in the post-Sputnik period has been substantially reduced in the face of competing social needs, increasing national economic problems, changing governmental fiscal policies, and an apparent drastic decline in the demand for the product of graduate schools. This has resulted in a decrease in the level of support available to American higher education--either in terms of actual dollars or at least in rate of budgetary increase in comparison to increases in the costs that the budget must meet.

At the same time, funding agencies are demanding that
universities justify their budgetary requirements and expenditures to an extent that has not been required for many years.
Continuing as well as new programs are under careful scrutiny.   Capital expenditures for expansion and even maintenance are meeting increasing resistance.   There is growing
insistence on the application of cost-effectiveness analysis,
program budgeting, and other similar management techniques
within institutions of higher education.   Universities are being required to demonstrate that they are maximizing the use
of their resources, that their operations are efficient, and
that their programs are developed in response to social
needs.

Faced with the prospects of declining levels of support
and rising demands for accountability, universities are being
forced to reexamine their own operations and priorities.
Long-established programs are being reduced or even eliminated.   New programs are forced to justify their support in
competition with those that already exist, and are frequently
funded only at the expense of reductions in other areas.
Academic planning, involving choices and priorities for the
expenditure of increasingly-limited resources, has a growing
critical importance.

Within this context, the university library finds that
it must compete with other segments of the academic community for diminishing resources in the face of rising costs.
This has a number of substantial implications, which are already being felt in academic libraries across the country.

First, acquisition budgets will no longer increase as
they have in the past.   Recognizing that world publication
continues to expand and that the inflationary rate for books,
journals, and other library materials has averaged 6.5 percent per year between 1951 and 1969, [3] it may well be that
the purchasing power of university libraries will actually
decline fairly substantially in the years ahead.

In the past, university libraries have sought to develop research collections which would fully meet the needs
of present and future instructional and research programs
at their parent institutions.   No university library in the
country has fully met this goal, and few have even approxi-
mated it.   In recent years, it has become increasingly evident that selectivity rather than comprehensiveness must be
the hallmark of collection development in university libraries,

supported by increased effectiveness in the sharing of resources at regional and national levels.

Second, library operations will have to become more
efficient and cost-effective. Just as acquisition dollars will
become more difficult to increase, so too will the budgets
that support staff, equipment, and supplies. Furthermore,
as external funding agencies and higher education institutions,
themselves, devote increasing attention to reducing operational costs, university libraries will undoubtedly undergo considerable scrutiny in this area.

In the face of these pressures, university libraries
will have to insure that their basic operations--acquisitions,
cataloging, circulation, and stack maintenance--are functioning as efficiently and inexpensively as possible. Many procedures will have to be improved, duplicative effort eliminated, and standardization adopted and implemented. It will
be increasingly important to insure that various levels of
staff--student, clerical, and professional--are each functioning in their proper capacities, consonant with their education, experience, and salary levels.

Automation has long been viewed as a significant potential means of reducing library operating costs, although
there has been little evidence of direct operating savings in
most academic library applications. Some recent developments, such as circulation systems and cataloging applications utilizing machine-readable data bases, do seem to
promise significant potential savings. This is particularly
true if standardization, such as acceptance of Library of
Congress catalog copy, can be implemented. Obviously,
such developments will continue.

Unquestionably, there will be increasing stress on
interlibrary cooperation in these operational areas as well
as in collection development. The success of the Ohio College Library Center is a clear indication of the value of cooperation and of the value of automation and standardization
in increasing library cost-effectiveness.

Finally, like the universities of which they are a
part, academic libraries will be required to demonstrate
sound and effective management. Until very recently, little
explicit attention was given to the theory and practice of university library management. Academic library administrators were drawn primarily from among the faculty, with

little formal experience in library operations, or from librarians who had little training in administrative and managerial techniques. A review of the literature of librarianship quickly reveals a remarkable lack of attention to this area of the profession.

Within the last two or three years, however, this has changed dramatically. Substantial management studies have been carried out at two major university libraries. The Association of Research Libraries has launched a major program to encourage and support such studies in other university libraries and to develop resources and techniques for improving library management among its members.

If university libraries are to prosper in the years ahead, they must develop the managerial and administrative competence to maintain and even upgrade their operations and services in the face of diminishing resources. Furthermore, they must be able to participate effectively and productively in university-wide administration and planning.

In reviewing the major challenges that confront the university library, it seems clear that the immediate future will be a period of budgetary retrenchment, during which the maximization of limited resources, increased operational efficiency, and effective administration will be the major ingredients. To many librarians, this may present a rather bleak forecast. However, there are other prospects in store for higher education which hold considerable promise for the university library.

In addition to the fiscal pressures that are presently confronting higher education in the United States, there are a number of substantial social and pedagogical pressures. During the 1960's, American higher education came under considerable scrutiny from students and faculty. One of the major issues raised by students in the campus turmoils that began in Berkeley was the relevance and quality of higher education. Partially on the basis of their own concern and partially as a result of student criticism, faculty also directed their attention to this issue. As a result, the late 1960's and early 1970's have been a period of considerable reevaluation of the programs and practices of higher education.

This reevaluation has directed its attention to three substantive areas: the social relevance of educational pro-

grams, the classic disciplinary divisions within the university, and new instructional and learning techniques. Out of
the first concern has developed a broad range of educational
and research programs directed at social problems, environmental studies, and the particular needs of social groups.
The second concern has given substantial impetus to a great
range of interdisciplinary studies. The final concern, which
may be the most critical in the long run, has sparked a growing reevaluation of standard educational methods leading to
more emphasis on faculty-student contact and individual study
at even the undergraduate level.

       These developments are beginning to have a substan-
tial impact on academic libraries. The new program areas
present some obvious demands with respect to library collections. Not only are university libraries now acquiring many
materials in areas that were of marginal concern previously,
but much of this material is highly specialized and even
ephemeral, posing significant problems with respect to collection development, bibliographic control, and effective use.
Further, as cross-disciplinary interest develops, patterns of
the use of collections are also changing, causing particular
problems with respect to the location of materials and effective access. Finally, as more and more students are becoming involved in individual research projects, they are becoming less dependent on a few texts and research materials
and more dependent upon sophisticated assistance in locating
highly specialized sources of information.

       If these trends continue, it seems inconceivable that
they will not have the effect of involving the library more
centrally in the academic life of the university. Specialized
materials, interdisciplinary study, and specialized library
research will require the involvement and assistance of
qualified librarians who can guide the student, and even the
faculty member, through the maze of information in library
collections to the material that is needed. In addition, more
formalized assistance through library orientation programs
and even courses in bibliographical instruction, taught by librarians, will probably become increasingly necessary. Indeed, some clear trends in this direction are apparent, as
evidenced by courses in library research taught by librarians
which are being offered at an increasing number of universities. The programs being mounted by a growing number
of university undergraduate libraries, involving classroom
lectures or full courses geared to the undergraduate, are a
significant aspect of this development. Similar programs of

a more sophisticated nature are being developed for graduate
students in an increasing number of disciplines.

Furthermore, recognizing the need for more selectivity in collection development as a result of decreasing acquisition purchasing power, the librarians responsible for these
programs are being forced to deal more continuously and directly with the departments to whom they relate. Such librarians must develop a full and intimate knowledge of the
programs and plans of these departments as well as the individual research interests of faculty and graduate students.
There seems to be a decided and necessary move toward the
development of a corps of subject librarians within the university library, each one of whom is related to a department
or group of departments, and who develop the collections to
meet instructional and research needs, provide sophisticated
reference services including formal instruction, and are involved in the academic planning of the department. Such developments also coincide with the continuing thrust for faculty
status for academic librarians.

Viewing these several trends together, it seems evident that changes are taking place in higher education and
the university library which will make the latter significantly
different from what it is today. In the university library of
1980, operations will be more cost-effective, more processes
will be automated, standardization will be more accepted.
The allocation of responsibilities among the staff will be substantially different, with student and clerical staff handling
the routine housekeeping operations and the bulk of the librarians functioning as subject specialists, in close cooperation with faculty and heavily involved with students. Collections may expand more slowly, but with more care and
knowledge of clientele needs expended in their development.
There will be increasing interlibrary cooperation and sharing
of resources. Finally, administration and management will
be more sophisticated, with considerable attention to cost-
effectiveness in relation to basic operations and to fuller direct participation by the library in university-wide planning
and instructional and research programs.

In the past, university libraries have been judged in
essentially quantitative terms: the size of collections, staff,
and operating budget. Despite frequent verbal recognition
that "the library is the heart of the university, " it has been
seen essentially as a repository of printed material, and its
functions have been recognized as essentially routine, cus-

todial operations connected with the acquisition, storage, and
circulation of this material.   In the future, university libraries may well be judged in qualitative terms: the degree
to which the assembled collections meet academic program
needs, the level of sophisticated service that is provided to
faculty and students, the contribution that is made to the educational programs through bibliographic instruction, and the
efficiency of basic operations.

It is perhaps ironic that the new depression in higher
education is one of the forces impelling the university library toward this new role.   How long this depression will
last is, of course, uncertain.   It may well be that the
present critical fiscal problems will be significantly allevi-
ated before the end of the present decade.   On the other
hand, it is very doubtful if the halcyon affluence of the
1960's will ever return.   It seems more certain that higher
education will have to struggle harder for, and make maximum use of, limited resources for many years to come.
If so, the university library will have to participate in this
struggle and maximization, which will bring with it an opportunity for the library to become a more active participant in
the university and its educational mission.   If the future is
recognized in these terms and seized as a challenge, it
should truly be bright for the university library.

References

1.   Cheit, Earl.   The New Depression in Higher Education:
      A Study of the Financial Condition at 41 Colleges and
      Universities.   New York, McGraw-Hill, 1971.
2.   Dunn, Oliver C., Tolliver, Don L., and Drake,
      Miriam A.   The Past and Likely Future Growth of
      58 Research Libraries, 1951-1980:   A Statistical
      Study of Growth and Change.   9th Issue.   West
      Lafayette, Instructional Media Research Unit, Univer-
      sity Libraries and Audio Visual Center, Purdue Uni-
      versity, 1973.
3.   Baumol, William J. and Marcus, Matityahu.   Econom-
      ics of Academic Libraries.   Washington, D.C.,
      American Council on Education, 1973, p. 47.

THE COLLEGE LIBRARY RESPONDS
TO CHANGE IN HIGHER EDUCATION

H. Vail Deale

By the first decade of the 21st century it is quite
possible that the academic library will be obsolete. The
ivory towers of higher education are crumbling so fast that
there is scarcely time to mourn their passing or, for that
matter, to evaluate the experimental and innovative programs
which are taking their place. Dr. Clarence J. Leuba, emeritus professor of psychology, Antioch College, has written:
"It is easy enough to find faults in our institutions of higher
learning, but vested interests in long-existing educational
procedures and content are so strong that it might seem
foolish to question them ... yet, the drawbacks of conventional educational methods and content have become so evident that new possibilities need to be explored."[1] He might
well have added that it may be the imaginative and innovative changes within individual institutions that will save them
from early extinction.

Innumerable and knowledgeable individuals have for
some time acknowledged that life is now so complex and
fast-changing that we can no longer think in terms of "finish-
ing one's education." Thomas Carlyle anticipated the situation when he referred to libraries as "the people's university." Today's educators speak of continuing education.
Once upon a time we used to try to stuff learning experiences into neat little boxes. The spatial boxes were classrooms; the time boxes were labeled grade school, junior
high, senior high, and college; and libraries were the information boxes. For more than a decade we have been breaking out of these boxes, discovering new learning patterns,
building new boxes, and experimenting with new ways of
collecting, storing, and disseminating information. "Innovation" has become the prestigious word in education, at all
levels. The successful college of the future will have elim-

inated structured classes, courses, course credits, grades, rigid admissions criteria, organization of its students by year, the traditional graduation or commencement--and possibly its library. In England, and in isolated islands of education in the United States, the concept of the "open university" already exists on an experimental basis. As long ago as 1967, Louis Shores, then dean of the graduate library school, Florida State University, made the following prediction: "Look for the carrel to replace the classroom as the learning locus in American colleges."[2] Though carrels are part of every college library today, they need not be located there in the future.

Television documentaries, book clubs, paperback editions, correspondence courses, facsimile transmission, portable cassettes, the microbook, and mobile museums--all are part of an "invisible university" that is permitting the motivated individual to share in the joy of discovery with scientists, social scientists, and humanists. And the wave of the future continues to stretch the imagination! Heresy of all heresies: we are discovering anew that you do not even have to get a college degree to be an educated person, and you don't have to stop educating yourself after you get a degree. This fact alone is increasing the options in post-secondary education; many struggling, self-centered institutions are disappearing, others will consolidate, and still others will be forced to experiment, innovate, and radically change their philosophy of what education is all about, if they have any hope for survival. In the final quarter of the 20th century, private colleges are fighting for their lives in competition with state-supported institutions, while community and junior colleges proliferate as never before.

Since the literature of education can document the drastic changes that are occuring in higher education, how are such changes affecting the academic library, and how is the academic library responding to change? The role of the library in the American college has achieved increasing significance with the evolution of higher education since the end of World War II.[3] According to Robert S. Taylor, the college library has served five purposes: 1) direct support to undergraduate instruction; 2) support for independent student honors work; 3) support, in many cases minimal, for faculty and graduate research; 4) space where students may study their own materials or meet a date; and 5) a context for browsing in the literature in the expectation that, by osmosis, students will absorb the great thinking and creations of

Western culture. [4] While there may be nothing wrong with
these purposes, they do not speak fully to the present generation of youth, nor to the potential of what a college library
can be. "The shift from a book- and print-oriented to a
communications- or media-oriented institution is one part of
the extended library concept, an attempt to make the library
more central to the total educational process and to obliterate
the line between what happens in the library and what happens outside. "[5] Sister Helen Sheehan, librarian emeritus,
Trinity College, Washington, D.C., recognized the wave of
the future with her comment:

> The student is, or should be, the pivotal figure in
> a college's planning and organization. In the under-
> graduate college, at least, all other elements--
> faculty, curriculum, library--should exist only for
> the student. In actual practice, however, the stu-
> dent is peripheral on the college scene, from the
> viewpoint of those who support and administer aca-
> demic institutions. [6]

Not only are librarians being forced to acknowledge
the changes within higher education, and to respond to them,
but institutions of higher education throughout the civilized
world are looking to the library profession for ways to enhance teaching, the learning process, and research. [7] The
number of new and exciting college library buildings each
year is but an outward and tangible recognition of the essential role which libraries (in whatever form they ultimately
become) must play in the academic community. Other factors
which have already begun to affect the future direction of the
college library are: 1) interdependence of libraries at the
local, regional, and national level, which affects the size
and subject content of individual libraries; 2) microform
technology, which already permits a student to scan material, find the exact page that interests him or her, punch a
button, and walk away with his or her own copy to be used,
marked, and stored when and where he or she wants; 3) paperback editions, already so pervasive, which will provide
increasingly imaginative ways to serve students, save staff
time, and give the patron the option of borrowing or buying
the material he or she wants; 4) and finally, not to be overlooked or minimized is the role of automation. Successfully
utilized in the business world, such routines as accounting,
filing, ordering, and cataloging will have standard computer
programs, and individual libraries will not have to bear the
expense of designing and starting their own systems. It is

already happening. It has been predicted that by 1980 libraries will be one of the major users of computer centers
for routine inventory and control, [8] not to mention the design
of computer-assisted instruction and other experimental programs not widely known about at this stage in their development.

Robert Jordan, formerly of the Council on Library Resources, and one of the core group of Library-College associates, succinctly characterizes today's experimental colleges:

> Most of the following criteria are characteristics
> of the experimental college: newness, a campus-
> wide pattern of experimentation, institutional will-
> ingness to take risks, faculty and student 'commit-
> ment' to moral and social purposes, institutional
> research, emphasis on out-group hostility, limited
> life expectancy, machinery for self-renewal, sense
> of community, identification with the world commu-
> nity, concern for the individual, concern for the
> 'whole man,' large areas of student initiative and
> choice including participation in campus planning
> and decision-making, respect for minority rights
> and ideas, viable size, faculty commitment to stu-
> dents and teaching; and reduction of emphasis upon
> grades, credits, degrees, faculty rank and depart-
> ments. [9]

While some colleges are responding to many of the criteria
which Jordan lists, and the new breed of college librarian
is a participant in such change, it is in the less tangible
areas of service to students and faculty that the basic conservatism of college librarians tends to hold back the future.
Dr. Logan Wilson, president of the American Council on
Education, commented:

> A common task of teachers and librarians ... is
> to stir the curiosity of young people and to show
> them how to satisfy that curiosity. In short, I be-
> lieve that the student activists who really want to
> change the world would be well-advised to 'invade'
> the library instead of the office of the President. [10]

The new breed of librarian, seeking closer rapport with students as well as his faculty colleagues, recognizes that future solutions to the role of the library in the academic

community will not be more buildings, more books, and
more librarians, but a change in the basic concept of what
a library is.   The library of the next century will not be
primarily a building, or a collection of materials, or a
staff of trained professionals; it will be an evolutionary concept that breaks down barriers between student/teacher, li-
brarian/faculty, and such arbitrary compartmentalization as
classrooms, faculty offices, library building, and so forth.
It is impossible to predict the unlimited possibilities.

        In an article for Library Journal in 1966, Dr. Louis
Shores, that venerable futurist of the library profession, began with the statement: "When a college is a library and a
library is a college, it is a Library College."[11]   The learning center of the future may well rest upon such a concept,
wherein "... the dominant learning mode is independent study
by the student in the library, bibliographically guided, intellectually aroused, and spiritually stirred by the faculty."   In
other words, today's college library will be transformed into
a true learning center, with librarians and instructors sharing their traditional but separate functions.   Forerunners of
such a concept have been such institutions as Jamestown College, Hampshire College, and Oklahoma Christian College,
which operates an electronic learning center in connection
with its more traditional library.   Each student is provided
with an individual carrel, fully equipped with audio and visual hardware.   Lectures and class notes, as well as other
more traditional materials, are available at the main desk
(first floor level) to be charged out for use in the student's
own individual study unit (second floor level).   One of the
encouraging signs in higher education has been this break-
down of the formalized structure of learning.   No longer is
the classroom sacred.   No longer is the textbook copy par-
roted back on examinations.   Perhaps we are witnessing a
return to those elementary ingredients of the learning process wherein the learner and the raw clay of knowledge are
brought together in an environment conducive to study, medi-
tation, and assimilation.   In such an environment the library
becomes the true learning center.

        In Dr. Alvin C. Eurich's popular volume, Campus
1980, Harold B. Gores writes:

                The physical campus will respond by becoming
                mostly library and living room.   To be sure,
                there will be other facilities accommodating the
                students' creature needs to exercise, socialize,

> fraternize, specialize, and eat and shop. But the
> dominating facilities will be library--where the in-
> formation is--and the living rooms--where the
> meaning of the information is determined. [12]

Such a concept parallels the one suggested earlier: that the
"library" may well become a part of the student's living unit,
or at least conveniently adjacent to it. It also suggests that
both the college administrator and college librarian should
"hang loose" when planning for the future, "to build no wall
or roof or fence which cannot, another day, serve another
purpose."[13] Dr. Gores, who was at the time president of
Educational Facilities Laboratories, predicts that "... whole
colleges will develop based on the 'library-college' concept
and new programs with a similar accent will sprout and
bloom in older institutions."[14] In his opinion, too, library
or learning center will replace traditional classroom; independent study will become the normal mode for all students,
regardless of their abilities; the closer relationship between
teaching faculty and librarians will lead to a single physical
facility joining faculty offices, classrooms, and study carrels
under one roof.

    In the continuing and controversial battle for recogni-
tion and status, the academic librarian would do well to learn
what is happening in some of the more progressive institutions, where teaching faculty are encouraged to have their
office hours in the library. "At Stephens College [Columbia,
Missouri], to make the library the natural center of the instructional program, each teacher is part of the library
staff, and the librarian and dean of instruction are combined
in the same person."[15] With such integration of instructors
and professional librarians, the troublesome distinctions between teaching and non-teaching faculty disappear, and the
student benefits.

    Robert Gaylord, associate dean, Oakland University,
Rochester, Michigan, has suggested that the college librarian
can best respond to change in higher education by putting
students in touch with the tools of learning, viz, the generic
book. "As used here, " says Gaylord, "the 'generic book'
is meant to be all instruments, or media, or instruction,
including such devices as teaching machines, filmstrips,
programmed learning, computer assisted instruction, projectors, recordings, and books per se."[16] The term "generic book" originated with Dr. Louis Shores, and in our present complex and multimedia culture includes a wide variety

of forms, as Gaylord has suggested; yet some people are concerned that somehow the new kinds of material will eliminate the importance of the book.   One among many who feels otherwise is Dr. Logan Wilson, who writes:

> Despite progress in making mechanical communications devices inexpensive and portable, I still know of none that can be purchased in paper cover for less than a dollar [!], borrowed without cost from a library, carried in one's pocket, used anywhere without plugging in, and then be placed back on a shelf to be always ready for later use. [17]

Dr. Dan J. Sillers, president of Jamestown (S.D.) College, feels that the library

> ... has a unique role to play in showing, or displaying, how the generic book is applicable to the learning of individual students.   This display should be a major factor in motivating, or stimulating, the development of one's personal library or resource center.   To maximize this potential, the library should be prepared to make materials even more available by allowing students to purchase them. [18]

This suggests that the campus bookstore might well be located in the library building.   The ideal learning center, in my opinion, would be a well-balanced collection of books, an attractive bookshop, and a coffee shop--all within the same physical location.

In summary, there is recognition today that education is a lifelong, continuing process, in or out of college. Innovation is the prestigious word of the present in higher education, and progressive educators and imaginative librarians are responding to the inevitable winds of change that appear to be the only hope of survival for many institutions.   College librarians and administrators must examine, evaluate, and experiment if they seriously wish to keep abreast of the changing trends in higher education and the role of the academic library within the college community. In the foreseeable future the student will be the pivotal figure in planning and organization.   Librarians cannot afford to wait for change, but must be participants in engineering the concepts already appearing on the horizon.   Independent study, microform technology, imaginative use of

paperback editions, and automation are some of the present
and future modes of learning that are being demonstrated in
certain experimental colleges that are not satisfied with traditional patterns. There is a new breed of academic librarian seeking more viable solutions to the problems of
college libraries, and searching for pragmatic recognition
of libraries and librarians within the changing framework of
higher education. Though the future may be unpredictable,
in spite of the unlimited possibilities, no better concluding
statement can be made than Louis Shores' utopian edict of
nearly a decade ago: "When a college is a library and a
library is a college, it is a Library College." It is for the
fulfillment of such a dream that college librarians are responding to the changes in American higher education in this
last quarter of the 20th century.

References

1.   Leuba, Clarence J.   "Thoughts on an Ideal College,"
       Library-College Journal, 1:38, Winter 1968.
2.   From notes made at a Library-College Conference,
       Drexel Institute of Technology, Philadelphia, Decem-
       ber 18-21, 1966.
3.   Deale, H. Vail, ed.   "Trends in College Librarian-
       ship," Library Trends, Vol. 18, No. 1, July 1969.
4.   Taylor, Robert S.   The Making of a Library: the
       Academic Library in Transition.   New York, Becker
       & Hayes, Inc., 1972, p. 36.
5.   Ibid., p. 40.
6.   From notes made at the Library-College Conference,
       op. cit.
7.   Wilson, Logan.   "Library Roles in American Higher
       Education," College & Research Libraries, 31:98.
8.   Taylor, op. cit., p. 44.
9.   From notes on a concluding talk at the Library-College
       Conference, op. cit.
10. Wilson, "Library Roles...," op. cit., p. 99.
11. Shores, Louis.   "The Library-College Idea," Library
       Journal, 91:3871-75, 1966.
12. Eurich, Alvin C., ed.   Campus 1980:   The Shape of
       the Future in Higher Education.   New York, Dela-
       corte Press, 1968, p. 298.
13. Ibid.
14. Ibid., p. 288.
15. Gores, Harold B.   "The American Campus ... 1980."
       In Alvin C. Eurich, ed., op. cit., p. 290.

16.   Gaylord, Robert.   "The Philosophy of the Last Fron-
       tier," Library-College Journal, 2:35, Summer 1969.
17.   Wilson, "Library Roles...," op. cit., p. 98.
18.   Sillers, Dan J.   "What Library for the Educated Man?,"
       Library-College Journal, 1:39, Fall 1968.

ON THE CUTTING EDGE OF CHANGE:
The Community College Library/
Learning Resource Center

Louise Giles

During the last decade or so, the impetus of social,
political, and educational change has inevitably led to change
in the field of librarianship. The steadily flowing production and publication of a variety and volume of print and
nonprint media, too, has perhaps been just as great a factor
in causing change in library practice. Since this decade of
"newer media" paralleled a decade of rapid growth and development in community colleges, community college libraries
have tended to be on the "cutting edge" of change.

Today, everyone preaches "change" and "innovation"
in library practice, though the majority of us still do not
practice it. However, I do not agree with Paul Wasserman,
who feels that "Libraries are failing because they are tied
inexorably to the past. . . .   They fail as they identify with
the status quo rather than with the forces of change sweep-
ing our planet. "[1]

Always conservative, librarians have been slow to
espouse change, but in recent years, perhaps sparked by the
enthusiasm of the younger generation of professionals, many
librarians have begun to realize the necessity of abandoning
solely traditional objectives and replacing them with objectives which will enable them to meet the changing educational, social, and political needs of the present day.   Librarians have come to this realization slowly and are in the
tortuous process of coming to grips with it.   I do not feel
we can say we have failed; rather, we have not yet finished
trying to meet the challenge.

Formerly, libraries existed as separate entities.
Then, audiovisual departments stated to develop either
separately or as a part of the library.   It was still possible

for a while for librarians to think, "That is not my responsibility," and shove the newer and stranger-looking educational
materials over to the AV man.   Today, it is no longer possible to avoid the responsibility: for better or for worse,
we now share the "turf" of educational technology with the
media specialists, and there are sometimes "territorial tensions."

Greater involvement with the newer media has made
undisputed impact on the work of the community college librarian and of other librarians.   There has been a radical
change in the materials and equipment that they handle.   In
addition to being responsible for the traditional books, periodicals, recordings, and films, librarians are now responsible for handling media production services including slides,
audio tapes, transparencies; video services such as videotape
recorders, video cassettes, television studios; individualized
instruction services such as dial access, computer-assisted
instruction, and learning laboratories; and the selection,
purchase, distribution, maintenance and storing of same!
Community college librarians and other librarians are now
"into" computerization of various library operations, including cataloging, test administration, individualized instruction,
instructional design, external degree programs, and many
other heretofore unheard-of areas.

Far more important than amassing an inventory of
hardware and software, though, is librarians' responsibility
for the development and implementation of a learning resources program or system to support the utilization of
media and facilities in a manner consistent with the curriculum.   Brown, Norberg, and Srygley aptly state:

> Contemporary education requires a systematically
> administered and technologically oriented media
> program that is considerably more than a simple
> combination of library and audio-visual resources.
> The key to this approach is not found in merely
> bringing together various educational media ser-
> vices under a new organizational title; it lies in
> the effective integration of those services with the
> processes of planning and implementing the entire
> instructional program. [2]

Most community college librarians today will agree
with B. Lamar Johnson that: "The saturation of junior college campuses with multimedia instructional facilities is

clearly an important aid to stimulating faculty members to
creativity in teaching.   This is completely consistent with
the role and responsibility of the library in the instructional
program. "3

Community college librarians and/or media center
administrators who wish to know specifically the basic components of a learning resources program are advised to refer to the "Guidelines for Two-Year College Learning Resources Programs, "4 which appeared in the January 1973
issue of Audiovisual Instruction.   Also, copies may be ordered from the American Library Association or the Association for Educational Communications and Technology.
This document was developed over a period of several years
with the joint cooperation of the American Library Association (ACRL/CJCLS), the Association for Educational Communications and Technology, and the American Association of
Community and Junior Colleges.

Implicit in the development of any learning resources
program, of course, is the assumption that the developer
will ask: What are the goals of the institution?   What is
the institution's commitment to learning resources?   Does
the program meet the needs of curriculum and instruction?

The prevalence and abundance of new media, it can
be seen, has influenced the materials that we handle, and
it has influenced our learning resources programs.   It has
also influenced our services, staffing and organization, and
standards and role.

Services

In 1960, the "Standards for Junior College Libraries"
described the functions of the library as: serving as the
center for curricular materials; being the focal point for
cultural life on campus; providing bibliographic and reference
services for faculty and students; and providing a "teaching"
function by giving instruction in the use of books and the library to students and faculty. 5   The avalanche of print and
nonprint media on the market has had its impact on services that librarians perform or are expected to perform,
and today the functions of community college and other librarians defy such facile synthesis.

Brown, Norberg, and Srygley list, for example, the

following functions typically assigned to educational media units in higher education:

Participation in [but not full responsibility for] the design of instructional systems, a process involving the comprehensive analysis of human and non-human factors and their interrelations in teaching and learning

Circulation of printed materials, involving the use of modern information storage and retrieval systems

Circulation of motion pictures and other audiovisual materials and equipment for on-campus instructional purposes

Off-campus circulation of educational materials through extension services and/or by means of cooperative 'service-area' programs

Customized production of instructional materials such as motion pictures, graphics, and photographic materials

Provision of facilities and coaching for faculty members and students to prepare their own inexpensive instructional materials, such as overhead transparencies, slides, and charts

Provision of services and facilities for large-group instruction, including open- and closed-circuit television and special classrooms designed for use by groups of varying sizes and equipped for the use of various media or for multimedia presentations

Television and radio broadcasting for regional and community education [in the broad sense] and for off-campus instruction of enrolled students

Provision of language laboratories and other electronic teaching or learning facilities for independent study and automated instruction

Monitoring of programmed instruction, including the use of teaching machines

Technical services such as the design, installation,
maintenance, and operation of instructional equipment of all kinds, including television and radio
transmitters, electronic components for language
laboratories, classroom communication and stu-
dent-response systems, projectors, magnetic recorders

Assistance in planning and designing new buildings
and instructional facilities to promote efficient
use of educational media

In-service education and dissemination of information regarding instructional media developments,
techniques, and research findings

Experimental development and trial of instructional
devices, techniques, and materials

Professional education of specialists and generalists
qualified to assume positions of leadership in planning and directing educational media programs and
research in this area. [6]

For community college librarians, however, a more
succinct list of commonly-provided services is found in the
"Guidelines":

1. Instructional development functions, which include task analysis, instructional design, evaluation, and related research.

2. Acquisition of learning materials, including
   cataloging and other related services.

3. Production.

4. User services which include reference, bibliographic circulation (print and non-print material), transmission or dissemination, and assistance to both faculty and students with the
   use of learning resources.

5. Other services, such as the computer operation, bookstore, campus duplicating or printing service, the learning or developmental
   lab, various auto-tutorial carrels or labs,

telecommunications, or other information networks might be included within the functions
and purposes of the college's overall organization and objectives. [7]

One of the newer services being provided by community college librarians is instructional design ("I.D."). Previously, when it existed, this service was most often found
in a separate department, such as Research and Development
or Instructional Development, but now it is not uncommon to
see "I.D." being provided by the community college library /
learning resource center. The involvement in media, in individualized instruction, and in instructional systems flows
inevitably into involvement with instructional design. Instructional design is, essentially, the "systematic planning
and development of instruction."[8] There are many types of
instructional design, and these are utilized with many types
of teaching methods and a wide variety of media.

Staffing and Organization

The unit which provides educational media services
in community colleges bears a varying array of names:
Learning Resource Center, Learning Media Center, Learning
Materials Center, Instructional Resources Center, Instructional Materials Center, Educational Media Center, Media
Center, and so forth. Usually, in a community college,
this unit includes a library, but the library is sometimes a
separate administrative entity. In other cases, the library
serves as a kind of umbrella to shelter the unit. When the
library and media unit are separate, the administrators are
usually separate but equal (though not always) and report to
the same boss.

When a library is included in a learning resources
unit, the chief administrator is very often not a librarian.
The most essential qualities in the head of such a unit are
management ability, the ability to relate to people on all
levels, and the ability to view the role of the LRC in relation to the total educational program.

Not surprisingly, the variety of positions in community college library/learning resource centers has increased.
The LRC administrator's staff includes not only librarians
and clerks, but media specialists, library technicians, audio-
visual technicians, television engineers, teachers of individu-

alized and/or developmental instruction, and, in some cases, research specialists and computer programmers. A whole new range of "media people" has emerged, and the LRC administrator must now employ a broader set of criteria in the recruiting, selection, and supervision of personnel.

The role of the media technician is still being defined. The May 1973 issue of Audiovisual Instruction was devoted to a discussion of the definition, certification, and accreditation of educational media personnel. Jobs in Instructional Media by C. James Wallington and others (Department of Audiovisual Instruction, Washington, D.C., 1970) is a helpful basic reference which analyzes the work performed by media support personnel and identifies some schools in the country which provide media support training.

The Role of the Community College Librarian

The gap is a large one between the 1970 "Standards, "[9] which referred to staffing mainly in terms of librarians and clerks and to functions in rather cautious definitions, and the 1973 "Guidelines, " which address themselves to "well-qualified and experienced staff" in "areas of specialization" who perform duties relating to "learning materials" and "instructional systems. " In order to cross this gap, a lot of soul-searching and role-searching had to take place in the community college library world. Some faithful and persistent librarians worked hard to distill the essence of community college librarians' views of their professional responsibilities toward print and nonprint materials, instructional systems and equipment, learning resources programs, and ultimately, their role in the community college field. They also worked with other media and education professionals to develop and re-edit "Guidelines" which would be flexible and comprehensive enough to be embraced and supported by all related fields.

Though some community college librarians felt let down when we backed off the quantitative references in the "Standards" to the qualitative ones in the "Guidelines, " many feel that the latter document represents a step forward. The "Guidelines" provide enough flexibility to meet the special needs of individual institutions and to deal with whatever new media may emerge in the future. In the publication of the "Guidelines, " we have sought, as Wasserman recommends, "a role positively linked with the achievement

of specific and viable ends identified with human needs and
with human aspirations. "[10]   Community college librarians
need to bring the "Guidelines" to the attention of their presidents and boards as they ponder together the types of educational media programs to be developed and/or maintained
at their institutions.

Physical Facilities

Evans and Neagley comment that "new media has impact on the planning and building of the total educational facility. "[11]   Too often, building specifications for instructional facilities are developed by others, perhaps even outsiders,
and the learning resources administrator is not called on the
scene until after the fact.   The involvement of the learning
resources administrator in the specification of campus instructional facilities is most important.

Libraries are also extending out into the campuses.
B. Lamar Johnson advises community college librarians to
"Take all steps possible to extend the fingers of the multi-
media library to all sections of the campus.   It is important
that the multimedia library not become a place, a single lo-
cation--but that rather it become a service which permeates
the entire college. "[12]   This is, in fact, happening in many
community colleges today, and a number of learning resource
centers have the assignment of equipping, maintaining, and
supervising one or more mediated, large-group instructional
facilities, not to mention learning laboratories and satellite
libraries.

It is evident that abundant utilization of media greatly
affects the campus physical facilities with regard to the design of electrical power systems; size, location, and types
of buildings; furniture and equipment.   Furthermore, the
combination of new media and new practices has a radical
effect upon the LRC itself.   More libraries are beginning to
catalog print and nonprint materials and to interfile both in
a common card or book catalog.

Richard L. Ducote, dean of learning resources at the
College of DuPage, says:

Librarians have been their own worst enemies in
regard to cataloging nonbook materials.   Of course
we catalog books, label them, and put them on

shelves, but we have continued to think of other
types of materials--films, recordings, transparencies, tapes, etc.--as widely diverse entities in
regard to their physical format. We have not
properly focused on the similarity of content. As
a result, the average library patron is confused,
disturbed, and mystified. But in the cataloging of
nonbook material, we have been dominated by format and not by content. A book or a film or a
tape may all have a similar message on the life
of Michelangelo, and yet because of our cataloging
and housing systems, the book will be out on the
shelves, the tape locked away in a storage cabinet
on another floor, and the film over in another
building. Even if the material is all cataloged in
a single place, the task is still a formidable one.
If it is not cataloged, it is an impossible one.
Our approach to processing has been pretty much
the same. Here, to a degree, we have been vic-
tims not so much of the format or the medium itself, as we have been of the agency or the manu-
facturer producing the material. [13]

The decision to catalog both print and nonprint materials, naturally, influences the interior design of the technical processing area and the selection of furniture and
equipment therein. In the case of the College of DuPage,
the decision to integrate the cataloging of materials led to
the next logical step: the intershelving of materials. Intershelving, in its turn, had impact on the selection of shelving and, for some media, necessitated specially-designed
cartons for more convenience in labeling and shelving.

After experiencing several years of integrated cataloging and shelving, Robert A. Veihman, a learning resources
staff member at DuPage, wrote:

In the three years of operation, our collection consists of 32, 000 books, 600 filmloops, 1, 200 filmstrips, 6 kits, 370 motion pictures, 2, 300 phono-
discs, 24, 000 slides, 440 study prints, 2, 300
tapes, 900 transparencies. Even though it has
been a long, difficult and expensive task to catalog and process all these items, we feel that it is
the only way to make all materials easily accessible and retrievable to faculty members and students. We do not hesitate to shelve a small book

next to a large book. Why should it concern us
to shelve a small filmstrip next to a large book?
Because we at the College of DuPage feel that
learning may result from numerous means, we are
trying to make all materials available to everyone.
After all, this is our main function.[14]

DuPage also successfully instituted "media browsing."
Richard Ducote describes the student reaction to this unique
service:

Once all of the intershelving had taken place, we
set up in carrel alcoves, or little carrel arcade
areas interspersed throughout the stacks, carrels
that had permanent tape recorders, record players,
film strip viewers, etc. The result of this was
immediate and fantastic. It was and is quite exciting to see students browsing at a section of material, to find them selecting a book, a film loop,
and perhaps a set of slides, and going over to one
of the wet carrels to sort of program themselves.
It has been highly accepted and received by the students and our use of nonbook material has simply
skyrocketed.... Because of the intershelving, the
students are having a rather interesting impact on
classroom teaching. A number of faculty members
have remarked that when they discussed a certain
topic or dealt with a particular issue in a classroom situation, the students were making reference
not only to books that they had read, but were
citing a segment of a film, or referring to some
charts that had been represented by a transparency.
These were things that they had discovered themselves and were using as a questioning of or a reaction to what the faculty member was presenting.
This can only have, in my opinion, a rather positive effect on the teaching that takes place at the
College of DuPage, as well as on the quality and
level of learning.[15]

Dimensions of the Future

What of the future? We have recently been hearing
doleful prophesies that "the bloom is off higher education."
It might be more appropriate to change that to "the boom is
off higher education," for though sharp enrollment increases

will probably abate, community college enrollments, for
varying reasons, are expected to continue increasing, though
at a slower rate during the next five- to ten-year period.

What might happen in community college library/learn-
ing resource centers during that period? I think there will
be more and better kinds of individualized instruction methods
and materials; instructional design will be seen more often
as a function of the LRC. Computerized cataloging, circulation, and acquisitions operations and computerized information retrieval systems will improve, and become more economical and more accessible. Computer output microfilm
(COM) may become more available to the average agency.

LRC's may become involved in more and better external degree programs, such as Lifetime Learning and College Without Walls. They will have more community use
and will, themselves, venture more often into the community.
There will be more use of television and telecommunications;
cable television will come into its own--including two-way
response systems. There will be more pressure for existing LRC's to become involved in cooperative systems and
networks and for new LRC's to develop without the traditional, fixed, and expensive physical facilities. And the river
of new media materials will continue to flow unabatedly.

Anna Mary Lowrey says:

> Educational technology has provided an outside im-
> petus for librarianship to take an inside look at
> itself. The library profession must now address
> itself to objectives based on function performance,
> the learning it takes to accomplish these objectives,
> and the methodology to best achieve them. New
> theories will continue to emerge with impact for
> library leadership roles in technologically sup-
> ported media centers. It is up to those in the li-
> brary profession to determine whether technology
> will make us more mechanical and task oriented
> or will truly assist us to facilitate, personalize,
> and humanize the library function. [16]

The community college librarians who absorb this message
will be able to deal effectively with the future.

References

1. Wasserman, Paul. The New Librarianship: A Chal-
    lenge for Change. New York, Bowker, 1972, p. xi.
2. Brown, James W., Norberg, Kenneth D., and Srygley,
    Sara K. Administering Educational Media: Instruc-
    tional Technology and Library Services. 2nd ed.
    New York, McGraw-Hill, 1972, p. 1.
3. Johnson, B. Lamar. "Toward the Multimedia Library"
    (Paper presented at the Preconference for the Commu-
    nity and Junior College Library Section, ALA/ACRL).
    Detroit, Michigan, June 1970, p. 5.
4. "Guidelines for Two-Year College Learning Resources
    Programs." Prepared by the American Library As-
    sociation (ACRL), the American Association of Com-
    munity and Junior Colleges, and the Association for
    Educational Communications and Technology. Audio-
    visual Instruction, 18:50-61, January 1973.
5. American Library Association. Association of College
    and Research Libraries. "Standards for Junior Col-
    lege Libraries," College & Research Libraries,
    21:200-206, May 1960.
6. Brown, op. cit., pp. 102-3.
7. "Guidelines for Two-Year...," op. cit.
8. Brown, op. cit., p. 125.
9. American Library Association, "Standards..." op. cit.
10. Wasserman, op. cit.
11. Evans, N. Dean, and Neagley, Ross L. Planning and
    Developing Innovative Community Colleges. Engle-
    wood Cliffs, New Jersey, Prentice-Hall, 1973, p. 165.
12. Johnson, op. cit., p. 9.
13. Ducote, Richard. "The Storage and Shelving of Audio-
    visual Media." In Jordan M. Scepanski, ed. Plan-
    ning Libraries for Media Services (Presentations
    made at the LAD Buildings and Equipment Section
    Program, Dallas, Texas, June 22, 1971). Chicago,
    ALA/LAD, 1972, p. 18.
14. Veihman, Robert A. "Cataloging and Processing Non-
    Book Materials--A True Instructional Resources Cen-
    ter Concept," Audiovisual Instruction, 15:59, Decem-
    ber 1970.
15. Ducote, op. cit., p. 20.
16. Lowrey, Anna Mary. "Staffing Patterns and Education
    for Media Center Personnel: Relevant or Regres-
    sive?" Library Trends, 19:518, April 1971.

THE CHANGING ROLE OF THE UNDERGRADUATE LIBRARY IN UNIVERSITIES

James Davis

One of the most pressing problems facing undergraduate libraries is the need to develop a general definition of their proper activities, functions, and responsibilities. This problem may largely be a result of the tendency to assert the "uniqueness" of undergraduate libraries without placing them in some kind of administrative context. They are, after all, an integral part of the over-all campus library systems that serve the needs of everyone from the undergraduate to the most advanced researcher. For years, special campus libraries have been established to offer in one place the materials of a particular discipline or related disciplines to a specialized clientele; the creation of libraries in art or economics has not been considered a revolutionary development. An undergraduate library may blaze new service trails or perhaps goad older library units into some kind of greater response to reader needs, but essentially it is merely one library unit among many.

Undergraduate libraries attempt to be (or are thought to be) generalists' libraries; to be, within the confines of space, staff, budget, and reality, all things to all undergraduate students. They represent selective microcosms of their university libraries; whereas the research facility strives for depth and comprehensiveness in its collection, the undergraduate library aims for breadth and quality. Whereas the research library emphasizes the scope of its resources, the undergraduate library attempts to instruct its users in methods of making good use of more limited services and provides a sort of laboratory for study.

Changing educational patterns are making it impossible to categorize the clientele of an academic library, and the undergraduate library must be considered an integral part

of the library service offered to all people on its campus.
One undergraduate library reports that more than 30 percent
of the use of its open stack collection is made by graduate
students, staff, and faculty who apparently find the availability of its multiple copies, standard editions, and recent acquisitions an attraction. At the same institution undergraduate students represent more than half of those who use the
open stack research collection. The point, then, is that an
undergraduate library is to be differentiated from the research
library not so much by who uses it but by what they use it
for.

Irene Braden was concerned with separately housed
facilities in her study, The Undergraduate Library. [1] She
listed six basic ways they were to differ from traditional
academic libraries, [2] but these ways were essentially techniques that would be observed by any reasonably progressive
library. Billy Wilkinson tried to distinguish undergraduate
libraries by the scope of their activities, [3] and while this is
rather closer to the mark, there is still no clear differentia-
tion between the activities of an academic library and the
functions and programs of an undergraduate library.

At UCLA, an attempt was made recently to delineate
what makes its undergraduate library an essential part of
the library's activities on campus, and to explain what, if
anything, justifies the need for and existence of this special
facility for undergraduate students. In the course of discussions with a faculty committee, the following general concept
was evolved:

> Perhaps the best description of an undergraduate
> library is that it represents an intermediate stage
> between the school and public library and the re-
> search collection. ... Undergraduate libraries pro-
> vide both the basic materials students require and
> the basic assistance with bibliographic procedures
> that undergraduates may need. This combination
> represents a unique service on the campus since
> the staff of most academic libraries are unable
> for a variety of reasons, most particularly time,
> to work repeatedly with students at a basic, even
> remedial, level. [4]

Acknowledgment is made here of the continuum of the educational development of a student and of the various levels
of service an academic library must offer.

The development of undergraduate libraries has been traced back as far as 1608, at which time Sir Thomas Bodley dismissed the notion because of the additional staffing it would require and because much of the material in such a library would also be of interest to more advanced readers. [5] Little more was done until 1907, when Columbia University opened a reading collection of 6,000 volumes in an attractive area specifically designed for the needs of undergraduate students.

The precedent for a complete library especially designed for the needs and interests of undergraduate students existed, but it was not until 1949 that the Lamont Library was created at Harvard. The basic goal of an undergraduate library was established at Lamont: "That undergraduates will make more and better use of a library designed expressly for them."[6] Lamont "tried to make the collection as accessible to the students as possible.... The catalog [was] minimized"[7] to the extent that no systematic approach by subject was provided. It was, by implication, very much a self-service operation, following the pattern established by its spiritual predecessor at Columbia. At the same time, "it was clearly understood that undergraduates would always be welcome in Widener whenever they needed material not available in any separate library established for them."[8] This critical aspect of Lamont's role at Harvard, this essential interrelationship of any undergraduate library to its total campus library system, seems now rather clouded by time and practice.

The physical plant of the Lamont Library has worn well, but certain of the fundamental concepts of service have had to be changed. The simplified call number system created for its collection is now being replaced by Library of Congress cataloging, and the lack of scheduled reference personnel is soon to be remedied. The "minimized" catalog might rightly be considered a condescending approach for a facility that should ideally be a stepping-stone to knowledgeable, self-assured use of other, larger libraries by students.

Although the Lamont Library was the first, the University of Michigan Undergraduate Library may with some justification be considered the prototype of most undergraduate libraries. The classification system there follows more closely the one that prevails in other libraries on the campus, and a comprehensive program of reference assistance is provided. New buildings have been constructed for most undergraduate libraries, including those at the Universities of California at Berkeley, Illinois at Urbana, and Washington (as well as those at Harvard and Michigan). A variation on this approach was made at Cornell, where the decision was reached that the old library building would be renovated and refurbished to house the undergraduate service. An intelligent and sensitive remodeling followed, and a building resulted that has far more character--and idiosyncrasies-- than most new ones. A few institutions, including the University of Hawaii and UCLA, have followed this pattern and consider it more than satisfactory.

Another approach has been to incorporate the undergraduate library in a corner, floor, or wing of the basic campus library building. Northwestern has housed its Core Collection in this way; Indiana University has provided its undergraduate library with an entire wing, joined to the research collection by a common circulation point. A number of undergraduate libraries share a building with other campus activities: the University of Maryland and UCLA also have their respective library schools under their roofs; the Moffitt Library at Berkeley and the College Library at Wisconsin have classroom annexes; Indiana and Washington are both above underground cafeterias.

Whatever the arrangement of the building, it is relatively less important than the services offered by the undergraduate library. Each has, for the most part, certain activities in common with others: an open stack collection that more or less duplicates titles in other libraries on the campus, a reserve service, reading rooms, reference assistance, audio materials, etc. These services have been thoroughly discussed by Wilkinson, [9] though his proposed inclusion of moving pictures in an undergraduate library seems fiscally a bit unrealistic.

The undergraduate library should be defined as a service operation, and all of its resources (including staff) should be directed toward actively meeting the needs of its users. These needs fall into three basic categories: resources for academic studies; information for preparing class assignments; and, lastly, materials for students' extracurricular interests and pursuit of happiness. Two products should ideally emerge: students who can eventually work in any library with a minimum of difficulty, and people who consider the library an integral part of their life style. Because of this commitment to public service, it is appro-

priate that most undergraduate libraries not process the bulk
of their materials themselves, but rely on other library
units for most of this preparation. This freedom from processing of materials enables the undergraduate library staff
to concentrate on working with those who need assistance.

Generally, an undergraduate library collection is not
a comprehensive or fully rounded one; it reflects the academic programs of the institution and the interests of its
users. The reserve service of any library directly supports
the teaching program of its institution. Through reserve requests for materials to be used by students in conjunction
with course assignments, faculty often become the most important (or largest) developers of the undergraduate library's
collection. Multiple copies are generally purchased, but because of exiguous financial allocations, the traditional provision of one copy for every ten or 15 students in each class
is now rarely practiced. Some libraries rely on paperback
copies, when they are available, for reserve use and do not
bother to bind them. This unquestionably extends the book
money, but it does not provide copies that can be subjected
to heavy or extended use.

It is a pleasurable responsibility of the undergraduate
library staff to augment faculty requests with additional material to meet other needs of undergraduate students. Book
selection is one of the critical matters that every undergraduate library must face; the more imaginative the combination
of sources, the better are the chances of having a lively,
current collection for readers. Basic, traditional listings
can be extremely useful, but they are used in combination
with journals that students read. Rolling Stone, Playboy,
and alternative press sources should be reviewed at least
as carefully as Choice. It is essential that selection be
made title by title for an undergraduate library. Approval
plans seem particularly inappropriate; delegation of selection
of materials to individuals not directly involved in a library's
activities, especially in an undergraduate library, is an ab-
dication of professional responsibility.

Much has been made of the duplicate status of undergraduate library collections, indeed it is one of Braden's
six criteria.[10] Most undergraduate libraries no longer attempt to assure that materials they order are available elsewhere on their campus; this seems remiss in terms of the
needs of both users of the university library's collection and
the undergraduate students. Faculty frequently include titles

on reserve lists that are not a part of the library's collection, and not ordering a copy for the appropriate part of the research collection deprives the library of that academic's expertise as a book selector.   One undergraduate library found that 20 percent of the titles it ordered in 1972-73 would have been unique to the system.   If it had not placed simultaneous orders for the main collection, the impact on the demography of that undergraduate library would probably have been considerable, for faculty and graduate students would tend to exercise their droit de seigneur over many of those titles, and undergraduate students would have difficulty extricating them from those more privileged borrowers.   Although faculty committees on some campuses have passed resolutions stating that faculty should not have their usual preferential treatment in the undergraduate library, their constituencies frequently do not concur with this principle. Maintaining a duplicate collection is one way to assure that faculty have no reason to demand or expect more latitude than an undergraduate student in an undergraduate library.

The information explosion and the vagaries of the publishing world have caused non-book materials to become particularly important in many undergraduate library collections.   As much as 20 percent of the money available to an undergraduate library is used for the purchase of serial publications; periodicals are among the most heavily used parts of many of these collections.   Pamphlets complement periodicals as sources of current information; some libraries have dramatically increased the use of these materials by adding form cards to their card catalogs, indicating subjects on which pamphlets are available.   Past examinations and even lecture notes are now generally available within an undergraduate library and can be useful study guides as well as specific aides to passing a course.   A survey made in 1971[11] showed that six of 25 responding undergraduate libraries had microform material.   Although this figure has no doubt increased, microforms in an undergraduate library might perhaps be largely limited to the New York Times.[12]

Provision of audio material is another service which many undergraduate libraries have developed to a significant degree.   Although musical recordings are often included, most facilities tend to emphasize spoken records and consider them an extra dimension to the library's book collection.   A number of undergraduate libraries, particularly those at the Universities of Maryland and Washington, have extremely sophisticated listening facilities.   The UCLA Audio

Room began with a collection of spoken recordings, but now maintains a representative sampling of the current popular musical scene. It is literally up to its collective ears meeting student needs not only for Shakespearean and other literary recordings and the listening requirements of non-music majors in survey courses of music appreciation and the development of jazz, but also supplying selections of interest to audio browsers. A main entry for each title in this collection has been incorporated into the college library's public catalog to increase the accessibility of the material. This main entry supplements the complete listings by title, selection, performer, etc. that are located in the Audio Room.

It is in the area of reference assistance, although not all undergraduate libraries offer it on a regular or scheduled basis, that librarians are perhaps most appreciated; it is here that librarians most obviously complement the activities of their colleagues on the faculty. Their work in locating information and giving advice is, for the most part, done with the materials in hand, and their method is to explain the procedure to the student as they progress, rather than direct the student to sources and assume that he or she will find the information required. This active assistance, moving with the student and explaining routines through each step of the search and through each part of the library in that search, is probably the most distinctive aspect of undergraduate library reference work. [13] Undergraduate librarians might well be compared to general practitioners, and their broad general knowledge of materials and resources is at least as important a specialization as a more thorough, but narrower, background in a specific area. Since most undergraduate students are prohibited from requesting materials on interlibrary loan, their referral to other resources on the campus and in the community is an essential element of the service an undergraduate library extends to them.

One of the problems most common to academic libraries is centered on the undergraduate library: the continuing lack of library expertise of entering--and continuing--students. It is a frustrating fact that after 12 years of school, most students still have only the barest idea of the various approaches to and uses of a card catalog, know of few bibliographic resources beyond the Readers' Guide to Periodical Literature, are so locked in to Dewey Decimal that they cannot comprehend the principles of another classification system, and are intimidated by library staff. A

basic responsibility of any undergraduate library is to try to
overcome these liabilities, but this sort of repetitious remedial work can sometimes be stultifying, even for the most
energetic, dedicated librarian.

One undergraduate library has reached out to tackle
this problem in the high schools themselves. It got in touch
with high school librarians in its community to explain how
it can support the schools' activities, and has recruited the
school librarians to screen the high school students, determine their actual needs, and advise them of proper bibliographic procedures before referring them to the undergraduate library for further assistance. This program appears
to be greatly appreciated by the students as well as by the
school librarians and it is being extensively used. This
same undergraduate library also requires the school librarian to explain the general principles of classification systems
and to have scheduled a visit to the local public library before it will give a tour of the library to any school class.

Recent Developments

Library developments in the past five years have been
of great significance to undergraduate students. During this
time the ACRL meeting in Detroit discussed aspects of service in undergraduate libraries, an institute on the topic was
held in San Diego, and a two-day preconference on undergraduate libraries was a part of the ALA conference at Dallas.
Critical evaluations of the roles and activities of undergraduate libraries began to appear, and the whole concept of special library services for undergraduate students came under
real scrutiny.

In Detroit, Billy Wilkinson gave a preliminary report
of his comparisons of reference assistance and instruction
at two undergraduate libraries, [14] Kenneth Tooms detailed
the reasons for discontinuing a third, and Norah Jones
described the creation and functions of a fourth. [15] The unusual frankness of each of the speakers caused many people
to begin reassessing the practicality of an undergraduate library. Possibly the most important week in the development of concepts regarding undergraduate libraries was the
one in August 1970 following the Detroit ACRL meeting.
An Institute for Training for Service in Undergraduate Libraries, conducted under a grant from the U.S. Office of
Education, was held at the University of California, San

Diego.   Representatives from undergraduate library services
at 30 institutions in 18 states met with six recognized author-
ities on various aspects of undergraduate libraries to discuss
the unique attitudes and potential of undergraduate libraries.
As a result of the papers and inquiries covering basic aspects
of planning and developing undergraduate library programs,
it became clear that until that time many of the participants
had been somewhat parochial in their concerns.   In many
ways, the institute represents the high water mark of the
undergraduate library movement.   A follow-up preconference,
"Librarians Confront the New Undergraduate Environment, "
was held in Dallas, and librarians, faculty, and administrators discussed the present state and future possibilities of
librarians and libraries concerned with service for undergraduate students.

        Perhaps the most interesting review of undergraduate
libraries yet made appeared recently.[16]   It reiterates the
basic premises of the Lamont Library, that by siphoning off
undergraduate students to their own facility the Widener Library would become a better facility for research, and points
out that "the distinction between graduate and undergraduate
needs is becoming increasingly obsolete."[17]   The rationale
for the elimination of 11 existing or proposed undergraduate
libraries is given, and a tabulation of the opinions of undergraduate librarians as to whether their facility should be
separate from or incorporated with the research collection
is reported: "a majority preferred what they did not have."[18]

        Whither, then, the undergraduate library?   Ideally,
toward oblivion.   However, given the realities of academe
today--and of elementary and secondary education--this cannot be considered.   A more positive approach might be the
evolution of undergraduate libraries, with the second-rate
status the adjective often connotes, into student or service
libraries.   In a recent report it was stated "... the UGL
resembles a public library, and several UGL librarians
have, in fact, expressed the view that the UGL is the public
library within the university library."[19]   This concern with
serving the disadvantaged, both students and faculty, must
be nurtured.   Many undergraduate libraries represent to
their constituencies a haven, both physical and intellectual,
and advantage must be taken of this fact.   Materials relating not only to academic programs but also to reality must
be provided somewhere, and what better place than the undergraduate library, the one egalitarian library service on the
campus.

One of the particularly difficult aspects of an undergraduate library is that its resources tend to be inadequate
for its assigned responsibilities. This situation is worsened
when it is assumed that an undergraduate library can be--or
should be--all things to all undergraduate students. In 1971 a
tabulation was made of the statistics from an arbitrary selection of eight of the largest or oldest undergraduate libraries
then existing[20] (there is little reason to believe that the situation has changed significantly since that time). These
undergraduate libraries were allocated from 1.94 to 7.45
percent of the total library's book budget. Their collections
provided from 3.47 to 29.36 volumes per undergraduate student. They had from 5.12 to 10.11 percent of the library
staff; the ratio of undergraduate library staff to undergraduate students ranged from one per 236 students to one per
1,305. The ratio of librarians to undergraduate students
went from one for every 776 to one for every 8,099. Undergraduate students comprised between 50 and 80 percent of
the total enrollment at these institutions. Obviously, most
undergraduate libraries lack the resources to fulfill their
essential mission of enriching undergraduate students' lives.

It would not seem unreasonable for an undergraduate
library to receive 10 percent or $100,000, whichever is the
smaller amount, of its institution's book allocation, for it is
in theory serving the greatest single group of library users
at the institution. This would yield a considerably larger
selection of available materials and would promulgate the
Harvard theorum of improving the research facility by reducing demand there for basic sources. Along with this, a
marked increase in staff support would be required to cope
with the increased use that would result from the growth of
the collection.

Instruction in using the academic library has mani-
festly been a hit-or-miss affair. Too often students are in-
structed what to produce but not how to do it; frequently, no
systematic approach to bibliographic procedures is given
students until they reach the graduate level. Although the
serendipity factor is one of the most important elements in
research, a logical approach to resources greatly increases
the chances of its occurring. Because undergraduate students represent the largest single group of users of an academic library, and the undergraduate library one of the
smallest parts of it, it is obvious that education in the use
of the library must be an activity that involves all members
of the campus library staff. It is critical that library in-

struction be considered not solely the responsibility of the undergraduate library, but rather as one of many important activities in which it actively participates with other library units.

Improved relations with the faculty are essential. Adversary roles are rarely productive, and although some librarians eat, drink, play volleyball and the cello, and even sleep with the faculty, working with them professionally is a critical necessity for any academic library and every academic librarian. Anticipating their needs (and those of undergraduate students), rather than discovering them too late, is probably the single most significant element in the successful operation of an undergraduate library. Rapprochement with the faculty generally leads to greater mutual understanding and possibly to greater participation in the educational process. Incorporating library instruction into departmental courses is far more productive than offering them apart from the educational mainstream.

Using the undergraduate library as a proving ground for procedures being considered for implementation could be the undergraduate library's most important contribution to academic libraries. Its clientele is generally more tolerant of change and experimentation, and should a procedure prove successful there, it probably could be less painfully adopted subsequently by other library units. Examples of this sort of proven usefulness include automation of the undergraduate library's circulation records, using library school students as interns at the undergraduate library's reference desk, and not fining borrowers for overdue books from the open stack collection that have not been requested by others. Each of these has been successfully tried by undergraduate libraries and is now implemented or under consideration for adoption by other parts of their respective systems. Undergraduate libraries have also begun investigating the practicality of administrative stipends and collegial management.

Libraries are concerned with communication, but only a few really encourage any input from their clientele. Suggestion books or boards are used in several undergraduate libraries and are notable for being "heavily used by the students and producing an excellent channel of communication and sounding board for the librarians."[21] Additionally, it is difficult to consider a truly responsive library without at least one television set available for viewing events of campus interest or national importance. What better way to disseminate information than while it is happening?

        Finally, it is vital that the library staff, and particu-
larly the undergraduate library staff, become involved to a
far greater degree in the ongoing activities of its campus.
Space is a great problem, but providing an office for various student activities is a useful ploy.   Ideally, an undergraduate library would occupy the center portion of the student union building and be surrounded by offices of student
officials and organizations.   The interaction and increased
appreciation on both sides that would occur would change beyond recognition the traditional student/library roles.

        The basic aim of every library should be institutional-
ization, described by John Haak as "the degree to which a
system of action obtains support for its decision or goal
from the environment."[22]   Undergraduate libraries are not
a nostrum for many of the ills presently besetting academic
libraries.   Many undergraduate libraries have needlessly
been established as unrealistic solutions to problems unrelated to service for undergraduate students.   But judiciously
conceived and properly supported, both administratively and
fiscally, they can infuse all components of the community of
an academic library with a new spirit of enthusiasm and
interest.

References

1.   Braden, Irene Andrea.   The Undergraduate Library
        (ACRL Monograph, no. 31.).   Chicago, American Li-
        brary Association, 1970.
2.   Ibid., pp. 2-3.
3.   Wilkinson, Billy Rayford.   "A Screaming Success as
        Study Halls," Library Journal, 96:1568-69, May 1,
        1971.
4.   California.   University, Los Angeles.   Library.   Col-
        lege Library.   Staff Report on UCLA's College Li-
        brary, 1972, p. 3.   [Mimeographed]
5.   Wagman, Frederick Herbert.   "The Case for the Sepa-
        rate Undergraduate Library," College & Research Li-
        braries, 17:150, March 1956.
6.   Metcalf, Keyes Dewitt.   "Harvard Faces Its Library
        Problems," Harvard Library Bulletin, 3:187, Spring
        1949.
7.   Ibid., p. 188.
8.   Metcalf, Keyes Dewitt.   "The Undergraduate and the

Harvard Library, 1937-1947, " Harvard Library Bulletin, 1:299, Autumn 1947.

9. Wilkinson, "A Screaming Success...," op. cit., p. 1569.
10. Braden, op. cit., p. 3.
11. UgLi Newsletter, no. 5, November 1971, p. 7.
12. Memorandum from James R. Cox to Everett T. Moore,
    August 7, 1973, discussing use of microform materi-
    als by UCLA undergraduate students; 53.4 percent of
    the use of The New York Times (15.1 percent of the
    total use of microforms) was by undergraduate stu-
    dents.
13. This is discussed in greater detail and from a some-
    what different perspective in Wilkinson, Billy Rayford.
    Reference Services for Undergraduate Students.   Me-
    tuchen, N.J., Scarecrow Press, 1972.
14. Wilkinson, "A Screaming Success...," op. cit.,
    pp. 1567-71.
15. Jones, Norah E.   "An Undergraduate Library for Un-
    dergraduates: The UCLA Experience, " Wilson Library
    Bulletin, 45:584-90, February 1971.
16. Keever, Ellen Hull.   "Reassessment of the Undergradu-
    ate Library: A Personal Critique, " The Southeastern
    Librarian, 23:24-30, Spring 1973.
17. Ibid., p. 24.
18. Ibid., p. 25.
19. Memorandum from Yoram Szekley to Eldred Smith,
    SUNY at Buffalo, September 14, 1973, p. 2.
20. UgLi Newsletter, op. cit., pp. 4-5.
21. Memorandum from Szekley to Smith, op. cit.   Addi-
    tional testimonials to this endeavor in academic li-
    braries include articles in California Librarian,
    33:42-45, January 1972; RQ, 9:144-46, Winter 1969;
    and Wilson Library Bulletin, 47:493-96, February
    1973.
22. Haak, John R.   "Goal Determination, " Library Journal,
    96:1578, May 1, 1971.   This article (pp. 1573-78) is
    an extremely perceptive view of the interrelationship
    of librarians and readers and of the responsibilities
    the former have toward the latter.   It is also one of
    the best general descriptions of a library to appear
    recently.

PART II

NEW APPROACHES IN SOLVING
ACADEMIC LIBRARY PROBLEMS

LIBRARY ORGANIZATION IN ACADEMIA:
Changes from Hierarchical to Collegial Relationships

Evert Volkersz

The nature of education and the function of the library are among the fundamental issues in academic librarianship which demand continuous attention. More specific agenda items concern the process of learning, collegial relationships, and the practice of librarianship and its cultural manifestations. Although they are elements in the larger academic community, academic libraries have often followed separate paths of their own. Discussions concerning academic libraries have primarily focused on managerial problems as a consequence of rapid growth and the size of collections. Such developments have caused neglect of the natural dialogue which helps to define and clarify the basic issues confronting librarians in higher education.

In breaking out of the hierarchical structure librarians have renewed the dialogue while challenging the authoritarian nature of academic library life. Collegial involvement encourages individual growth and development in concert with other faculty. This interdependence contrasts with the traditional relationship, in which most librarians neither shared responsibility for, nor participated in, making the crucial decisions shaping their contributions to teaching, research, collection development, and community involvement.

The more notable studies on the state of higher education in recent years have been made by the Carnegie Commission on Higher Education and the Center for the Study of Democratic Institutions.[1] As one example, an article by educational innovator Robert M. Hutchins should provoke response from librarians. Beginning a paper entitled "Desperation in Education," he writes, "The future of education depends on the future of everything else. The conditions and desires of a society are decisive, and desires seem more important than conditions."[2] Hutchins makes a very pessi-

mistic assessment of the possibility for change in the educational establishment.   If conditions and desires of a society
are decisive, what do they portend for education and librarianship?   In the light of such questions, and with the many
reports made for the Carnegie Commission, a beginning can
be made to study the implications for librarians and libraries
and their publics.   The massive growth of higher education
and libraries following World War II has created new academic and institutional dimensions for librarians; e. g. , the
relationship between the size of collections and the quality
of education has never been established.   Numbers, unfortunately, have become synonymous with excellence, and these
numbers have created bureaucracies.

     The bureaucratic vision of librarianship is being
challenged.   Library bureaucracy ideally exists to facilitate
the educational process, but in actuality the reverse is true.
Bureaucracies have a leveling effect, demanding conformity
in thought and action.   Instead of professional determination
of programs, institutional life circumscribes the duties and
responsibilities of its staff.   Libraries have identified the
duties and responsibilities of library faculty with the building, its collections and services.   In rejecting this faulty
logic, librarians are rediscovering the elusive nature of
learning and teaching.   "The desire of the true teacher is
not to triumph but to teach, and in teaching to learn... , "
comments Mark Van Doren in Liberal Education.   About the
immeasurable qualities of education he writes: "When the
student has found his own way in the world he cannot recall
how much of his wisdom he owes to another.   It is his now,
and that is what his teacher had intended. "[3]

     Teaching and learning are solitary processes which
defy quantification and are therefore undervalued, especially
in libraries.   The academic functions of library faculty are
gradually earning their long-deserved recognition in the
classroom, in reference, in working with students and faculty, and in the quality of the bibliographic development of
collections and services.   Librarians are specialists who,
like their teaching colleagues, make individual contributions
within a programmatic context.

     Academic librarians have two clearly distinct respons-
ibilities, which are often closely intertwined.   First, there
is participation in the educational process--teaching the
techniques and substance of learning and bibliography and
providing the resources for the pursuit of self-knowing.

Secondly, librarians support writing, studying, and research by supplying factual items of information. In the informational function the librarian provides data which may or may not be of use to the patron; as a teacher, the librarian works with the learning person.

Participation in decision-making and integration with teaching faculty has freed librarians to accept responsibility for their professional futures. As colleagues, librarians can exercise their academic and intellectual freedom, becoming learners, readers, and teachers. This will be reflected in broadened subject expertise, bibliographical knowledge, and improved collections.

During the past five years librarians have entered into a much more complex world than they anticipated when they called for recognition of their academic contribution. As they gained entry in library and campus governance through membership in library consultative bodies and in the academic senate and its committees, the election of collective bargaining agents started to alter the nature of campus governance itself. In this time of transition librarians have the opportunity to review their professional obligations as members of the library department, as members of the faculty senate, and as members of a collective bargaining agent.

The stresses and strains on library directorship have been chronicled by McAnally and Downs in their farewell to the remarkable post-Second World War era in librarianship.[4] After identifying and itemizing many changes which took place in this period, their recommendation is that future library directors do-more-of-the-same-better to avoid the high administrative mortality rate of their own generation. This contradicts their understanding and compassion, because the authors make it abundantly clear that the old methods failed to yield to new demands. The tensions between the requirements of the management of libraries and their educational mission have not been adequately and properly acknowledged. The flux and interaction between the educational and administrative aspects of libraries cause antagonisms which are not necessarily destructive. The awareness must exist that

> Participation, while difficult to initiate and sustain, can no longer be safely avoided ... there is a conflict between democratic expectation and the ability and opportunity to share in the decisions

that affect an individual's role in his organization. [5]

This describes the classic conflict between faculty governance
and academic administration, a conflict librarians are joining
of necessity.

University and library administrations are responsive
to the desires of society. Some change has been brought
about through management studies, budgetary regimens,
fluctuating enrollments, the questioning of the value of education, the relative status of the library within the university, and the high turnover rate of presidents and library
directors. Further, library administrators are beginning to
be aware of their problems and are attending seminars and
workshops for library executives. In fact, many of these
workshops teach management skills without giving a clear
understanding of the real purpose of educational administration. Few libraries are responding creatively to calls for
change. The administrative character changes reluctantly
under pressure, and then in ways to absorb the librarian in
the administrative rather than the policy and educational decision-making process.

There are clear differences between participative
management, committee consultation, delegation, decentrali-
zation, self-governance, staff organization, and other forms
of staff involvement. The basic distinction is between involvement in an administrative-hierarchical model (which
participative management often turns out to be) and a more
democratically oriented collegial structure. This does not
in any way contradict the need for committee consultation
and recommendation, but it should not occur to the exclu-
sion of individual professional activity.

The different structures can serve their purposes effectively. Acquisitions, cataloging, and circulation lend
themselves more easily to traditional organizational patterns.
Their major thrust is routine processing of materials, often
requiring minimal continuing intellectual contribution once
policies and procedures have been defined and implemented.
Collection development and reference services, on the other
hand, do not lend themselves to performance and productivity measurements; they bear directly on the educational
mission of the institution. Close analysis of these activities
may suggest the need for organizational restructuring of the
library, freeing faculty with academic responsibilities from

administrative burdens, and streamlining the activities of
production-oriented departments.

The impact of library faculty collegial governance is
starting to have far-reaching effects. Review of candidates
for appointment, promotion, and tenure is seriously affecting personal and professional relationships. The requirement
of a subject master's degree is putting a severe strain on
younger, untenured librarians. Added to this strain are the
imposition of rank and tenure quotas, which in turn will be
affected by higher education equal employment opportunity
programs. In rectifying inequities and balancing staff, col-
legiality will be seriously tested if promotions and rewards
are made on political rather than meritorious grounds.
Automation of technical processes and bibliographic data
bases seriously challenges librarians now engaged in marginal professional duties, and may also lead to reassignment
of experienced librarians.

Collegial involvement has a mixed effect. For some
it has meant accelerated advancement, including appointment
to major administrative positions. For others it has fore-
closed advancement and caused professional dislocation,
termination, and withdrawal. The miseducation of librarians
and the technocratic rather than humanistic attitude fostered
in traditional working relationships bear some responsibility
for this inability to change.

The focus of collegial activity is a reorientation
toward the needs of library users, toward people. Such
activity concerns library programs, communications, and
orientation; library collections and services; professional
development; and the rights, privileges, and responsibilities
of librarians. Decisions on vital issues can no longer be
ordered unilaterally for staff implementation. Issues must be
defined and clarified by library faculty for review and adoption. It brings library education and service back to its
proper source: the reader of books and user of library materials.

Collegial activity is having a tonic effect on professional library organizations. The Association of College and
Research Libraries and the Library Administration Division
of the American Library Association, for example, have
adopted several policy statements and action programs supporting the welfare of academic librarians and library programs. The Association of Research Libraries has com-

missioned studies to investigate management problems and
cooperative development.   The net result is a growing awareness of professional responsibility at all levels; organizational activity has reinforced and stimulated campus efforts.

Integration with classroom colleagues has often been
slow and difficult, but is an essential consideration in attaining academic recognition.   Librarians know that academics
participate in a modified hierarchical organization under a
governing board, president, and departmental chairpersons.
Faculty senate and committee membership permits participation in the consultative and governance activities of the campus.   It has given librarians an opportunity to work on academic planning and deliberation, increasing the effectiveness
and visibility of library programs and services.   Many
studies have shown that personal contact between librarian
and classroom instructor is one of the most effective ways
to introduce bibliographical concerns.

Developing contacts with teaching colleagues requires
constant effort.   Among positive results are that some librarians teach in academic departments and join in departmental deliberations.   Such exchange of expertise and knowledge keeps librarians and teachers aware of changes in
fields of academic pursuit and bibliographic services.   It
encourages librarians to develop collections in anticipation
of research needs.   Collective bargaining is transforming
internal administrative and collegial library faculty relationships and campus academic governance.   The most profound
change is the diminution of campus administrative responsibility in favor of the governing board, which negotiates and
signs the contract with the bargaining unit.

For most academic librarians unionization is usually
not a matter of choice, because they constitute a part of a
larger bargaining unit.   David Selden, president of the American Federation of Teachers, has asserted that present academic senates and departmental organizations could not cope
with the problems facing universities.   In a speech sponsored
by the AFT-Affiliated United Professors of California on
"The Future of Academic Government, " he said:

> There can be no faculty life, no community of
> scholars, no interdependent relationships among
> faculty members without the support of an organi-
> zation, independent of the faculty senate, the de-
> partmental structure, or other official apparatus.

He declared that a teacher's union "could tackle not only the economic needs of the professors, but their professional responsibilities as well. "[6]

In a number of institutions library administrators and library faculty now meet in three overlapping and interrelated structures.   The library administrator is ineligible for union membership and represents "management" in a labor dispute; the administrator is a member of the central campus administration and is responsible for the administration of the library; the librarian, as a member of the library or campus faculty, or as local union representative, may meet the library administrator as an equal or an adversary.   So, while the library has been democratized, the development of collegial hierarchies is overlaid by egalitarian union positions negotiated and executed in an adversary relationship with the governing board.

Benefits and obligations of librarians in collective bargaining units are highly dependent on institutional conditions.   Since higher education collective bargaining has taken hold only in the last decade, its impact is not clear.   Original faculty opposition to unionization has turned to support; however, many faculties are attempting to retain their exclusivity by refusing to include librarians.

The primary aim of collective bargaining is the establishment and improvement of the terms and conditions of employment of its members.   An immediate result is to deny campus administrators the opportunity to bargain for individual salaries, merit increases, or bonuses.   While certain arbitrary administrative practices are eliminated, they are sometimes replaced by others as a result of a negotiated contract.   In terms of programs and support, librarians may be able to gain more personal independence and influence through the local union chapter.

An attempt to avoid collective bargaining and still meet the demands of campus restlessness is being attempted by several private institutions of higher education.   Under this plan campus personnel is divided into three units: officers of instruction, officers of the library, and officers of the administration.   Such a structure may very well strengthen library administrations at the expense of the faculty. Differential salaries and treatment can result from such classification, as decision-making power remains in administrative hands. [7]

Librarians are becoming more respectful of their colleagues' bibliographic contributions and their public's needs.
Recent discussions in the literature indicate a growing intelligence about the dilemmas in librarianship.   We need to
probe deeper to justify and codify the changing relationships.
J. Krishnamurti has said that "Self-knowing is the beginning
of wisdom and it does not lie in books, in churches or in
the piling up of words. "[8] The process of self-knowing fur-
nishes a continuing beginning of the wisdom needed to make
libraries more useful tools for peace and understanding.
This awareness will define the relationship of students to libraries and librarians to learning.

References

1.   For information and reports on its studies, contact the
      Carnegie Commission on Higher Education, 1947 Cen-
      ter Street, Berkeley, California 94704.   For an im-
      pression of the activities of the Center for the Study
      of Democratic Institutions see MacDonald, Donald.
      "A Six Million Dollar Misunderstanding--The Carnegie
      Commission's Study of Higher Education, " Center
      Magazine, 6:32-52, September/October 1973.   Also,
      "Follow-up/The Carnegie Report, " Center Magazine,
      6:46-55, November/December 1973.
2.   Hutchins, Robert M.   "Desperation in Education, "
      Center Report, 4:26, December 1973.
3.   Van Doren, Mark. Liberal Education.   Boston, Beacon
      Press, 1959.   In MacDonald, op. cit., p. 51.
4.   McAnally, Arthur, and Downs, Robert B.   "The Chang-
      ing Role of Directors of University Libraries, " Col-
      lege & Research Libraries, 34:103-25, March 1973.
5.   Kaplan, Louis.   "Participation: Some Basic Considera-
      tions on the Theme of Academe, " College & Research
      Libraries, 34:240, September 1973.   CRL and its
      News issues have published noteworthy and informa-
      tive reports on advances in academic status, partici-
      patory management, collegial governance, and profes-
      sionalism.   The letter columns are lively and fre-
      quently passionate.
6.   "Campus Unions Take Initiative; Colleges Spur Bargain-
      ing Drive, " American Teacher, 58:1, 14, December
      1973. The terms of the three-year CUNY contract are
      outlined in "College Faculty Wins Contract.   New York
      Sets the Pace, " NEA Reporter, 12:8, December 1973.
      A significant study is Ladd, Everett Carll, Jr., and

Lipset, Seymour Martin. Professors, Unions, and American Higher Education. Prepared for the Carnegie Commission on Higher Education, 1973. Distributed by McGraw-Hill.

7. After completion of this article several useful titles appeared on this, and other topics discussed. The reader may wish to consult: Booz, Allen & Hamilton. Organization and Staffing of the Libraries of Columbia University: A Case Study. Westport, Conn., Redgrave Information Resources Corp., 1973. Also, Gotwals, Joan. "Review of Collective Bargaining Activities in Academic Libraries," ARL Management Supplement, 1, no. 3, 1973.

Interesting examples of library faculty governance structures are the Constitution of the University of Minnesota University Libraries, Twin Cities Campus, adopted and approved in 1972, and the Southern Illinois University--Edwardsville Library Operating Paper, adopted by the Lovejoy Library Faculty August 15, 1969.

8. Krishnamurti, J. "Parenthood and the Young Generation," Krishnamurti Foundation of America Bulletin, 20:5, Winter 1973.

COMPUTER APPLICATIONS
IN ACADEMIC LIBRARY OPERATIONS

Mohammed M. Aman

During the past decade, the computer in higher education has grown from a powerful but infrequently used tool for data analysis in limited areas of research and administration to become an integral part of the normal research, administrative, and instructional activities on most college and university campuses. Computing has become very much a part of the academic scene in spite of its relatively short life.

The computer in American universities is no longer confined to the business operations of the university or to science and technology. Computer applications in social sciences and humanities gained professional attention as new areas of computing, such as text processing, bibliographic organization, and other related activities began to emerge.

As computer facilities began to be available to professors and administrators, librarians began to contemplate the possibility of utilizing computers to help them control the flood of literature caused by the information explosion. Libraries were quick to observe that manual practices were no longer sufficient to cope with the increased numbers of library materials received, the rapid growth in student enrollment and faculty and staff numbers; and the demand for better and more personal methods and procedures of library work. The old manual methods are increasingly inadequate, slow, costly, difficult to use, frustrating, and incapable of providing the kind of service librarians want and users expect.

New and successful experiments in the field of library automation prompted many academic libraries to adopt computer techniques to solve their library problems in such frus-

trating areas as circulation control, ordering and billing
procedures, and more recently for bibliographic control of
information. A general survey of automation activities on
American campuses, published in 1967, reveals that "many
libraries have begun to make use of automated processes
for ordering, acquisition, cataloging and distribution. "[1]

The report of the panel that surveyed the operations
of the Library of Congress, with library automation in mind,
revealed that:

1.   Automation can, within the next decade, aug-
     ment and accelerate the services rendered by
     large research libraries and can have a pro-
     found effect upon their responsiveness to the
     needs of library users.

2.   Automation of bibliographic processing, cata-
     log searching, and document retrieval is tech-
     nically and economically feasible in large re-
     search libraries.

3.   The retrieval of the intellectual content of
     books by automatic methods is not now feasible
     for large collections, but progress in that di-
     rection will be advanced by effective automa-
     tion of cataloging and indexing functions.

4.   Automation will enhance the adaptability of li-
     braries to changes in the national research en-
     vironment and will facilitate the development
     of a national library system.

5.   Automation will reduce the cost-to-performance
     ratio; however, the library should aim at the
     expansion of services rather than the reduction
     of total operating costs. [2]

Cataloging

The first recorded attempts to introduce computers
in academic libraries were in the production of book catalogs. Librarians have always retained their affection for
the book catalog which existed before the invention of the
3 x 5 catalog card. They view the book catalog as having
advantages in terms of its mobility and the user's ability to

browse through its pages, the card catalog as stationary and
cumbersome.

Proponents of the card catalog have maintained that
it has the advantages that the file may be easily updated by
inserting new cards in their proper alphabetic or classified
sequence or by pulling out cards for discarded or lost material.   Computer advocates discovered that updating can
easily be performed by computers, that filing and updating
by machines is faster and more accurate than by humans,
that print-outs can easily be produced if and when the library chooses, that deterioration or destruction of the card
catalog can be avoided by having a master file that can always be safely kept, that special bibliographies can be produced by simply making copies of segments of the catalog,
and that it is more convenient for the user to examine a
book format with many entries per page than it is to use a
card catalog.   The academic environment in higher education also encouraged the adoption of computerized book catalogs because many academic libraries began to have branch
libraries on the regional campuses, and separate undergraduate and graduate departments require not only a catalog of
their own collection but also immediate access to the main
catalog of the university libraries.

As experimentation with computerized cataloging increased and the results became known, librarians and computer specialists began to develop new by-products of computerized cataloging.   Once the cataloging information is
converted into machine language, computer programs can
then be used to update, merge, and arrange the file in alphabetical sequence by author, title, or subject; the entire
catalog or parts of it can be printed out, and manipulation
for subject search becomes possible.   Book labels can also
be produced as a by-product of machine-readable cataloging.

The advent of the MARC (Machine Readable Cataloging)
experiment in 1966 marked the beginning of a line of development which successfully affected computer applications in
library operations, including the standardization of computerized cataloging. [3]   The MARC project proved that the
library profession can periodically produce machine-readable
catalog data for commercial distribution.   As academic librarians rely heavily on the MARC tapes for their cataloging routine, they also enrich their collection by incorporating in their computerized file bibliographies of interest to
their local academic community.   Examples are: the Bibli-

ography of Faculty Publications at the University of Rochester Library and a list of M. A. theses at San Francisco State
College Library.

Technical Services

The impact of the computer has been greatest in the
clerical aspects of library technical services.   A computerized acquisition system searches outstanding orders, handles
ordering, receiving, and notification, and provides statistical information.   The first reported attempt to computerize
an acquisition system was put in operation at the Pennsylvania State University Library in 1964.   In June of the same
year, the University of Michigan Library introduced a computerized acquisitions procedure which was more sophisticated than its predecessor. [4]   Such systems feature a list
of items produced by computer from punch cards in which
order information has been recorded.   Claim notices are
automatically produced for items which remain on order for
longer than the predetermined period.   In addition to creating and maintaining full financial records and compiling selected statistics, the system produces specialized acquisitions lists on demand.

A well-publicized acquisition system is LOLITA (Library On-Line Information and Text Access), used by the
Oregon State University Library.   Another system is BAL-
LOTS (Bibliographic Automation of Large Library Operations
Using a Time-Sharing System), at Stanford University.   It
has as its essential goals the minimizing of manual filing,
the elimination of many clerical tasks now performed by professionals, increasing self-service efficiency, and providing
mechanisms for recording users' suggestions.

The effect of these computer capabilities will be to
reduce drastically errors associated with manual sorting,
typing, and hard transcription; to speed the flow of material
through library processing; to aid book selection by providing fast access to central machine files; and to enable librarians to advise a patron of the exact status of a work
about which he or she is inquiring.

Serials Control

The continuing explosion in serial publications, the

necessity of constantly changing entries, the uneven receipt
of some titles, and the arrearages that result from the increasing number and complexity of serials are a few of the
major problems faced by the serial records administrator.
Most of the functions in handling and internal control of
serials are of a repetitive and clerical nature, thus lending
themselves to automation.

Automated serials systems include four main functions: acquisition, fiscal check-in, display, and public service. The acquisition and fiscal functions usually include
accounting, subscription renewal, subscription records (historical), and at least some aspects of budget control. The
check-in system should achieve at least the following goals:
1) provide efficient, inexpensive, over-all control of serials
receipts; 2) provide rapid check-in; 3) provide efficient and
dependable retrieval of holdings information; and 4) comprise
a simple operating procedure.

Current efforts in computerized serials control systems are aimed at producing the following information:
lists of currently received materials actually in the library;
claim reports for issues that have not been received by a
prescribed time; producing of tags for bindery use; orders
of new subscription lists; financial records showing categories of expenditures by funds, by subject, by language;
and lists of materials not owned by the library that are
needed to fill gaps in holdings. Other by-products that can
be provided by a serials system are: routing slips for
journals circulated among staff members; receipt notices
for staff members who are to be notified when new issues
of serials that are of special interest to them arrive in the
library; lists by branch or departmental library of serials
received within some certain period of time; and lists for
the circulation desks of volumes at the bindery.

The greatest activity in the field of serials automation, however, has occurred in the production of lists of
holdings. The style of the lists is very varied and standardization has not yet begun to appear. The amount of detail
which is given in computer-generated book catalogs differs
appreciably, but the principle underlying all of them is that
the data adequate for the checking of records are also adequate for a bibliographical listing in a book catalog. Once
the bibliographic data on a library's serial holdings are recorded in machine-readable form, continuous updating and
expansion of holdings can be made in almost any combination

of time periods and subjects. [5]

Computerization of serial operations and lists of serial holdings have been tried and implemented in such academic institutions as the Linda Hall Library, the Medical Library Center of New York, M. I. T. , the University of California at Los Angeles Biomedical Library, and the University of California at San Diego, to mention only a few. [6] A published list containing the titles of all periodicals received in all units of the State University of New York was compiled under the direction of Irwin Pizer of the Upstate Medical Center at Syracuse. [7]

New communication devices and data processing equipment offer tremendous potential for tying together the holdings of one library with those of another, within regions or nationally. With the addition of the capability of transmitting facsimile copy through communication links, it becomes possible to consider centralizing, on a regional or national scale, serial holdings of lesser-used materials.

Computerization of serial title and title holdings lists and the production of serial book catalogs in multiple copies have facilitated the provision of ready information to main and branch libraries on serial holdings. Direct user inquiry is feasible, and very soon users may have access to the computerized serial file to determine where a specific issue of a periodical is located and to place their order at the same time.

Circulation

Circulation in any type of library involves a regulated movement of materials from the shelves to borrowers who request them. These materials must be properly recorded and monitored to insure their return. In a manual system, this process has been a constant problem to librarians, especially with the increase in materials published and acquired by the library annually. Through the development of computers and data processing, the efficiency of circulation control has been maintained to some extent.

The new systems proved that it was possible to eliminate tedious manual filing of book cards; they speed up the return of books to the shelves; and they offer the promise of providing, with relative ease, a detailed analytic record

of the use of books, which would be a useful management
tool for several purposes, including the identification of
titles which should be duplicated because of heavy use.

Current computerized circulation projects seek to perform the following functions: produce lists of materials actually in use and identify their location; produce lists of materials in use by individual borrowers; produce overdue notices automatically; collect circulation statistics by borrower,
subject, or any other category of interest to the library.

These functions may be performed by on-line or off-
line.   Academic libraries, even those with limited funds,
have found it feasible to develop automated off-line systems
utilizing their institutions' computer facilities.   Off-line is
the most common approach because basic charging and dis-
charging operations can be performed in an economical
manner.   Input requirements of this system are: student
badges and book punched cards for individual books.
Hollerith-coded badges are embossed with the bearer's name
and a nine-digit student or social security number followed
by a tenth digit indicating the bearer's status, i.e., undergraduate or graduate student, faculty, etc.   The 80-column
card in a pocket in each book bears the book's call number.
In addition to accepting badges and cards through separate
slots for optical reading, the units will accept input data,
instructions, and queries through a numerical keyboard and
function keys.

At the end of the day, transaction information is formatted by the computer and transferred onto a magnetic
tape.   It is then processed by a computer which prepares a
master tape to update the master circulation file with all the
new transactions.   Regularly, the computer will check the
circulation list and prepare data which can be used to print
overdue notices ready for mailing.   Circulation statistics
will be automatically tabulated and made available at the
circulation desk.

In large academic libraries with scattered branches,
data concerning circulation activities are automatically recorded on tape and collected from the local libraries on a
frequent update basis.   Data concerning withdrawals and returns are entered onto this tape on a real-time basis by
circulation personnel using keyboard entries on a console
and prepunched or premarked user cards and book cards.
Success with computerized circulation systems has prompted

many academic librarians to automate the reserve book room
circulation system also.   This was effectively done at the
University of Wisconsin Library.

Reference Services

Reference departments in academic libraries have so
far made little use of technology, with the exception of communication devices.   Few attempts have been made to automate information and document retrieval functions.   One of
the major obstacles to effective computer application is
caused by a technical limitation that prevents the rapid conversion of printed matter into machine-readable form.

Private and non-private publishing organizations and
research centers, such as Chemical Abstracts Service and
the Institute of Scientific Information, are beginning to gene-
rate machine-readable text as a by-product of manuscript
preparation.   As the number of these machine-readable bibliographies, catalogs, texts, indexes, and abstracts increases,
the prospect of establishing an inter-academic information
network connecting libraries becomes more feasible.   The
academic library will then be able to transfer data via communication lines and various dial access systems.   Traditional reference functions will then be handled by man-machine interaction, on interactive, question-answering information systems.   One operational system which has a large
data base and on-line search formulation dialogue capabilities
is the SUNY (State University of New York) Biomedical Communications Network.   A similar system is the Medical
Communications Center at the University of Wisconsin Medical Center, where doctors in the state can dial some 200
brief and up-to-date practices.   The center also offers regularly scheduled telephone-radio conferences on important and
timely topics.

As a by-product of the availability of automated data
bases, libraries in some colleges can also initiate selective
dissemination of information (SDI) programs by developing
profiles of individuals, interests, and technical programs
on campus, and by providing a bi-weekly computer print-out
of selected document accessions received and indexed during
the previous two-week period.   The information contained in
the print-out is the same as for comprehensive searches.

Although the practice of SDI is not new, its applica-

tion in academic libraries has been irregular, informal, and
very limited, depending variously on the memory, willingness,
and free time of the librarian, and contingent on the desire
and ability of the patron to make his or her interest known. [8]

A number of information dissemination services performed by various types of libraries are often labeled as
"current awareness" services.   Some make use of electronic
data processing (EDP) equipment but the majority are carried out manually.   In addition to SDI this current awareness
category subsumes such activities as the routing of periodicals, abstract bulletins, indexes, and digests, and the distribution of various types of new accessions lists.   With the
advent of MARC tapes, dissemination services are becoming
increasingly feasible in college, university, and large public
library systems.   Some MARC-based SDI systems are already operational, at least on a test basis, at Georgia Institute of Technology, which is providing an SDI service to
faculty members based on the PANDEX tape service.

As the time-sharing concept in computer networking
gains wide publicity on college campuses, more and more
academic librarians are utilizing it in their dissemination of
information.   At M. I. T., where project MAC began, Dr.
M. M. Kessler of the M. I. T. Library has had the articles
of a number of physics journals cataloged and inserted in
the memory of the central MAC computer.   Thus a user with
a teleprinter can contact the central computer, call up a
given computer program, insert input data into the computer,
have the data processed, receive the results back at his or
her terminal, and, if he or she wishes, can also query these
stored physics journals for bibliographic references. [9]

With the advent of machine-readable data from local
cataloging, from MARC, and from other centrally produced
tapes, the opportunity exists for producing bibliographies
and lists for student and faculty use and for special activities and programs.   Project SPIRES at Stanford University
was developed to support the research and teaching activities
of the library, faculty, students, and staff, through a generalized automated storage and retrieval system.   According
to the design of this system, each user will be able to define his or her requirements in a way that automatically
tailors the system response to fit his or her individual needs.
The SPIRES system stores bibliographic, scientific, administrative, and other records in machine-readable form.   Collections range from large public files, created from central-

ly produced machine-readable data, to medium-small files,
created from user-generated input (faculty and student files).
The system provides the capability for searching files inter-
actively (on-line), via a computer terminal; on batch basis,
by grouping requests and submitting them on a regular
schedule; and on a standing request basis, in which a search
query is routinely passed against certain files at specific intervals.

Library Cooperation

      Academic library cooperation, thanks to computers,
is spreading fast through the country in the form of library
and information networks.   These networks consist of either
a group of participating libraries or a group of regions.   Information networks are different from library networks in
that an information network usually employs a data base that
a single institution has constructed and to which queries are
put.   Automation of academic library operations by means
of an interinstitutional cooperative--more particularly, a
regional association involving medium sized university li-
braries--has enabled librarians to establish new substantive
and economic goals.   Computerized cooperation has also
contributed to uniformity of library processes.

      The combination of cooperation and the computer
makes possible the fulfillment of library objectives such as
economic viability, sharing of resources, shared cataloging,
and cooperative acquisition, among others.   The combination of computers and other electronic advances such as
transistors, printed circuits, microreduction, reprography,
microwave transmission, facsimile transmission, television
recording, and similar advances have made academic library
networking a reality.

      Cooperative library programs on the regional level
can be exemplified by the New England Library Information
Network (NELINET), which is a regional center for the provision of computer-aided services in New England libraries.
NELINET, through the support of the New England Board of
Higher Education, the Council on Library Resources, and
the U. S. Office of Education, has progressed from an initial
systems analysis of the six New England State University
Libraries to a pilot operation in which five of these libraries
receive customized cataloging products, conventional catalog
cards (with all numbers and overprinted headings), and book

labels.   Additional services now being developed or planned
include acquisitions (searching, order control, processing,
and accounting); accession lists and book form catalog production; circulation and interlibrary loan control; library
management information; and remote data base interrogation. [10]

The Five Associated University Libraries (FAUL) is an
example of a cooperative consortium comprising the SUNY
(State University of New York) units at Binghamton and Buffalo, the University of Rochester, Cornell, and Syracuse University.   It was formed in August of 1967.   The stated purposes of FAUL are to: "Work toward a coordinated acquisitions policies, shared resources, the development of compat-
ible machine systems, provision of easy and rapid communication systems among the membership, the provision of shared
storage facilities, and exploration of other areas of cooperation. "[11]

The Ohio College Library Center (OCLC) at Columbus,
Ohio, was formed on July 6, 1967, to "establish, maintain
and operate a computerized, regional library center to serve
the academic libraries of Ohio (both state and private) and
designed so as to become a part of any national electronic
network for bibliographical communication. "[12]   OCLC con-
templates development and implementation of six subsystems:
1) an on-line union catalog and shared cataloging system;
2) an interlibrary loan communications system; 3) serials
control; 4) technical processing with initial emphasis on acquisitions; 5) remote catalog access for users and circulation control; and 6) user access by subject and title.   The
on-line union catalog and shared cataloging system began to
operate at the end of August 1971.   Forty-eight libraries in
Ohio academic institutions participate in the system, as well
as a sprinkling of libraries in other regional centers.   The
data base consists of MARC II records from the Library of
Congress and OCLC MARC records input by participating institutions. [13]   The entire system, including shared cataloging,
bibliographic information and retrieval, circulation control,
serials control, and technical processing, will be used on
one file, thereby achieving a truly comprehensive system.

The colleges of the State of Maryland are in the process of implementing the Maryland Academic Library Network.   The project is being developed by the MALCAP
(Maryland Academic Libraries Automated Data Processing
Center).   The group has as its goal the creation of a computerized library services and circulation control network

serving the state's universities and colleges. Member libraries will thus have ready access to their respective materials, while centralized cataloging of new books will eliminate repetitive cataloging in each library.

The SUNY (State University of New York) Biomedical
Communication Network was conceived in the fall of 1965 by
a committee of librarians, medical faculty members, and
administrators from the three State University of New York
medical centers. The network was designed originally to tie
the four medical centers of the State University together in
order to amplify their sources and thus provide vastly improved services to the medical community of the participating schools. The network has now evolved into a facility
with connections between Federal, state, and private institutions.

Management

Computers are used, on a very limited scale, in the
decision-making process in academic libraries. Mathematical models and computer simulation techniques are used to
measure physical situations. Research work involving mathematical models and computer simulators has been reported
in progress at Purdue, the University of Chicago, and the
University of California at Los Angeles. The computer
makes it possible to use a model for testing a hypothesis in
compressed time. A director of a college library can exercise his model on the computer, observe the consequences
of his decisions, alter his strategy accordingly, and repeat
the process until he is satisfied with the results. Combined
with intuitive judgment and experience, these techniques can
give the librarian increased confidence in deciding which
course of action to take in the real world.

A computer program was written at Johns Hopkins that
was capable of predicting the self growth of a classified collection. It used a random-number generator to simulate the
pattern of book receipts in the library by class, and another
sub-routine kept track of the number of times various segments of the collection had to be moved to make room for
new materials. By assigning an average weight to each book,
it was also possible to calculate the number of pounds or
tons which had to be lifted by a page to fill the stacks to
capacity. A mathematical model of this type enables a library director to interpret and judge the effects of various

courses of action--such as new construction, large-scale
weeding, or extensive reshelving--long before things reach
the crisis stage![14]

Conclusion

In spite of recent advancements in computerization in
academic libraries, the academic library scene, in general,
relies heavily on manual systems. Applications of the computer to academic library operations are sporadic, and computerization in libraries has also created many problems
which are currently under investigation.[15] Such problems
are caused by: a) lack of well-tested and immediately operational computer programs; b) lack of standardization, which
is a natural outcome of (a); c) the need to develop library
oriented computer hardware; d) the severe shortage of well-
qualified personnel who can combine expertise in both data
processing and librarianship; e) lack of proper training of
academic librarians in the areas of computation and library
data processing; f) reluctance on behalf of library users to
use non-traditional medium of information transfer; g) the
unavailability of accurate figures on the cost of operating
fully- or semi-automated systems.

Computerized library operations, however, will be
implemented in the academic library of the future. It will
also be possible to combine technological elements such as
computer storage, microreduction, and remote transmission
to develop a national or regional research library system
the aim of which will be to place in the hands of every
reader the text he wants instantly and at the least cost.
New and anticipated changes in storage, handling, and publication of texts, as well as a new attitude in the library profession, will make effective library automation a reality.

References

1. Caffrey, John, and Mosmann, Charles. Computer on
     Campuses; a Report to the President on Their Use
     and Management. Washington, American Council on
     Education, 1967, p. 57.
2. King, G. William, ed. Automation and the Library of
     Congress. Washington, D.C., Library of Congress,
     1963.
3. The MARC Pilot Project Final Report. Washington,

D.C., Library of Congress, 1968.
4. Dunlap, Connie. "Automated Acquisitions Procedures
    at the University of Michigan Library," Library Re-
    sources and Technical Services, 11:192-206, Spring
    1967.
5. Allen, Walter C., ed. Serial Publications in Large Li-
    braries. Urbana, Illinois, Graduate School of Library
    Science, 1970, pp. 120-45.
6. Osborn, Andrew. Serial Publications; Their Place and
    Treatment in Libraries. 2nd ed. Chicago, American
    Library Association, 1973, pp. 174-89.
7. The Union List of Serials in the Libraries of the State
    University of New York. Syracuse, N.Y., State Uni-
    versity of New York, Upstate Medical Center, 1966.
8. Studer, William Joseph. "Computer-based Selective
    Dissemination of Information (SDI) Service for Faculty
    Using Library of Congress Machine-Readable Catalog
    (MARC) Records." In Louis Kaplan, ed. Reader in
    Library Services and the Computer. Washington,
    D.C., NCR Microcard Editions, 1971, pp. 101-7.
9. Kessler, M. M. The M.I.T. Technical Information
    Project - I. System Description M.I.T. Report, No-
    vember 2, 1964. Cambridge, Mass., M.I.T. Press,
    1964.
10. Goldstein, Samuel. New England Library Association
    Newsletter, January 1969.
11. Kaser, David. "FAUL: A Consortium Approach to Li-
    brary Automation." In Paul Fasana and Allen Veaner.
    Collaborative Library Systems Development. Cam-
    bridge, Mass., M.I.T. Press, 1971, pp. 106-7.
12. Kilgour, Frederick. "Library Networks." In EDUCOM.
    Proceedings of the EDUCOM Fall Conference, October
    11, 12, 13, 1972. Princeton, N.J., 1973, pp. 38-41.
13. Ibid.
14. Becker, Joseph. "The Future of Library Automation
    and Information Networks." In A. L. A. Library Auto-
    mation State of the Art Review. Chicago, 1969, p. 1.
15. Planning Conference on Information Transfer Experi-
    ments, Woods Hole, Mass., 1965. Carl F. J. Over-
    hage and R. Joyce Harman, ed. Intrex; Report of a
    Planning Conference on Information Transfer Experi-
    ments, September 3, 1965. Cambridge, Mass.,
    M.I.T. Press, 1965.

COORDINATION OF COLLECTION BUILDING
BY ACADEMIC LIBRARIES

Richard C. Quick

Of the many avenues to interlibrary cooperation which initiative and resourcefulness have opened for academic libraries, coordinated collection building is one of the most alluring and, at the same time, most tortuous routes. Known variously as cooperative collection development or shared acquisitions, coordinated collection building is, at the ideal working level, a symbiotic relationship between two or more libraries in which each accepts designated responsibilities to build collection subject strengths of predetermined breadth and depth which will be mutually useful and accessible to their several constituencies. The object has usually been that of reducing needless multi-campus duplication of expensive, lesser-used resources.

The rigor and complexities of the times have demanded that libraries learn to function cooperatively if they are individually to meet all the needs of all users. Much of present day librarianship is predicated upon a sharing of resources and services which far transcends earlier neat concepts of geographic and political boundaries, set clienteles, and self-contained adequacy. In less than a decade coordinated collection building has won gathering favor with academic librarians as a significant area for experimentation within an interconnected range of cooperative undertakings.

The mix of coordinated collection building measures which have so far seemed workable includes such relatively uncomplex expedients as: pre-purchase consultation among consorting libraries when a major and expensive acquisition is contemplated by any member; joint compilation of union lists or catalogs to assist both in the location of specific materials and to enable purchase decisions based upon area availability/non-availability; exchange of catalog card sets

representing major works or sets acquired; or, the clearing-
house approach most recently exemplified at the University
of California at Berkeley, where all University of California
campus libraries and that of Stanford University are invited
to centrally list expensive purchases.   There has been the
cooperative combination of fragmentary sets and transfer of
these to a single repository, and there have been jointly sub-
sidized purchases of expensive series and sets for retention
in one member library.   Such measures have been adopted
singly or in combination.   There are doubtless others.

Considerably more complex and ambitious coordinating
agreements, presently practiced or proposed, begin with development of a written action program detailing a series of
recommended goals usually including: the assessment of collection strengths and weaknesses among participating libraries;
definition of areas of mutual interest; suggested assignment
of collection development responsibilities; assessment of subject weaknesses in the cooperating region and recommendations for assigned collecting responsibilities in desirable new
subject areas; and identification of specialized collections
which may be unique in the cooperating region and which
should be developed on a non-competitive basis.   More sophisticated proposals for coordinated collection building and
resource sharing are apt to include consideration of the desirable concomitants of teletype communication among members, scheduled delivery service, and the central storage or
warehousing of lesser-used materials.   Some planners look
toward a future interface of regional coordinately developed
resources that may assemble into a national network for
comprehensive assigned acquisition and retention.   And there
is some optimism concerning the utilization of consortial
electronic bibliographic data bases in the process of acquisition rationalization, systems for electronic facsimile transmission for speedy user access, and the long-term implications of these for coordinated collection development.   Most
practitioners and commentators would agree that exploitation
of the coordinated collection building aspect of interlibrary
cooperation is still in an early developmental stage, with
some theorists tending to reach for the outer limits of the
cooperative universe while others experiment tentatively on
home ground.

The idea of mutual dependency through shared acquisitions is not new.   It has evolved naturally from the thought
process that conceived and perfected interlibrary loan.   One
early evidence of a linkage between these two cooperative

expedients appears in Fremont Rider's 1943 summary of proposed action for six college libraries of the "Connecticut
Valley Project" which had not only agreed to create a union
catalog of holdings and to develop the full potential of interlibrary loan through daily delivery service, but had also
agreed to "Avoid the unnecessary duplication of little-used
research items already held by one or more member libraries."[1] That the program was not carried through was
attributed by Rider to "a lack of unanimity among the librarians concerning the real worth and workability of the
proposals."[2] In retrospect it would appear also probable
that in the 1940's motivating pressures were not yet sufficiently extreme to induce a joint action requiring some very
difficult collecting compromises on the part of each participant.

       In the 1960's and 1970's a much harsher circumstan-
tial climate has forced the issue of cooperative interaction.
Reacting to economic pressures and service demands of
greater magnitude than ever before, academic librarians have
increasingly understood that exhaustive collections are not
possible to achieve, that full self-sufficiency cannot exist in
any single library, and that even collection adequacy is difficult to maintain in the face of uncertain economic conditions and the runaway production of published knowledge.

       The stimulus to effect agreements for coordinated col-
lection building has been supplied most often, but by no
means always, by academic librarians. The motivating force
has been almost purely economic. Backed into a tight economic corner by a critical rise in book and periodical costs,
acquisitions budgets which have tended to stabilize, increased
user demands, and a bewildering multiplicity of world publishing output, librarians have, with mixed enthusiasm and
reluctance, sought the escape hatch which cooperative action
affords.

       The combined effect of inflation and devaluation upon
increasingly steady-state library acquisitions budgets is sur-
facing with greater frequency as a major concern of college
and university administrators. In his recent report, "Berkeley in a Steady State," Chancellor Bowker discloses that the
library's book budget has increased by 15 percent since
1969-70, but that the budget's purchasing power has de-
creased 33 percent in the same period.[3] Acknowledging that
the library is in a desperate situation, Bowker notes that
"Any possible solution will require effective cooperation and

coordination among several campuses. "[4]

While library purchasing power has been eroded, the vast increase in available published materials has continued unabated, and has become too widely familiar to require extensive definition. An estimate of several years ago, however, retains its shock value and, if firmly based, encapsulates a major problem which can hardly be less serious in 1973:

> More than 2, 000 pages of books, newspapers, or reports come off the worldwide press every sixty seconds.... While the United States is annually producing over 30, 000 new books, titles, or new editions, the world's annual production of books has been estimated as 320, 000 separate titles. These are in addition to 30, 000 newspapers, 70, 000 periodicals, and millions of research reports, not to mention nearly 100, 000 scientific and technical journals being published in more than sixty languages with new journals being born at the rate of two per day. [5]

Other significant factors compelling academic librarians to seek cooperative solutions to a common problem have included: the expansion and diversification of academic programs, requiring user access to expanded and more diverse library resources; increasingly sophisticated library-oriented approaches to learning, noticeable especially in undergraduate instruction; and cross-disciplinary, intense research specialization among both budding and mature scholars. These and similar considerations have had a general effect in mandating that quantitatively and qualitatively superior library resources must be placed at the disposal of a larger, more versatile and, perhaps, more intellectually aggressive generation of library users. And these factors, combining with an advanced rate of publication and an inflated economy, have snowballed into an avalanche of circumstance crushing most remaining pretense to self-sufficiency among individual academic libraries.

While the idea of coordinated collection building has been acceptable in theory for a number of decades, its acceptance in practice has not been easy or especially rapid. For the process leads inevitably to concession and compromise in collecting activities. And, owing to the geographical-logistical problems encountered when shared resources

are located remotely in space and time, there is the disturbing truth that users may no longer have access to some
needed resources upon the moment of demand.

Traditional resistances hindering development of
shared acquisitions programs are frequently noted in the recent literature of coordinated collection building.   Robert
Balliot finds that "Cooperation between and among academic
libraries is more studied than practiced and more praised
than analyzed."[6]   Faye Simkin cautions that "Any scheme of
cooperative acquisitions must be carried out with great tact.
All librarians pride themselves on their selection policies
and the right to determine their own needs."[7]   Donald Hendricks suggests that "librarians are so acquisitive and faculty members so insistant on campus availability that progress
is slow on cooperative acquisitions."[8]   Robert Houze says,
"An on-going program of library cooperation is dependent
largely on the attitude and dedication of the librarians themselves, and not altogether on funding or lack of funding, administrative support or indifference, or other such reasons."[9]
In his recent post-mortem commentary, "The Death of the
Farmington Plan," Hendrik Edelman found that, among other
deteriorating influences, "Libraries never fully understood
the extent of their commitments."[10]   Again, on the demise
of the Latin American Cooperative Acquisitions Program
(LACAP), Edelman remarks that "There are many different
reasons for LACAP's death, some of which find their origin
in attitudes of librarians."[11]   Hendricks holds that, "Although the literature speaks highly of the attractive economics
of such arrangements, few accounts are able to document
much success in the implementation of a cooperative acquisitions program."[12]   In her Guidelines For Library Cooperation, Ruth Patrick concluded that few library consortia,
among those studied, were involved in the cooperative development of resources, and that consortia would seem to
favor instead commitments requiring less investment and
compromise and which yield more discernible benefits.[13]
Although human and systemic failures have been demonstrated
in some past attempts at coordinated collection building,
most commentators would probably agree with Hendricks that,
"Despite the discouraging lack of significant progress noted
in the literature, this concept still seems to be of promise
and one that justifies continual effort."[14]

Most often, coordinated collection building plans at
the "neighborhood" or limited region level have aimed at
achieving the most elementally obvious benefit for partici-

pants: that of avoiding costly duplication of expensive lesser-
used materials while at the same time assuring that these
will be readily available somewhere within the inclusive geographic area.

Spatial relationships of participating libraries have
played a significant role in delimiting the inclusive area in
which programs for coordinated and shared acquisitions may
effectively function.   Research materials retained in one library should be enabled to reach the user at another library
rapidly by conventional surface transportation or, conversely,
the user should be able to travel readily and inexpensively to
the desired materials.   Lapsed time during the request/de-
livery turnaround period is always an important consideration
where independent faculty research is concerned, and may be
critical in the case of students locked into a tight academic
year schedule or for faculty engaging in sponsored research
with deadlines to meet.   The Council of Research and Academic Libraries (CORAL), San Antonio, established in 1966,
determined early that membership should not extend beyond
the distance to which the farthest flung of 12 original participating libraries were removed from San Antonio; a matter
of 50 miles at most.

However, there may be a tendency for localized consortia to "creep" geographically and to include adjacent libraries when the opportunities for mutual benefit seem good.
Connecticut Valley Libraries (CONVAL), originally including
Amherst, Smith, Trinity, and Wesleyan as members, agreed
in 1967 to

> extend the topographic province of the Connecticut
> River Valley westward to the Berkshires and east-
> ward to the Atlantic; although dispersed geograph-
> ically, the individual and collective wealth of the
> bibliographic resources and cooperative services
> and efforts in which the libraries participate war-
> rant a potential for development that overrules the
> obvious limitations imposed by distance. [15]

And so the libraries of Bowdoin, Dartmouth and Williams
became participants.

While neighborhood and limited regional arrangements
for academic library cooperation have tended to emphasize
cooperative acquisitions and resource sharing at the local
level, the history of coordinated collection building among

academic and research libraries includes also a continuing
undercurrent of concern for the development of a comprehensive national resource. This was evident in the goals of
the Farmington Plan in the late 1940's, and was perpetuated
in the later Latin American Cooperative Acquisitions Plan
and in the so-called Public Law 480 Plan. In all of these
the objective was to secure important foreign publications on
a regular basis, depositing them in participating academic
and research libraries to insure that at least one copy of
each selected publication would be available for research
use in the United States. Concern for the ultimate development of a comprehensive national resource--as opposed to
strictly local and regional arrangements for inclusiveness
and economy--was expressed in Edelman's action program
produced in 1969 for the New York Metropolitan Reference
and Research Library Agency, Inc. (METRO) SHARES project. Among other considerations Edelman recommended
the cooperative purchase of material "to be considered essential for the region or the nation, "[16] and advised that
METRO "should study the necessity of support for specific
subject collections in the METRO region, " seeking outside
funding with emphasis "on those collections which are to be
considered of vital regional or national interest and for which
the burden of upkeep and servicing becomes too much for the
responsible institution. "[17]   Marion Wilden-Hart, in her commissioned study for the Five Associated University Libraries
(FAUL) in New York State, cautions that this group "should
not develop its own networks alone, even in areas of ex-
ceptional interest and competance, but should link itself to
the national and government sponsored organizations by every
means available, " for, "It seems fairly certain that much of
the basic intellectual work of bibliographic control and analysis of research materials will increasingly be generated by
a national network of documentation centers. "[18]

   In summarizing the findings of his 1970 study for
CONVAL, Balliot stresses CONVAL's potential for network
interaction with numerous other consortia:

> The basic conclusions are that the potential exists
> for significant cooperation among the CONVAL li-
> braries because of the quality of their bibliographic
> resources, and that such a network of independent
> college libraries would form a strong and vital
> link with other similar institutions, including the
> state universities, colleges and state libraries,
> and with regional and national cooperatives. [19]

It is evident in Simkin's 1970 evaluation of SHARES'
ongoing acquisition projects that involvement on a national
scale may also be advisable in terms of more adequate funding:

> The prospect of financial aid on the federal level
> looks bleak when sought for the enrichment of
> local resources. METRO's cooperation with exist-
> ing national networks is essential for any federal
> backing. [20]

That major academic libraries are actively exploring
toward a national system of cooperative acquisitions programs is seen in a recently reported project of the University of California at Berkeley's library to attempt calculation
of the growth of library collections by Library of Congress
classes for as many as 30 large research libraries during
a trial year. It is anticipated that if the project can be continued on a national scale in years to come, it can be shown
annually "where library collections are growing and could
provide data on which to base wide-ranging cooperative acquisitions policies and programs."[21]

While some academic consortia do--and should--antici-
pate their broader involvement in systems or networks which
promise some degree of universal coordinated collection
building and sharing, it seems clear from recent tradition
and current practice that achievement of this goal will depend in large measure upon solid grassroots development.
Functional vitality in local programs and well-defined regional agreements must precede consolidation into larger networks. And, at the local and limited regional level, development proceeds slowly.

Essential to the launching of a program for coordinated acquisitions is the requirement that all parties agree
to agree. In the past, more often than not, agreement was
apt to result from casual discussion of mutual problems
among neighboring library administrators who might then
proceed to form loose agreements committing their libraries
(and parent institutions) to designated collecting responsibilities within an initially limited subject area. With one sharing objective successfully realized, the consorting libraries
might then move on to one or more additional subject areas
for development, building shared resource strength piecemeal in response to suddenly recognized needs, or to budgetary or other stresses.

An early experiment by the libraries of the University of Florida and Florida State University was simplicity itself, demonstrating a "limited objective," piecemeal approach which may still be the most practical and immediately beneficial for small groups of small academic libraries whose parent institutions exhibit similarities in philosophy, instructional goals, and curriculum.   Orwin Rush[22] recounts that in the collection area of 19th century English literature, both Florida libraries were agreed on their need to individually hold complete files of certain periodicals.   Comparing notes, they identified 42 additional periodical backfiles comprising a desirable backup resource not held by either library and with not enough foreseen frequency of use to warrant duplication on both campuses.   The two university libraries then divided responsibility for acquisition of the backfiles.

The limited objective approach to coordinated collection building, especially when it involves acquisition of retrospective files, appears to offer a distinct advantage in that it isolates and then assures the addition and availability of specified titles, but purchases are terminal and participants are not committed to continuing subscription or developmental costs.   Also, little preliminary study or assessment would appear to be undertaken in such cases; the cooperating libraries almost intuitively recognize resource gaps and together set about filling them at something like half the cost to each library in purchase funds, staff time, and storage space.   Simple and effective, limited objective shared acquisitions arrangements between pairs or very small groups of neighboring academic libraries have probably been more widespread and have existed longer in time than has been generally recognized.

In the mid-1960's the academic libraries of CORAL began to explore what might be called an "expanded objective" approach to coordinated collection building, with a larger number of participants and a greater fragmentation of collecting responsibilities.   The nine college and university libraries "agreed to direct their acquisitions in such a way as not to overlap unnecessarily with one another."[23] Acting within this general framework of cooperative agreement, the libraries distinguished 33 areas of subject concentration for collection development, not necessarily focusing upon known strengths or weaknesses in participants' collections, but rather upon fields where parent institutions were known to concentrate teaching and research efforts.

The proposed effect would be to enable development of collection strengths in support of established institutional teaching and research strengths while relieving individual libraries
of the financial burden of acquiring other excessively expensive and less frequently used materials in subject areas of
lesser curriculum emphasis.   Initially the consorting libraries
depended to a considerable degree upon funding through basic,
supplemental, and special purpose grants under the Higher
Education Act, Title II-A, receiving more than $260,000
from this source in 1968.   While Federal funding has since
declined, the CORAL academic libraries have continued to
discharge their assigned collecting responsibilities.   The libraries communicated by exchanging acquisitions lists, or
submitting titles monthly to the Notable Acquisitions Clear-
inghouse for acquisitions costing $50 or more.

As exemplified by the CORAL libraries, the expanded
objective approach to coordinated collection development appears to be a successful regional experiment.   Participating
libraries are formally associated within a climate of general
cooperative agreement through membership in their Council
of Research and Academic Libraries and are committed
under its by-laws to a variety of interacting cooperative
goals.   Their coordinating agreement--in contrast to a
limited objective agreement--is of a continuing and more
binding nature.   Initial decisions concerning subject responsibility, while not absolutely binding, become less easily re-
versible with the passage of time as collection strengths
grow.   So long as the parent institutions will rationalize
curricula in consideration of concentrated collection strengths
in their individual libraries, the corporate future should remain secure.   However, an institution's decision to de-emph-
asize or discontinue a program of teaching or research concentration, with consequent curtailment or discontinuance of
its library's special collecting responsibility, could mean
that others with some degree of dependency upon it would
either have to reassign collecting responsibility, revert to
individually acquiring materials, or go more frequently outside the cooperating region for needed materials.

In the 1970's, planning and early action stages for
groups such as CONVAL, SHARES, and FAUL have seemed
to signal a third generation approach to coordinated collection building, and transition to an "extended objective" outlook.   Like the libraries in the earlier CORAL, members
in these three are confederated and jointly committed to exploring a number of means for cooperative interaction; they

have agreed to agree. Each consortium has recognized cooperative acquisitions as one component in a logical sequence
of sharing activities, and, toward this end, each has undertaken a feasibility study developing recommended objectives.
While they represent somewhat different constituencies,
Balliot (CONVAL), Edelman (SHARES), and Wilden-Hart
(FAUL) have sorted out some understandings and goals
which, taken together, suggest several trends in thought concerning coordinated collection building.

As has been noted, the three consortia commonly
take an "extended objective" view of resource building and
resource sharing, both among themselves and in interaction
with other consortia. There is an understanding that, just
as neighboring libraries may realize strength and economy
in the coordination of their collection activities, so may
their joint economy and sufficiency be additionally strengthened as they develop their specialized local and regional
resources in light of what may or may not be already accessible through their group liaison with other consortia in
the larger community of regional or national cooperating
networks. One of Wilden-Hart's many imperatives is that
"FAUL must determine the many roles it can play as a consortium and potential national resource, and formulate objectives for liaison with all outside bodies."[24]

There is a tendency in thought, then, to see an ultimate national system, pyramidal in form, with localized
consortia such as CORAL or SHARES as base blocks with
members mutually dependent for retention and rapid availability of some expensive less frequently used library materials, and depending for more comprehensive, specialized
collections upon access to these where they are developed
within such regional groups as FAUL. In a national system
the pyramid apex might comprise the sum of highly specialized, exhaustive subject collections developed according to
a nationally coordinated scheme aiming at complete coverage.
In looking toward a future interdependency in resource acquisition and resource sharing, consortia are faced with a
major problem in sorting out those resources or blocks of
resources which should be present locally, and those which
need not be locally present so long as they are accessible
somewhere. Here, decisions on what not to collect may be
as important as decisions on what to collect. This is but
one reason for the National Commission on Libraries and
Information Science's recent concern that library cooperation be coordinated now. Wilden-Hart concludes her study

for FAUL with:

> We are led toward national and subject based sys-
> tems, not by the attractiveness of centralization
> but by quantitative and qualitative changes in our
> media. The continuing increase of output of pub-
> lications, the complexity of languages, the varieties
> of interdisciplinary needs, the multiplicity of origi-
> nating bodies and the cost increase in all library
> activities leave us with an urgency for increased
> and better structured cooperation. [25]

Another tendency evident in recent feasibility studies
toward coordinated collection building is to see that, as Balliot notes, "Academic libraries are not autonomous, and can
achieve only limited success in cooperation if working in
relative isolation of the central authority of their institutions."[26] His basic recommendation is that

> CONVAL librarians participate actively in the plan-
> ning and deliberative sessions of the Fourteen Col-
> lege Program, the Pentagonal Colleges, the Four
> College Program, and other such groups in which
> one or more CONVAL is involved, and that the in-
> dividual librarians participate to a greater degree
> in their local administrative and educational plan-
> ning. [27]

Edelman, for SHARES, sees that "The development of a
written acquisitions policy, jointly produced by library staff,
faculty and college administration is considered indispens-
able."[28] Wilden-Hart obviously finds that library acquisition
policies must accurately reflect the needs of the institution
or institutions served, and agrees with Fussler that such
policies can be instrumental in the institution-wide planning
process:

> Acquisition policy statements, whether of single li-
> braries or consortiums, are of fundamental im-
> portance for any planned expenditure and evalua-
> tion of performance. Policy statements can also
> 'focus attention of the faculty and the university
> upon the need for basic decisions of the institution,
> i.e., what can the institution do, what should it
> not attempt, and what are the implications of
> changes in scope or direction. '[29]

In its 1973 report, the Advisory Committee on Planning for the Academic Libraries of New York State concurs with Balliot and others in finding that the objectives of consortia and their parent institutions are not separable:

> The uniform experience of libraries everywhere and in all ages has been that if they attempt to rationalize their collecting efforts cooperatively before, rather than after, interinstitutional rationalization of curricula, they are likely to be ineffective. This is true because librarians determine only in a very superficial sense what goes into their collections. [30]

In their feasibility studies CONVAL, SHARES, and FAUL would seem to confirm an older precept that consortiums should attempt to build resources non-competitively upon existing strengths, while defining subject areas in need of development. Prior to the writing of its action program CONVAL had undertaken a quantitative count of its members' collections, a qualitative analysis of special or unique holdings, and an assay of subjects felt to be not adequately represented in the collections. Through the survey it was established that the collections exhibited considerable homogeneity, but were also quite diverse in special and unique holdings. Balliot found that the major non-duplicating interest of consortium members was "probably in the curriculum related subject areas,"[31] but sensed that little could be accomplished in the way of assigned collecting responsibility until there was some coordination of academic and library planning. Analysis of the survey data did reveal some existing strengths and some inadequately developed peripheral subject areas, and it was recommended that:

> Trinity collect exhaustively in the popular American fiction genres including science fiction, detective stories, and 'Western' stories; that Wesleyan collect exhaustively in current American literature, especially during the period of 1950 to the present, and including the underground press publications and all other materials of possible research interest; that Trinity begin a comprehensive collection of folk music recordings and that Williams assume the responsibility for collecting related works on musicology and biography. [32]

Balliot also recommended relocation of some collec-

tions and judicious weeding in all collections to both con-
serve space and combine scattered subject weaknesses into
useful centralized collection strengths. These expedients,
however, were considered so closely related to the requirement that there should be a general rationalization of academic and library planning among the parent institutions that
they would need to be deferred until such intra-institutional
coordination was effected.

For FAUL Wilden-Hart sees that "The only possible
way to meet the resource needs of research is to build when
possible on existing research resources and to link these resources to each other by an extensive and well-ordered program of cooperation."[33] Unfortunately, it was not the purpose of her report to detail a technique for comparative
identification of FAUL's existing research resources. Edelman notes in a general way some area collections in the
fields of science and technology in need of improvement, and
recommends that "a detailed survey of the present holdings
in the humanities and social sciences be done to evaluate the
quality and accessibility of the already available collections
and to make recommendations for support."[34]

Progress toward viable systems of coordinated collection building has been slow, and there remains a significant gulf between what is envisioned and what, in fact, may
be accomplished. Of the 125 academic consortia identified
and studied by Carlos Cuadra and Ruth Patrick, only 28
were actually engaged in some form of assigned subject
specilization in acquisitions; 33 other groups were planning
or developing this activity. Typically, coordinated acquisitions is only one aspect of consortial activity and may well
be assigned a lower priority than some quick-yield projects
such as union lists and catalogs, open access, and the perfection of delivery systems. FAUL, which has had Wilden-
Hart's study and ambitious recommendations in hand and
under consideration since late 1970, has not moved toward
implementation except for the recent appointment of a committee of acquisitions librarians to select a methodology for
establishing comparative strengths in collections among the
participants. The implications of Wilden-Hart's far-seeing
and far-reaching action recommendations may be too removed from immediate needs. Her recommended base
studies of users and user patterns, the nature of ongoing
research, the detailed codification of a spectrum of acquisitions objectives, and a rich assortment of feedback mechanisms and other desirable base data may be much beyond

the present capabilities of five busy university libraries
whose limited staffs and resources must perforce be closely
committed to the exigencies of the present. It has recently
been considered with some seriousness by the five libraries
that, given the existing broad disproportion between monies
expended for salaries and those spent to acquire library materials, they might better review individual staffing needs
and possible joint staff utilization with an eye to reducing
staff numbers and, in effect, turn "people" money into book
money.

This trend of thought is paralleled in the thinking of
the Advisory Committee on Planning for the Academic Libraries of New York State, which views library labor sharing as an important cooperative component which can enable
effective resource sharing:

> ... a major future for library sharing in the next
> decade will be in the area of labor sharing--labor
> sharing in cataloging, in developing lists of hold-
> ings both of books and serials, in designing and
> operating common larger systems wherein econo-
> mies of scale can inhere, and in interlibrary com-
> munications. Clearly there is a large core of
> such activity which is common to all libraries and
> where its accomplishment once should suffice for
> all. [35]

Most academic consortia are very recent corporate
ventures. Cuadra and Patrick found that of 125 such organizations studied, 96 had been established in the period 1966-
70. [36] The relatively few groups with operating programs for
coordinated acquisitions are still too young and too limited
in experience to produce a thoroughgoing body of evaluative
literature to guide the profession. Lacking such assessment,
it seems too early to read future trends with any great certainty, although there is some evidence of tendencies in
thought toward identified, separable working arrangements
which naturally sort and group participant institutions in
closest liaison according to known mutual similarities in
purpose and clientele; such are the FAUL libraries. Thus,
academic libraries in New York State's South Central Research Library Council, in a recent Statement of Policy on
Coordinated Acquisitions, endorse the need to achieve collection coordination while cautioning, "it is a function which
may not be feasible or one which may be implemented through
a variety of programs. "[37] The statement holds that:

It must be recognized that in the South Central Research Library Council and possibly in other Coun-
cils, the variation in the sizes of the collections
and in curriculum offerings as well as geographic
scattering of the academic institutions, are factors
which create problems in designing a program of
coordinating acquisitions. It is not feasible for
instance, for the Cornell University Libraries to
coordinate an acquisition program with two year
community colleges and/or four year undergraduate institutions. They might better work out a
deal with Harvard, Yale, New York Public Library,
etc. On the other hand, it is feasible for Alfred
Agricultural and Technical College and Delhi Agricultural and Technical College to work out a program of coordinated purchasing because of the similarity of their programs. It is also possible for
them to coordinate their policies with contiguous
libraries in their geographic area. In some instances, this geographic area might be designated
as one outside the boundaries of South Central.
Thus Delhi might want to extend its program to
Cobleskill. What is being said, in effect, is that
it might be more feasible for two or three institutions which have common interests to work out a
program of coordinated acquisitions within the
Council, rather than for a program to be worked
out for twenty or more institutions. [38]

That rationalization of collecting responsibilities among
cooperating libraries must also depend upon rationalization
of academic programs among parent institutions is a major
consideration of a thoughtful segment of the Report of the
Advisory Committee on Planning for the Academic Libraries
of New York State. In a deliberate consideration of cooperative acquisitions the committee recognizes that:

Some economies can doubtless be effected through
cooperative collection development policies, but as
pointed out by the Regents themselves in Education
Beyond High School, to be fully meaningful such
cooperative collection policies will have to await
interinstitutional rationalization of academic programs, and that may yet be some time away. [39]

The report acknowledges that libraries have often been forced
by their local circumstances to duplicate expensive resources

and services, and implies that this will probably continue
to be the case. The report concludes that "There doubtless
are ways in which cooperative collection development can aid
the academic libraries of New York State, even though to a
limited degree. "40

        One factor which may serve to influence academic
libraries, especially those of small to medium sized colleges,
to prefer local neighborhood associations is the lingering
danger that expansion of a cooperative acquisitions system
may result in members channeling funds equalling or exceed-
ing foreseen savings into added administrative and technological costs, even while sacrificing immediate availability of
materials to their users.   This seems to be illustrated in
the recent brief history of the Periodical Bank of the Associated Colleges of the Midwest.   Established in 1969 to pool
and store periodical resources of member libraries, the
Periodical Bank was to minimize the number of periodical
subscriptions maintained by members and to reduce dependency of these undergraduate institutions upon interlibrary
loan from large university libraries.   Participating libraries
were to transfer up to 15 percent of their periodical collections, sending $50,000 worth of materials to the bank.
Lehman, in 1969, noted the "irreversible nature of this venture. "41   In 1972 Beloit College announced its intended withdrawal from the project after evaluation by a faculty/student
committee concluded that "too few students and faculty were
making use of the bank's services to give grounds for its
annual cost to the college--over $9,000. "42   It was argued
that funds saved by Beloit in withdrawing from the project
would, if added to the library budget, enable the addition of
300 subscriptions to its own holdings.   At the same time,
it was reported that a majority of other participants were
finding the bank too expensive.

        The ACM Periodical Bank experiment may represent
an attempt to accomplish too much, too fast.   Certainly,
the reactionary reflex of one participant's faculty and students in suggesting the resumption of 300 periodical subscriptions should alert academic librarians to the near futility
which may inhere in a cooperative agreement which requires
remote location and administration of significant blocks of
materials.

        An overview of an area of academic library coopera-
tion which is so patently emergent as coordinated collection
building, and so without uniform structure in practice, is

necessarily superficial and selective. A "how to do it" manual has yet to be written, although some groups through
their preliminary studies and early experience have already
contributed toward that end. All that has appeared possible
up to this point is to note trends and tendencies, both in
planning and implementation, among a few isolated consortia
of the recent past.

Some academic consortia have obviously derived some
satisfaction and real benefit from programs of shared acquisitions. At the same time, there are planning groups not
overly sanguine about the future of such arrangements.
While a national system or systems for the coordination of
specialized research collection development may finally benefit large research libraries and their very specialized clienteles immeasurably, there is really little in it for thousands
of four-year college libraries and their users. And these
are the very ones so considerably in need of economic and
other reliefs through day-to-day sharing of collections and
collecting responsibilities in subject areas where expensive
resources can be identified as lesser-used but of peripheral
importance to their similar curriculums and instructional
goals.

The development of electronic bibliographic data bases,
reflecting fully or in part the collections of participating libraries, can provide a basis for pre-purchase searching and
acquisition rationalization for clusters of geographically adjacent libraries with or without a consortial agreement. But,
for a majority of libraries both great and small, this lies
in the undetermined future. Facsimile transmission of library materials holds much promise as an enabling device
in coordinated collection building, but remains too expensive
in operation for most libraries and is unlikely to benefit
small to medium sized academic libraries in this decade.
Until such time as a general application of developed technology is possible, it would appear that the greatest benefit
for the greatest number of students and faculty will derive
from intimate collecting and sharing arrangements at the
neighborhood and limited regional level.

It has been said that there are no real problems--
just challenges and opportunities. As a new dimension in
academic library service, coordinated collection building is
one component in an interconnected range of sharing activities which offers a surfeit of both.

References

1. Rider, A. Fremont. "Real Cooperative Cataloging--The
    Concrete Approach, " Library Quarterly, 13:99-112,
    April 1943.
2. Balliot, Robert L. A Program for the Cooperative Ac-
    quisition and Use of Library Materials of Seven New
    England Liberal Arts Colleges (CONVAL) Based on an
    Analysis of Their Collections. (ED 047 711). Cullow-
    hee, N. C. , Western Carolina College, 1970, p. 7.
3. Bowker, Albert H. Berkeley in a Steady State: A Re-
    port to The Board of Regents of the University of
    California. Berkeley, September 21, 1973, p. 60.
4. Ibid. , p. 62.
5. Lehman, James O. "Cooperation Among Small Aca-
    demic Libraries, " College & Research Libraries,
    30:493, November 1969. Lehman cites this estimate
    from: Lorenz, James G. "The Communication Net-
    work: The Academic Library and the Dissemination
    of Knowledge, " Dedication of the University Library,
    Bowling Green, Ohio, Bowling Green University,
    1967, p. 19.
6. Balliot, op. cit. , p. 8.
7. Simkin, Faye. Cooperative Resources Development; A
    Report on a Shared Acquisitions and Retention System
    for METRO Libraries. (ED 039 903). New York,
    New York Metropolitan Reference and Research Li-
    brary Agency, Inc. , 1970, p. 28.
8. Hendricks, Donald D. "Interuniversity Council Coopera-
    tive Acquisitions of Journals, " Texas Library Journal,
    47:269, November 1971.
9. Houze, Robert A. "The Council of Research and Aca-
    demic Libraries, San Antonio, Texas, " Texas Library
    Journal, 47:263, November 1971.
10. Edelman, Hendrik. "The Death of the Farmington
    Plan, " Library Journal, 98:1252, April 15, 1973.
11. Ibid. , p. 1251.
12. Hendricks, op. cit. , p. 269.
13. Patrick, Ruth J. Guidelines for Library Cooperation:
    Development of Academic Library Consortia. Santa
    Monica, System Development Corporation, 1972.
14. Hendricks, op. cit. , p. 269.
15. Balliot, op. cit. , p. 8.
16. Edelman, Hendrik. Shared Acquisitions and Retention
    System (SHARES) for the New York Metropolitan
    Area; A Proposal for Cooperation Among METRO
    Libraries. (ED 039 906). New York, New York

Metropolitan Reference and Research Library Agency,
Inc., 1969, pp. 13-14.

17. Ibid., p. ii.
18. Wilden-Hart, Marion. Cooperative Resource Develop-
     ment in the Five Associated University Libraries; A
     Study With Recommendations. (ED 049 768). Syra-
     cuse, Five Associated University Libraries, 1970,
     p. 2.
19. Balliot, op. cit., p. 68.
20. Simkin, op. cit., p. 28.
21. "Berkeley Acquisitions Study: Toward a National Plan?,"
     Library Journal, 98:1756, June 1, 1973.
22. Rush, Orwin. "Library Cooperation in the Florida
     State University Libraries--The Last Decade and the
     Next," Florida Libraries, 19:168-75, December 1968.
23. Houze, Robert A. "CORAL; San Antonio's Success
     Story in Library Cooperation," Texas Library Journal,
     44:185, Winter 1968.
24. Wilden-Hart, op. cit., p. 8.
25. Ibid., p. 58.
26. Balliot, op. cit., p. 9.
27. Ibid., pp. 69-70.
28. Edelman, op. cit., 1969, p. 8.
29. Wilden-Hart, op. cit., p. 18. Includes quotation from:
     Fussler, Herman H. "Acquisition Policy in the
     Larger University Library," College & Research Li-
     braries, 14:366, October 1953.
30. Report of the Advisory Committee on Planning for the
     Academic Libraries of New York State. Albany, The
     University of the State of New York, The State Educa-
     tion Department, 1973, p. 6.
31. Balliot, op. cit., p. 71.
32. Ibid., pp. 71-72.
33. Wilden-Hart, op. cit., p. 57.
34. Edelman, op. cit., 1969, p. 10.
35. Report of the Advisory..., p. 8.
36. Cuadra, Carlos A., and Patrick, Ruth J. "Survey of
     Academic Library Consortia in the U. S.," College &
     Research Libraries, 33:271-83, July 1972.
37. South Central Research Library Council. Minutes [of
     the] Development of Collections Committee Subcom-
     mittee on Coordinating Acquisitions. SUNY Agricul-
     tural and Technical College at Delhi, Delhi, N. Y.,
     May 9, 1972, p. 2.
38. Ibid., pp. 2-3.
39. Report of the Advisory..., p. 6.
40. Ibid., p. 6.

41. Lehman, op. cit., p. 496.
42. "ACM Periodical Bank Hit With Waning Support," Li-
     brary Journal, 97:1762, May 15, 1972.

ALTERNATIVE WAYS TO MEET USER NEEDS

R. Dean Galloway and Zoia Horn

      Libraries have long held a reputation for standardized ways of operating. Many of the economies and much of the progress of libraries have resulted from standardized equipment, tools, and procedures that have ensured interchangeability of staff as well as equipment. This standardization has been the pride of many well-organized members of the profession.

      One has only to look at the microform situation to realize the need for standardization in libraries. The great variety of microform publications and the equipment needed to read them and to print them introduces chaos into the otherwise good order of libraries. Yet, in addition to the need for standardization there is also a need to maintain a flexibility of attitude so that alternative ways may be introduced whenever it is appropriate to do so.

      It makes no sense to use a standardized or traditional way of providing services to users when some non-standard way will provide better. We should try to discover user needs and design appropriate ways to meet them whenever they occur. The traditional ways must, of course, be considered because they have proven to be efficient and adequate for most situations. Change should not be made for the sake of change but to meet specific needs. So we must first discover the needs of our students and faculty.

Discovering User Needs

      The techniques of discovering user needs in academic libraries are not highly developed, nor are they often used. The attitude of most academic librarians on this matter is that those needs are already known or, worse yet, that the

librarians know what the users <u>ought</u> to need.   Services are
provided for needs that are seldom examined in any systematic or rigorous way.

An examination of the standard texts on library administration reveals little, if anything, on discovering user needs,
and what exists is found under the heading of public relations.   Many of the techniques of public relations, such as
bulletin boards, student library committees, and other forms
of communications, are discussed as ways to provide information about the library rather than to gather information
about user needs. [1, 2, 3, 4, 5]

User needs in an academic library express themselves
in many ways.   No single technique or instrument will serve
to discover them.   The traditional way of keeping alert to
student and faculty requests at the reference desk and the
circulation desk, unfortunately, only discovers the needs of
those users who come to the library and have the courage to
state their needs openly to the reference librarian.   This is
a useful source of information, but it is very limited.

Faculty members are more vocal than students about
their library needs and are consequently better served, but
even faculty members do lots of griping to other faculty
members and to students about the inadequacies of the library services.   This is especially true if they have been
rebuffed by an insensitive librarian at some time.   It is essential to maintain a staff attitude of helpfulness and sympa-
thetic interest at all times so that user needs will be brought
to the library instead of grumbled to others who cannot meet
those needs.

Fay Blake has expressed the attitude that is required
to determine user needs:

> Most of all, perhaps, we have to learn how to be-
> come human beings.   We have to come away from
> the desks we barricade ourselves behind and mix
> it up with students and faculty.   We have to see
> them not only as library users but as people.   We
> have to resist becoming numbers or dossiers in
> an Army or FBI or university file.   We have to
> become convinced that everyone can help us or-
> ganize good and useful libraries--if we listen to
> what they have to tell us.   We have to recognize
> that the most important thing about a library is

> not how it's organized but why it exists and that
> it exists to put people in touch with each other.
> The only reason we collect books in a library is
> that a book is one way--only one way--in which
> people can talk to each other, and we have to look
> for ways, many ways, in which we can help people
> communicate with each other. [6]

If we approach the whole problem of communications with
this attitude, we will use a variety of techniques to ask questions, to invite responses and, most of all, to listen.

The Moffitt Undergraduate Library at the University
of California at Berkeley has a suggestion box in the library
which elicits valuable suggestions for improving library services.   Each suggestion is carefully considered and answered.
The suggestion with its answer is posted on the bulletin
board near the suggestion box.   George Jenks describes the
technique as it works at Bucknell. [7] The wit as well as the
insight in the communication provides interesting reading as
well as useful suggestions.

Questionnaires have been used to obtain student opinion about various library practices, study facilities, and
user behavior, but most of these questionnaires are limited
to the students who come to the library.   Unfortunately,
many students do not come to the library, and their needs
are therefore never discovered unless the questionnaire is
distributed more widely.   John Lubans used a questionnaire
technique to discover the needs of non-users at Rensselaer
Polytechnic Institute.   Though his results were not particularly productive and the effort expended was considerable,
the technique appears to be workable. [8]

Student library committees and student representatives
on faculty library committees sometimes offer useful insights
into student needs.   Oakland University in Rochester, Michigan, has provided an effective example of a functioning student library committee. [9] The chief difficulty with this technique is that the students who serve on these committees are
already favorably inclined toward traditional library practices.   If there is a way to get representation on these committees from groups who do not use the library, then the
results may be more useful.

Probably the most useful technique for discovering
user needs is to have library staff members involved in stu-

dent and faculty activities.   By getting acquainted with students, staff members can learn their interests and their
needs.   By attending classes they can learn how poorly students are served by the reserve book room.   By attending
meetings of students they can hear the complaints that would
never get to the library.   Though this is the most useful
technique it is also the most demanding in time, energy,
and sometimes patience.   To engage in these activities requires a high commitment to the importance of meeting the
needs of potential library users.

Robert S. Taylor's idea that librarians should spend
half their time outside the library building may seem excessive, but whatever the percentage of time, the librarians
should be out there listening.[10]

Responding to Needs

After discovering needs it is important to communicate immediately with those who have expressed them, even
though the ways to meet those needs may not yet have been
designed.   Assure them that an effort will be made to serve
them and invite further discussions to learn more specifically
what is needed!   It is essential that an honest effort be made
to serve the need.

Not all needs can be met immediately, and it is important to explain the reasons for this inability without re-
sorting to bureaucratic rules of the library's own making.
Even rules which come from the fire marshal or some other
outside authority should be challenged if the cause seems
worthwhile.

A paraplegic in a wheel chair complained at Cal-State,
Stanislaus, Library that the stack aisles were too narrow for
him to get into the stacks for browsing, and crowded conditions made an expansion of the stacks impossible.   There
was no alternative but to refuse his request.   Help in solving his problem was offered by suggesting that a library
staff member could put the materials needed on a book truck
and wheel them to him.   This was not a completely satisfactory solution, but it was the best that could be done at
the time.

Complaints about the need for longer hours, fewer
fines, more books, less noise, comfortable chairs, smoking

areas, and so forth, are common ones which can be handled
with understanding and a flexible, helpful attitude.   The emphasis should be upon serving the need and making it easy
for the user.   As long as no one else is hurt by granting
the request it should be done.

Noncurricular Needs

In recent years students have expressed many needs
which are not always related to the curriculum of the college.   It is easy to justify the expenditure of staff time and
budgeted funds for activities related to the curriculum, but
activities relating to the personal interests and needs of students do not usually rate such a high priority.   Yet, if we
intend to minister to the needs of the whole student, we
must attempt to provide information in a range of areas
shunned by the traditional academic libraries.

Collections of underground publications have developed
in academic libraries in direct response to student requests,
though they were not related to the curriculum at the outset.
Many libraries followed the leaders in collecting the better-
known underground publications, but often neglected the un-
official student publications of their own campuses as being
too ephemeral or too difficult to obtain.   Ruth Trager describes an attempt to collect these local materials at UCLA
during a crisis period in 1970. [11]

If students are involved in tutorial programs, the library should be willing to assist them in any way it can.
If there is need for a "hot line" where students can call to
get information on community services, the library should
provide it.   The Moffitt Undergraduate Library at U.C. at
Berkeley maintains a message center bulletin board which
helps students to communicate with each other.   The University of Washington Undergraduate Library has a Contemporary Issues Center which specializes in non-curricular
reading materials on many subjects that the students want.
Mary Cassata has discussed many of these services and
others in an article on student unrest. [12]   The important
consideration is that the academic library should be concerned with the interests of its users, and of its potential
users.   It should serve them because it has no higher duty.

Collection Development Policies

This essay can only discuss a few examples of the many alternative ways that have been designed to meet user needs. In the area of collection development it is essential to remember that the user wants the item that he or she requests and that item only. He or she may accept a substitute, but is unimpressed by the great size of the collection if it does not provide the material wanted when it is wanted. It is, therefore, necessary to attempt to anticipate demand for a particular title and supply it in a sufficient number of copies so that one copy is always available. This is an impossible goal but one which must be attempted. It requires continual monitoring of the use of the collection and the fast acquisition of additional copies of materials that are in demand.

The advent of automation will provide the information that is needed to know immediately which items are in demand and which are not. Until that kind of information is available automatically it is necessary to discover it manually.

Paperback copies of titles in heavy demand are often available and may be added inexpensively without cataloging for the time that the demand exists. Microform is often available as a backup for periodicals that are lost or out in circulation. Photocopies of periodicals from hard copy or microform provide an adequate substitute if the cost is kept low by library subsidy. Out-of-print materials may be photocopied from interlibrary loan if the library is willing to cope with copyright problems. Good and fast interlibrary loan arrangements can solve many of the pressing problems if the library is willing to give it a high priority.

All of these suggestions aim at the one function of making the information available to the user at the time it is wanted. Other functions of an academic library are secondary.

Circulation Policies

A relaxed attitude toward circulation of materials is essential to providing good service. A hard and fast rule in circulation should always be broken if in the judgment of the library staff member the material will not be needed by

someone else. All materials, except the most rare and
special treasures, should be circulated if there is a need
for it.

The reasons for a term loan period for the bulk of
the library collection at Cal State, Stanislaus, Library were
presented in an article recently, [13] the principal argument
being that most of the materials in any academic library
circulate less than once per year. A short loan period makes
no sense for seldom-used items which the user needs for a
long time. If the user must return or renew materials in
two or three weeks, or perhaps pay an overdue fine, when no
one else wants them, the user has been poorly served.

Similarly, it is often forbidden to circulate reference
books for even a short time, although they may have sat un-
used on the shelf for weeks or months. Books waiting for
cataloging are often backlogged in processing rooms for
months and are therefore prevented from circulating. In an
attempt to provide better services to the user, Cal-State,
Stanislaus, Library circulates most reference books for
short loans. Backlogged books in process are shelved in
the public area and are available for circulation. All books
on order or in process are listed by author in the card catalog. Those on order are available for circulation as soon
as they arrive, and those in process are available within 24
hours after a request is received. There are many variants
on these themes, but they all aim at making the maximum
amount of material available to the user so long as no other
user is discomfited.

Architectural Features

The architecture and equipping of library buildings
have probably been more innovative than other aspects of
academic libraries, but since this is adequately covered
elsewhere we shall only comment briefly upon it.

The undergraduate libraries with their inviting student-
oriented atmospheres are replete with alternative ways to
meet user needs. The " 'quadraphonic room' where four
speakers blare forth an assortment ranging from Jefferson
Airplane to the sound of a roller coaster in motion" is an
attempt to lure students into the undergraduate library at the
University of Maryland. Bean-bag chairs in a room with a
paperback browsing collection and a cafeteria in the under-

graduate library of the University of Washington at Seattle
is another example of the same.

At the other extreme some academic libraries have
attempted to reach out to the students by placing small
reference collections and recreational reading materials in
dormitory and college study areas, e.g., University of California at Santa Cruz.

The variations in architectural design, decoration,
and furnishing of academic libraries reflect an endless search
for ways to meet users' needs.   These attempts are highly
commendable, but it is somewhat disturbing to realize that
more innovations have occurred in the physical environment
of libraries than in the services that are provided within
them.

Reference Services

Some innovations have occurred in reference services.
They have not been as dramatic as the architectural and
equipment changes, but they do point a way for the future.
Probably the most important changes in reference services
are a result of changes in technology which have made possible a tremendous increase in indexing and abstracting.
The growth and improvement of indexes and abstracts through
automation and computers has greatly increased the availability of information for those libraries which can afford to
purchase the new reference materials.   The G. K. Hall publications have enabled many academic libraries to share in
the indexing that has been prepared by the great research libraries of the world.

The future development of information retrieval
promises to bring great changes in the ability to provide
S. D. I. --Selective Dissemination of Information--to users
with long-term research interests.   It also promises to aid
in the consolidation of indexed information so that a reasonably complete, automatically-created bibliography can be
produced upon demand.   This capability will surely be available to those who can afford it.   Whether these innovations
can ever be economically feasible is still a matter of great
controversy.

Other innovations in reference services have come
from the budding social consciousness of librarians.   These

new services have come more slowly in academic libraries
than in public libraries, which are providing services to all
kinds of groups that had not been reached before, from
prisoners to senior citizens.   In academia this social consciousness has manifested itself in library services to
groups peculiar to academic life, mainly minorities and the
handicapped. [14]

Robert P. Haro's article on service to Mexican-
Americans details the ways of discovering and meeting the
needs of Chicano students, and he cites the program at the
University of California at Los Angeles as a model of response to these needs. [15]   E. J. Josey and Barbara Foster
have written similar articles on service to the disadvantaged
student, describing some of the activities on the campuses
of The City University of New York. [16,17]   Carolyn Wolf
describes ways of serving blind students at Hartwick College.[18]

Cal-State, Stanislaus, employs a student member of
a class that is especially designed to assist students in the
Equal Opportunity Program.   This student, a Chicano, serves
as a liaison to the library.   She works in the library, learning its resources and practices so that she can assist the
E. O. P. students and serve as a bridge between them and a
librarian.   She is identified as the "library person" in the
class.   Through her the library also discovers the needs of
a group of students who would not otherwise use the library.

Though public libraries and student organizations have
established "hot-lines" that provide crisis information on a
24-hour basis, we know of no academic library that has yet
done so.   Cal-State, Stanislaus, Library has experimented
with a 24-hour emergency reference service that includes
some aspects of a hot-line, but it is primarily designed to
offer traditional telephone reference service.   The response
to this service has been negligible in the five months that it
has been in operation.

Louisiana State University uses a telephone answering
service which gives the hours that the library is open. [19]
Roger Palmer describes the use of graduate students in subject areas to provide reference service as well as to shelve
books and do other student assistant chores. [20]   D. A. Yanchisin tells of a free-wheeling reference librarian who is a
peripatetic floater wandering through the library looking for
people to help. [21]   These are a few of the ideas that have
been suggested to provide better service to users.   Whether

they are useful in any particular library will depend upon
the response that is received from the users, for that is the
ultimate test.

References

1. Lyle, Guy R. The Administration of the College Library. New York, H.W. Wilson Co., 1961.
2. Wilson, Louis Round, and Tauber, Maurice F. The University Library. 2d ed. New York, Columbia University Press, [1956].
3. Rogers, Rutherford D., and Weber, David C. University Library Administration. New York, H.W. Wilson Co., 1971.
4. Reynolds, Michael M. Reader in the Academic Library. Washington, D.C., NCR Microcard Editions, [1970].
5. Sheehan, Sister Helen. The Small College Library. Westminster, Maryland, Newman Press, 1963.
6. Blake, Fay, "The Useful Academic Librarian," Library Journal, 96:3732, November 15, 1971.
7. Jenks, George M. "Just a Suggestion: A Suggestion Box," RQ, 9:144-46, Winter 1969.
8. Lubans, John, "On Non-use of an Academic Library: A Report of Findings." In New York Library Association. College and University Libraries Section. Morrell D. Boone, ed. Use, Mis-use and Non-use of Academic Libraries; Proceedings of the ... Spring Conference held at Jefferson Community College, Watertown, May 1, 2, 1970. Woodside, N.Y., 1970, pp. 47-70.
9. Hovey, Joseph, and McKenney, Elizabeth. "Point of Increasing Returns," Library Journal, 91:6039-42, December 15, 1966.
10. Taylor, Robert S. "Orienting the Library to the User." In New York Library Association, op. cit., pp. 5-19.
11. Trager, Ruth, "Moratorium History Committee," American Libraries, 2:1157-58, December 1971.
12. Cassata, Mary B. "Student Unrest and the Library," Wilson Library Bulletin, 45:78-85, September 1970.
13. Galloway, R. Dean, and Parker, J. Carlyle. "The Quarter Loan/Recall System at the Library of California State College, Stanislaus," California Librarian, 33:231-35, October 1972.
14. Haro, Robert P. "Academic Library Services for Mexican Americans," College & Research Libraries, 33:454-62, November 1972.

15. Haro, Robert P.   "College Libraries for Students,"
    Library Journal, 94:2207-8, June 1, 1969.
16. Josey, E. J.   "The Role of the Academic Library in
    Serving the Disadvantaged Students," Library Trends,
    20:432-44, October 1971.
17. Foster, Barbara.   "Continuing Education," American
    Libraries, 2:776-77, September 1971.
18. Wolf, Carolyn.   "Hartwick Serves Blind," American
    Libraries, 2:1193-94, December 1971.
19. Perrault, Anna H.   "Eagle on the Moon," RQ, 11:217,
    Spring 1971.
20. Palmer, Roger C.   "Resident Reference," RQ, 12:339-
    40, Summer 1972.
21. Yanchisin, D. A.   "The Portable Librarian," RQ,
    12:340-41, Summer 1972.

A NEW LOOK AT ORGANIZING MATERIALS IN ACADEMIC LIBRARIES

Joan K. Marshall

The assumption inherent in the title is that the present organization of materials in academic libraries leaves something to be desired. I believe that to be a valid assumption. The organization of the materials, themselves, is one problem. But, even if we all agreed (and I am not at all sure that we would) upon an ideal organization of materials, few of us, given the limitations imposed by factors of space and budget, could attain the agreed upon ideal. Which is a wordy way of saying that I am not going to discuss the problem of the physical organization of materials in this essay.

The catalog access we provide to materials, however they may be housed, is a separate and far more serious problem. Some aspects of it vary from library to library-- how non-book material is handled (many academic libraries have avoided this aspect of the problem by refusing to acquire it); how committed the library is to following Library of Congress practice; whether the library has the professional and financial capability to recatalog or make other changes that are deemed desirable, and so forth. Other aspects of the problem, however, plague all of us equally, and they are the topic of this essay.

One basic problem that plagues us all arises from our refusal to recognize that the card catalog, since it imposes order, is inevitably complex. Academic librarians, particularly, have ducked the service implications of this fact by hiding behind the assumption that their users are either scholars accustomed to bibliographic conundrums or potential scholars who should be trained--i.e., should be left to flounder for themselves--in the use of the card catalog.

As librarians we look upon the solutions to imposing order upon author entries that are offered, for instance, by the Anglo-American Cataloging Code (AACR) as intellectually sound and, often, downright ingenious. But to the person untrained in the intricacies of the AACR our solutions often remain a mystery. Scenario: "What is to be done," asks the descriptive cataloger, "about the mass of cards accumulating under Tolstoy? The editions of War and Peace, in the original and in translation, are scattered; collected works and individual works, in the original and in translation, are interfiled; Tolstoy is messy!" The cataloger follows the advice of the AACR and (with the help of the Library of Congress Russian literature classification schedule and other reference books to assist in determining accurate uniform titles) organizes Tolstoy. When the organization is complete, the cataloger looks upon the corner-marked and cross-referenced author and exclaims: "Tolstoy is neat!" Later, a student who wants an edition of War and Peace is seen staring, obviously confused, at the cross-reference:

> War and peace.
> > Tolstoĭ, Lev Nikolaevich, graf, 1828-1910.
> > > see his
> > Voĭna i mir. English.

The student knows he does not yet have what he wants; he is fairly certain the library has it, but very uncertain about how to locate it.

Or, consider the case of an acronym cross-reference:

> U. N. E. S. C. O.
> > Abbreviation of
> > United Nations Educational, Scientific and
> > > Cultural Organization
> > Publications by or about this body are found under its name written in full in the form indicated above.
> > When this abbreviation occurs at the beginning of titles and other entries, it is filed as a word: Unesco

and write your own scenario.

The solutions offered by the AACR to the problems of organizing author access are, I believe, intellectually

sound and, often, downright ingenious. But where does that
leave the perplexed user? There have been, and there will
probably continue to be, myriad attempts at simplification of
the card catalog. Dividing it, for instance, has been popular. Leslie Morris has recently put the benefits of the divided catalog in proper perspective: "Why not offer the patron any number of access points including the following: a
dictionary catalog, a title catalog, an author catalog, a subject catalog, a people catalog, a places catalog, and (for librarians only) a corporate author catalog?"[1] The moral to
be drawn from Morris's overkill is that librarians are likely
to do almost anything rather than face the simple fact that
our catalogs--whether in card or book format, whether dictionary or divided--are difficult to use.

        The only way we can help the perplexed user is by
fully accepting as fact that the time invested in creating and
maintaining a good card catalog is wasted if we do not in-
vest time in adequately servicing it. And, in connection
with adequately servicing our catalogs, I suggest we examine
the present division of responsibilities between public and
technical services in our libraries. The everyday concerns
of the cataloger are knowledge of entry and filing rules, of
the pecularities of cataloging practice (imposed locally or by
the Library of Congress) that have been adopted and abandoned over the years, and of the variety of means employed
to handle changes in form of author and subject entries.
Why should the public services staff be expected to duplicate
this expertise? (That they are expected to is simply additional evidence of our refusal to acknowledge the complexity
of our catalogs.) Catalogers should be moved out of their
full-time haven in the back room and moved part-time up
front to interpret their arcane product to the public. Ideally,
the student who wanted War and Peace should have had the
cataloger who placed the reference in the catalog (and assumed the job was complete) at his or her elbow to interpret
it. We may not be able to achieve this ideal, but we should
aim for it.

        So much for inevitable complexities. What of those
that are not inevitable? The solution to most--if not all--
of our not inevitable problems rests with the Library of
Congress and upon its decision to close off its catalogs.
William Welsh, director of LC's Processing Department, in
response to an article by Walter Fraser,[2] remarked that
Fraser had overstated the impact of closing off the LC catalog.[3] Fraser may have overstated the case in terms of the

necessity of all other libraries closing their catalogs if they were to continue to use LC cataloging, and he may have overstated the possibilities for reform in matters not relevant to the organization of the catalog, but it is impossible to overstate the impact--in terms of service--of being given the opportunity to reconsider choice and form of entry, and subject heading terminology.

In respect to the impact reconsideration of choice and form of entry would have, consider superimposition a thing of the past. LC's policy of superimposition was, I am willing to concede, adopted out of economic necessity. But, however necessary it may be for LC, it creates a variety of problems in libraries which attempt, out of their own economic necessity and in the spirit of cooperation, to use LC cataloging. For instance, the decision to employ superimposition is based on LC's holdings, and it very often makes little sense, therefore, in a library which has a smaller (or simply different) collection. To cite a minor example of such senselessness: LC retained Arthur, King (Romances, etc.) as a superimposition-type main entry; all added entries in that form were changed to the subject entry ARTHURIAN ROMANCES. There was one main entry under the old form in the Brooklyn College catalog. And, since our catalog is divided and we had, therefore, separated the cards representing our Arthurian romances by about 40 feet (and since if we did not recatalog, the reference relating the old and new forms would have been quite complex), we recataloged. But in recataloging, we have committed the library to future recataloging of works entered by LC under the old form. If you multiply this minor example by others, the practical problems of superimposition begin to take on major proportions.

However, and although it may sound contradictory, superimposition has had its advantages. As the AACR was originally formulated, a symbiotic relationship between aspects of it and of LC past entry and filing practice can sometimes be detected. The policy of superimposition has permitted LC to examine and to revise the 1967 AACR without concern for the effect implementation of the rules would have on its catalog.

AACR Rule 73, for instance, now requires the addition of the appropriate larger geographical entity to all local place names. If superimposition were abandoned and the rule were implemented, it would greatly increase the effectiveness of catalogs which are filed according to ALA, rather than LC, filing rules.   For example:

LC Filing	ALA Filing	ALA Filing with Italy Added
Florence (i. e. the chief city of this name with Italy and (City) understood)	Florence FLORENCE Florence. R. Accademia de belle arti	Florence and her treasures Florence, Col. FLORENCE CO. , WIS. - BIOG.
Florence. R. Accademia de belle arti	Florence and her treasures	Florence, Italy FLORENCE, ITALY
Florence. Archivio di stato	Florence (Archdiocese)	Florence, Italy. R. Accademia de belle arti
Florence. Biblioteca nazionale centrale	Florence. Archivio di stato	Florence, Italy (Archdiocese)
Florence. Ordinances, etc.	FLORENCE - BIBL.	Florence, Italy. Archivio di stato
Florence. Ufficio di statistica	Florence. Biblioteca nazionale centrale	FLORENCE, ITALY - BIBL.
FLORENCE	Florence, Col.	Florence, Italy. Biblioteca nazionale centrale
FLORENCE - BIBL.	FLORENCE CO., WIS. - BIOG.	FLORENCE, ITALY - HIST.
FLORENCE - HIST.	FLORENCE - HIST.	Florence, Italy. Ordinances, etc.
FLORENCE - STAT.	Florence, Mass.	
Florence (Archdiocese)	Florence. Ordinances, etc.	Florence, Italy (Republic)
Florence (Republic)	Florence press	FLORENCE, ITALY - STAT.
Florence, Col.	Florence (Republic)	Florence, Italy. Ufficio di statistica
Florence, Mass.	FLORENCE (SCHOONER)	Florence, Mass.
Florence, S. D.	Florence, S. D.	Florence press
Florence, Synod of, 1478	FLORENCE - STAT.	FLORENCE (SCHOONER)
FLORENCE (SCHOONER)	Florence, Synod of, 1478	Florence, S. D.
Florence and her treasures	Florence, the parish orphan	Florence, Synod of, 1478
FLORENCE CO., WIS. - BIOG.	Florence. Ufficio di statistica	Florence, the parish orphan
Florence press		
Florence, the parish orphan		

The example above (in addition to illustrating one of the effects the absence of superimposition would have) illustrates a consideration which is germane, I believe, to the impact reconsideration of choice and form of entry could have: how the entries file.   If AACR entries could be filed with equal logic by either LC or ALA filing rules, it might be regarded as quixotic that American libraries have devel-

oped one standard set of rules for entry and two standard
sets of rules for filing; but the fact is that they cannot be
filed with equal logic.

In an ideal world, we would all get together and decide on one system (the advantage to the user of being able
to transfer skills learned in one library situation to another
is apparent); but which one? The LC rules have a certain
logic which the ALA rules lack (in the example of filing
under place above: works by a principal city, followed by
works about it, followed by other entries in a variety of orders). But it is not a readily apparent logic (note the position of Florence, Col.--another place with the same name
as the principal city--and Florence Co., Wis.--filed as a
phrase heading). The ALA rules use, in place of logic, the
alphabet which is, or should be, readily comprehensible.
But, as both examples of ALA filing above illustrate, the
use of the alphabet to impose order results in a somewhat
capricious, and therefore not readily comprehensible, arrangement. Alphabetical filing is, supposedly, easier; if so,
that is the only clear advantage of one system over the other.

In conjunction with closing the LC catalogs, the Library of Congress and the American Library Association
should formulate one set of filing rules that will be appropriate for all (realistically, most) libraries, and they should
assume a position of leadership in urging the general adoption of this single set of rules. If it is not possible to
achieve this ideal, it should at least be incumbent upon the
Library of Congress and the appropriate ALA committee to
review the AACR in conjunction with the two major filing
standards, and to revise either the AACR or the appropriate
filing rule wherever necessary to eliminate or alleviate il-
logic. (The revision of AACR Rule 73, for instance, permits a more logical arrangement of AACR entries under
place in an alphabetically filed catalog. But a further step
could be taken. If Rule 77 were re-revised to permit the
addition of a parenthetical modifier to entries for municipal
governments, the entry for Florence, Italy (City) and the
entries for the Archdiocese and Republic of Florence would
no longer interfile.)

Finally, if one filing system is not developed and accepted, the Library of Congress should consider, in the future, the relationship between the form of subject entries
and filing. In an alphabetically filed catalog, inverted subject headings, for example, successfully bring together all

the material on a narrower aspect of a general subject, but
they separate the material under the general heading: for
example, ART, AMERICAN and all of its subdivisions file
between ART - ADDRESSES, ESSAYS, LECTURES and ART -
BIBLIOGRAPHY. The arrangement of cards under art (and
many other subject headings) in an alphabetically filed catalog is disconcerting, to say the least.

In respect to the impact reconsideration of subject
heading terminology could have, the considerations are such
that, even if no other advantages accrued from closing off
LC's catalog, it should be closed. The obvious advantage
to closing the catalog is that we would be able to up-date
terminology and orthography: ELECTRONIC CALCULATING
MACHINES could be changed to computers, and AEROPLANES
could be changed to airplanes. This type of subject heading
change, however, is purely clerical; given enough people
with enough erasers, the changes could be made now. If
there are not enough people with enough erasers (as would
probably be the case in most libraries), the changes could
be made by closing the old heading and instructing the user
to see the new heading for material published after the date
of the change. (This method of handling subject heading
changes which require too much erasing is employed in
many libraries, and it is, in effect, what we would be doing in closing off the catalog.) It might be nice to up-date
terminology and orthography, but it hardly justifies so drastic a step as closing the catalog.

The significant--in fact, decisive--advantage to closing off LC's catalog is that it would provide an opportunity
to review the philosophical bases of our subject headings.
Our subject catalogs are, I firmly believe, educational tools
and, as such, should be constructed on egalitarian principles
rather than on the principle, as stated by Hayken, [4] of identifying the majority user (as if such a thing were possible)
and allowing references to serve the needs of the minority.
The application of this principle has led us into the use of
subject headings that reinforce, quite bluntly, ignorance and
prejudice. BUSHMEN is the derisive terminology of Dutch
settlers in South Africa; NEZ PERCE INDIANS is the terminology of French Canadian fur trappers; MAMMIES is the
terminology of southern slave owners; YELLOW PERIL is
the terminology of German racists; and (to toss in an event)
WOUNDED KNEE CREEK, BATTLE OF, 1890 is the terminology of the U.S. Cavalry.

In establishing subject headings for peoples the terminology of the people concerned should be used. It is educational, not a disservice, to direct the user who looks
under BUSHMEN or NEZ PERCE INDIANS to the terms which
these people use to refer to themselves: San and Chute-pa-
lu. In establishing headings relating to the condition of
people or to controversial events, we should aim for neutrality; too many of our headings now express a point of
view. The subject heading MAMMIES, in conjuring up a
happy Aunt Jemima-like image, reinforces the contented
mammy myth; Slavery in the United States - Condition of
Women would provide a neutral approach to the material on
the subject. If the subject heading for the massacre (my
opinion) at Wounded Knee Creek must be lengthier than the
name of the place and the date, why not make it Wounded
Knee Creek, Incident at, 1890--neutral. (YELLOW PERIL
is so outrageous that I cannot think of a substitute. I would
just like to point out that the Encyclopaedia Britannica,
which is often cited by LC as a source of subject heading
authority, does not use that heading either directly or in
its index.) I will not belabor this point with additional examples. (Anyone who is not convinced should consult Sanford Berman's Prejudices and Antipathies, [5] which ably and
amply illustrates the peculiarities of LC subject headings.)
But if, as I and many others are convinced, our subject
headings reinforce personal prejudice, and prejudice the materials they provide access to, they must be changed. And
with the advent of Cataloging in Publication, the need for
rapid change has become imperative; our labels--and that is
what our subject headings are--are now actually in many of
our books.

Assuming that the Library of Congress, a few years
hence, having taken into account the considerations mentioned here and many others, has closed its catalogs, and
the best of all possible library worlds has been achieved,
how are we to maintain that happy state of affairs? Must
we seriously consider the possibility of closing off our catalogs every ten or 20 years? I do not believe so. I have
every hope that computer technology will allow us (in addition to providing additional and easier access) to make
changes in the future that were never possible in the past.
The ease with which author or subject entry changes can be
made in a computer-based catalog is obvious. In addition,
it is possible to add 20 to 30 descriptors (for use in in-
depth searching) to any title in the MARC data base. [6] The
addition of these descriptors (LC does not yet add them)

would greatly facilitate making subject heading changes so
that the narrower term becomes a subject heading in its own
right.   Titles indexed in the data base under the narrower
term could be readily identified and a determination made
as to the appropriateness of assigning the new heading to
them.

Perhaps more should have been said about computer
technology in a paper titled "A New Look at Organizing Materials in Academic Libraries." (A more appropriate title
might have been "A Hard Look at the Present Organization
of...") But if we were to apply computer technology to our
catalogs in their present state (as was done with MARC), we
would be worse off than we are now; we would become even
more firmly locked into our present problems.   I have mentioned, for instance, problems with changing entries that
could be eased if all of us had a computer base for our catalogs, but many of the problems with changing entries in our
manual catalogs should never have arisen.

Why did it take LC 20 or more years to establish
LINGUISTICS and ten or more years to establish ROCK MU-
SIC? (In relation to their delay in deciding that the latter
heading was valid, Edward Blume, chief of LC's Subject
Cataloging Division, remarked at a meeting of the New York
technical services librarians last spring: "Today's horse
may be tomorrow's carrion." It might be more appropriate
for LC to establish today's horse, once it has run a short
while, rather than to allow today's horse to be buried under
yesterday's carrion.) Computers will be of only minimal
assistance if such time-lags in establishing new headings
continue to exist.   Nor will computer technology alone help
us to resolve the problems presented by superimposition
and filing.   Finally, and most importantly, computer technology cannot help us to eradicate the most serious fault in
our catalogs: the "majority user" subject heading access
we provide to our collections.   (Shall we use Kikes as an
access term--or as a cross-reference; the majority users
of many libraries might consider that direct access.   Kikes,
however, is a derogatory term; Bushmen, Nez Percé Indians,
and Mammies are equally--even if it is not immediately apparent to all of our users--derogatory terms.)

The solution to LC's problems and to the problems,
therefore, of most libraries (a few do have the means to
break from LC practice) lies, I am convinced, in a fresh
start.   Close the LC catalogs!   Perhaps with the aid of

computer technology, retrospective conversion, and adequate
funding (!) we will be able to merge our two catalogs some-
time in the future; perhaps not.   But should we allow the
mistakes of the past to limit the possibilities of the future?

> so much depends
> upon
>
> a red wheel
> barrow
>
> glazed with rain
> water
>
> beside the white
> chickens

It is not reasonable that so much should depend upon
a red wheelbarrow;[7] it is not reasonable, in terms of the
service we will be able to offer in the (hopefully immediate)
future, that so much should depend upon the Library of Congress.   But so much does.

References

1.   Morris, Leslie R.   "Why not Both?, " Library Re-
        sources & Technical Services, 17:25-27, Winter 1973.
2.   Fraser, Walter J.   "Closing the Catalog: The Library
        of Congress and the Future of Cataloging Practice, "
        Wilson Library Bulletin, 46:836-38, May 1972.
3.   Welsh, William J.   "Response to Walter J. Fraser's
        'Overdue,' " Wilson Library Bulletin, 46:139-40,
        October 1972.
4.   Hayken, David Judson.   Subject Headings: A Practical
        Guide.   Washington, D.C., 1951, p. 7.
5.   Berman, Sanford.   Prejudices and Antipathies: A
        Tract on the LC Subject Heads Concerning People.
        Metuchen, N.J., 1971.
6.   Wellisch, Hans, and Wilson, Thomas D., eds.   Subject
        Retrieval in the Seventies.   Westport, Conn., 1972,
        pp. 2-27.
7.   Williams, William Carlos.   "The Red Wheelbarrow."
        In William Pratt, ed. The Imagist Poem.   New York,
        1963, p. 79.

THE BLACK COLLEGE LIBRARY IN
A CHANGING ACADEMIC ENVIRONMENT

Casper LeRoy Jordan

Historians of higher education of blacks in the United States have identified Lincoln University in Pennsylvania (1854) and Wilberforce University in Ohio (1856) as the first colleges for blacks. This identification is valid in the sense that these two institutions were the first to remain in their original location, to imply the granting of bachelor degrees as their objective, and to evolve into degree-granting institutions.

However, long before 1854 institutions were established or attempted for the education of blacks. In line with the acceptable requirements of the day, these schools were founded to prepare urgently needed black teachers and preachers. They were sponsored by two basic groups which differed in their objectives concerning the place of the black in the American social milieu. The American Colonization Society held out for the education of blacks in order that they would migrate to Africa. The second group consisted very largely of abolitionists and members of the Conventions of the Free People of Color who argued strongly for the establishment of colleges for the preparation of blacks for greater service within the American social fabric.

Thus, from such contrasting points of view, higher education of blacks was attempted or established. As early as 1817 the colonizationists founded a school for blacks at Parsippany, New Jersey. A Quaker of Philadelphia willed the sum of $10,000 to a board of trustees for the education of "descendants of the African race"--the forerunner of Cheyney State College (1832). Other institutions aimed at higher education for blacks were established during the antebellum days: Avery College in Pennsylvania (1849), the academy of Miss Myrtilla Miner (1851), Ashmun Institute (now Lincoln University) in Pennsylvania (1854), and Wilberforce University in Ohio (1856).

During the antebellum period only 28 blacks were awarded baccalaureate degrees from American institutions of higher learning. Many other blacks obtained higher education of various types that were regarded as proper during the period: apprenticeship training, nondegree courses, training for teaching, training abroad, training in black institutions, and self-education. No attempt has been made to estimate the number of blacks who thus obtained higher education; however, the impression is given that many more than the above-mentioned 28 blacks obtained legitimate higher education during the pre-Civil War period.

In the assessment of blacks' higher educational efforts during the postbellum period, 1865-95, certain facts or circumstances need to be taken under consideration. In 1865 the status of the recently freedman changed radically with emancipation: five million became new citizens. However, it required the Fourteenth and Fifteenth Amendments to the Constitution to raise the black's status to that of citizen and elector. Approximately 92 percent of the blacks in 1860 lived in the Southern States, and even in 1900 the figure was as large as 90 percent. Aside from North Carolina and Kentucky, the Southern States had nothing even approaching a system of public schools prior to 1860. During the Civil War, Northern missionary groups had followed the path of the Union Army, establishing Sunday and elementary schools for blacks. The establishment of literally thousands of these schools by Northern missionary groups during the Civil War is an astounding story.

On March 3, 1865, Abraham Lincoln signed the act to inaugurate the services of a bureau for the relief of freedmen and refugees. Thus, the Freedmen's Bureau came into existence. There is evidence of cooperation between the bureau and missionary groups in education of blacks.

Right after the Civil War, the Baptists, Methodists, Presbyterians, and Congregationalists (mainly through the American Missionary Association) took steps to found higher institutions for blacks in the South. These groups were joined by the Freedmen's Bureau in the effort. During the period from 1865 to 1890 the largest number of black private colleges and universities, historically, was established. Literally hundreds were founded with "normal," "college," and "university" in their titles--titles selected to indicate their eventual goal.

These colleges were largely elementary and secondary
schools. Atlanta, Fisk, Howard, Leland, Lincoln, Shaw,
and Wilberforce, however, started collegiate departments by
or before 1872, and Fisk, Howard, Lincoln, and Wilberforce
had graduated 68 students before 1876. However, the black
private colleges remained largely elementary and secondary
schools until 1895. It has been estimated that by 1895 over
1,100 college graduates had emerged from these fledgling
institutions--as well as many nongraduates. From this
small nucleus came many of the outstanding blacks who contributed to American life during the period from Reconstruction to the early years of the 20th century.

About half of the 34 historically black public colleges
now extant were founded prior to 1890. The passage of the
Morrill Act of 1890 ("the second Morrill Act") provided the
impetus for the establishment of the remaining historically
black public colleges. Between 1890 and 1899, a black land-
grant college was established or designated in each of the
17 Southern and border states.

There were instances of blacks graduating from historically white Southern colleges and universities during Reconstruction, but the practice was discontinued toward the
end of the period. With the exception of Oberlin College in
Ohio, Northern colleges made no great effort to recruit
black students during the period of Reconstruction. The major contribution toward the higher education of blacks in the
United States came from the historically black private "colleges" and "universities."

Throughout the first 50 years of the 20th century
more than two-thirds of the blacks in the United States were
still residing in the Southern and border states. Because
of enactment of state laws which received Federal court
blessings, the higher education of blacks through the level
of the bachelor's degree, therefore, was provided mainly by
the black institutions of the South. The essential development of the black colleges during this period (1890-1953) was
their emergence as institutions of higher education after half
a century of poverty-stricken existence as primary and
secondary schools.

During the period organized philanthropy had both a
direct and an indirect effect upon the development of the

Southern black colleges.   The Peabody Education Fund, established in 1867, gave its major attention to permanent systems of public education in the South for all races, to
scholarships for students preparing to teach, and to normal
schools.   The John F. Slater Fund was established in 1882
specifically for the benefit of education among blacks.   The
General Education Board was founded by John D. Rockefeller in 1902 and continued until 1956.   The board expended
over $300 million to promote a variety of educational activi-
ties in the United States.   It contributed over $60 million
to black education and was the largest direct philanthropic
contributor to black higher education.   The Phelps-Stokes
Fund, founded in 1910, contributed about one-third of its resources to black education in its early years.   The fund's
greatest contribution to the development of black colleges
was, probably, its participation in the first two of three
general surveys of black colleges: the survey of 1914-15
and the survey of 1928.   The Julius Rosenwald Fund was incorporated in 1917 and liquidated in 1948.   During this period it expended a little more than $22 million in the areas
of education; health and medical services; fellowships; and
race relations aimed at the alleviation of the plight of blacks.
A group of presidents of historically black private colleges
met in 1943 to discuss the desirability and feasibility of organizing a cooperative effort to obtain funds for the colleges.
In 1944 the United Negro College Fund was organized, intro-
ducing a new concept of cooperative fund-raising in American
education.

        The Plessy vs. Ferguson decision of 1896 gave the
legal sanction of the Federal Government to local laws and
customs that had been adopted to relegate blacks to the position of a separate group within the country's social order.
As a consequence, the black colleges were charged with the
responsibility of educating the majority of the blacks of the
country.   So there developed in the South a separate system
of education for blacks from elementary school through higher education.

        By 1951 the National Association for the Advancement
of Colored People (NAACP), through a series of successful
court cases, had established the right of blacks to attend
white public graduate and professional schools of the South.

        Higher education of blacks since 1954 has occurred
within the framework of significant changes in the United
States.   One of the changes was the United States Supreme

Court's interpretation that segregation in public education
was unconstitutional.   This destroyed the separate-but-equal
doctrine which had produced a separate Southern system of
higher education for blacks.

The decade of the sixties will be most dramatically
remembered in the United States for rapid and enduring advances toward racial equality.   The Federal Government en-
acted legislation guaranteeing certain basic civil rights and
took steps to inaugurate political equality for all citizens regardless of race or color.   The conscience of Americans
generally was aroused to the enduring evils of segregation
and discrimination and its consequent violations of the moral
principles of a democratic nation.

The salutary effects of increased education opportunity
extend beyond employment and housing and suffrage.   Education also gives renewed strength to the entire movement for
equal opportunity.   Black college students dramatized this
role of education in the 1960's when they began demonstra-
tions for equal consumer services--first in North Carolina
and then in Alabama and Georgia.   The enrollment of the
first blacks in previously segregated public universities in
Mississippi and Georgia focussed the eyes of the world on
the colleges that these young blacks attended and brought
about a greater interest in the character of education they
provided.

It has been demonstrated that, except at the topmost
level of excellence represented by a few celebrated institutions, the black institutions run the gamut of quality within
American higher education.   Black schools lie all along the
line of the academic procession in America; they do not
form a separate unitary group at the tail end.   Some are
exceptionally far forward and others far behind, but parallel
with each of them stands some institution attended predominantly by whites.

Some educators have concluded that both students and
society would be better served if a number of black schools
closed their doors.   Contrary to the proposals for dises-
tablishment, many observers of higher education conclude
that the black institution ought to be preserved and strengthened.   The black presence in higher education is just as
viable as the Catholic presence of Notre Dame and Fordham;
the Lutheran presence of Concordia; the Jewish presence of
Brandeis and Yeshiva; or the Mormon presence of Brigham

Young. Student finances, educational preparation, and growing enrollments argue compellingly for preserving, strengthening, and integrating existing black institutions, and against
closing them or allowing them to wither on the vine of
academe.

To retain any validity today, the image of higher education must include books, journals, microforms--the library.
If a library is to be of high quality, college administrators
must understand and appreciate its role in accomplishing the
objectives of higher education. Faculty members must be
familiar with its collection in their own subject areas; be
active in helping to keep the collection current; and assure
its effective use. Finally, the financial support of the library must be both adequate and free from frequent and vio-
lent fluctuations.

The quality of any college library is determined first
by the extent and nature of its materials and human resources.
When its holdings are insufficient, outdated, or inadequately
housed; or, when its staff and services are unreliable, un-
imaginative, or ineffective, the library cannot accomplish
its objectives. The resources and services of black academic libraries vary from poor to excellent, but the curve
is skewed toward the lower end. Their problems are those
of most small college libraries, but they are more intense.
The need for library resources and services is accentuated
in the black college by the lack of sufficiently trained personnel and the larger than usual proportion of poorly prepared
students.

Eighty-five black, four-year, degree-conferring institutions were queried in 1969, and 51 of the questionnaires
were returned. If a library says anything at all about collections, it almost surely mentions size. The institutions
reporting their 1968 fall figures recorded the presence of
92, 911 students. These libraries reported holding 4, 290, 915
volumes. No black academic library reported a collection
even approaching one million; and only 11 held 100, 000
volumes. During the year 324, 487 volumes were added to
the collections. Bound periodicals numbered a little less
than a quarter of a million. In terms of per capita figures,
there were 46.1 volumes per full-time student, and 2.5
periodicals per capita. Comparative figures are available
from the U.S. Office of Education. For the academic year
1967-68, 2, 300 academic libraries reported holding over
300 million volumes and 43.3 volumes per students. Twenty-

two million volumes were added; less than a half-million to black library collections.

The Association of College and Research Libraries published "minimum" standards for academic libraries in 1959 (these are currently under revision). A collection of 50,000 "carefully selected volumes" is suggested for an enrollment of 600 students. Of the 34 United Negro College Fund-affiliated libraries under study, 23 did not meet the ACRL minimum standard. Another study revealed that it would take over $30 million to bring all black college libraries up to the ACRL standard.

Libraries have made real gains with respect to support in recent years, along with hard-won recognition and general acceptance of the services they provide. As a general rule, a college library should receive a budget of no less than five percent of the total operating budget of the college. Replies from libraries indicated that a little over $7 million was expended for library purposes--about half of this amount went for salaries and less than a third was spent on books. The five percent figure was being observed in most cases, but this is of little consolation when the overall college budget considered as a base for this calculation is itself desperately small.

ALA standards suggest a minimum of three librarians in an academic library. Eight libraries reported staffs of less than three, but there are no longer any one-man operations. Supportive staff did not fare too well in these libraries. A great deal of dependence was placed on student help--an unwise condition. Salaries are not competitive in black academic libraries.

Black academe is making a considerable effort by itself to overcome the deficiencies of its libraries. The present condition of the library services in most of the black colleges can be summed up in the statement that the physical facilities are in general more adequate than the books, journals, films, and records they contain--thanks to recent government programs. The buildings and facilities also outstrip small but dedicated library staffs. The collections and staff need extensive strengthening to rectify a long history of insufficient support.

Black colleges and their libraries have no functions different from those enumerated by Lyle, Wilson, Tauber or

other writers on academic library administration.   However,
over the century of their existence black institutions have
added to their traditional functions the responsibility of educating a race long deprived of excellence in education pursuits.   This bootstrap operation so dear to black academe
has been its strong point.   Almost single-handedly the black
colleges have fulfilled the words of James Weldon Johnson:

> You sang not of deeds of heroes or of kings;
> No chant of bloody war, no exalting paean
> Of arms-won triumphs; but your humble strings
> You touched in chord with music empyrean.
> You sang far better than you knew; the songs
> That for your listeners' hungry hearts sufficed
> Still live, --but more than this to you belongs:
> You sang a race from wood and stone to Christ.

The part that small, ill-equipped, understaffed libraries
played in all of this is a story in itself.   Perhaps the major
contribution of black academic librarianship is in this area
of "making do" and pursuing excellence.

There is one area in which the black college library
has excelled, and it offers scope for further expansion in
the preservation and servicing of the black experience through
special collections in Negroana.   With a few exceptions, this
valuable corpus of material by and about blacks has been
saved by black institutions.   Long before "black" was
fashionable these institutions, without extra money and with
overworked staffs, kept the heritage of a people long despised.   The account of this stewardship should go down in
the annals of American librarianship as equal to any movement in the discipline.

It is of interest to recount the formation of these
priceless treasure troves.   The Moorland-Spingarn Collection at Howard University Library had its inception as a
creation of the board of trustees in 1914 when the Moorland
Foundation, the Library of Negro Life and History, was inaugurated.   Earlier in the same year, the Reverend Jesse E.
Moorland, a YMCA official and a Howard trustee, gave the
university his private library of more than 3,000 items relating to the black man.   The Moorland gift was combined
with an older collection of anti-slavery literature, the gift
of Lewis Tappan in 1873.   These two gifts together formed
the base for one of the most important collections of such
materials in the country.   The valuable collection of Arthur

Spingarn, of over 7, 000 volumes, was purchased in 1946, further strengthening this collection.

The Negro Collection at Atlanta University goes back almost as far as the founding of the university. The first mention of a library was in the catalog of 1870, and in 1925 the library reported a "Negro Collection" of 291 books. In 1932 the acquisition of the original manuscripts of Thomas Clarkson, a noted British abolitionist of the 18th century, was announced; to this was added the collection of John Brown letters. In 1946 the collection was established as a separate entity with the purchase of the Henry P. Slaughter private library. Slaughter was a black bibliophile who, on a Federal civil service salary, amassed a collection of note. Other collections came to the university, making the over-all collection an outstanding one.

The Negro Collection at Fisk University in Nashville absorbed the collection of the defunct YMCA graduate school in Nashville and became, with additional gifts and purchases, one of the strongest libraries in the South for the study of blacks in the United States.

The George Foster Peabody Collection on the Negro is at Hampton Institute in Virginia. The collection had its beginning in 1905. The library is a large, old one and con-tains a magnificent collection of several hundred scrapbooks of clippings on almost every conceivable subject for the years 1898-1920.

There is a venerable, sizeable collection in the Hollis Burke Frissel Library of Tuskegee Institute in Alabama. The material from the Department of Records and Research, founded in 1908 by the famed black bibliographer Monroe N. Work, is an integral and priceless part of this collection, along with the George Washington Carver Museum which was set up in 1938 to preserve the work of this black chemical genius.

The black collections at Central State and Wilberforce Universities in Ohio share a common beginning. The collec-tion of materials on the black man at Wilberforce University goes back to the collection mania of its founder, Daniel Alexander Payne. Payne, as its historiographer, collected material on the African Methodist Episcopal Church, begin-ning in 1848. His papers, along with the papers of Martin Delaney, were stored in a special room. In 1947, when

Central State University was separated from Wilberforce University, a part of the collection was separated. To these materials were added the papers of Hallie Quinn Brown, outstanding educator and eloqutionist.

The Heartman Collection on Negro Life and Culture, housed at Texas Southern University in Houston, is the outstanding special collection of the Southwest.

A distinguished collection of material on the black diaspora is housed at New Orleans' Dillard University: the Amisted Research Collection. Other collections are dispersed throughout the many black institutions.

The essential conclusion one may draw is that the major contribution to black higher education in the United States was made by the black man himself. And the small, ill-prepared libraries of these brave, glorious institutions played a great part in the history of American higher education, recognition of which is still denied them.

PART III

UNSCRAMBLING CRITICAL ACADEMIC
LIBRARY ISSUES

CREATIVE LIBRARY SERVICE FOR THE
NEW LEARNERS IN HIGHER EDUCATION

Robert P. Haro

The academic library within the last 20 years has
been, mainly through circumstances beyond its control, the
target of close scrutiny by campus administrators, faculty,
and even students. The wave of change, both in terms of
economic necessity and pedagogic considerations, that has
faced the academic libraries has caused considerable anxiety,
planning, and rethinking on the part of librarians. The previous forms of library service that were traditionally provided by the academic libraries, defended by the practitioners, and taught by the academics in the library schools had
become little more than ritual. In the last 20 years the
priorities of higher education shifted first to the hard sciences with the "Sputnik" threat, then to address the growing
concern of our urban problems, then to the biological problems that confronted mankind and the environment, and now
to a growing concern for human needs in all aspects of our
social experience. Because of these outside pressures on
the academic library, new techniques and, to a lesser extent, new service programs were entertained by academic
librarians. The overriding concern of academic librarians
should have been a thorough understanding of the changing
educational objectives of our institutions and the development
of a planning mechanism to address those needs while building in the capability for change to accommodate new priorities. What does this process, then, mean for students, and
particularly for the new learners in our institutions of higher learning?

Before discussing the new learning concepts, it is
necessary to briefly define new learners. I choose to consider new learners as members of our society who in the
past would either have been excluded from the process of
higher education or would not have been satisfied by the tra-

ditional educational structure.   This category includes ethnic
minorities, vocationally-oriented people, and highly intelligent and independently-oriented students.   The new learners
were confronted with a traditional system of higher education
structured into three types of institutions that, while similar
in purpose, differed markedly in function.   These institutions were and still are the two-year community colleges
that specialize in vocation, terminal education, and some
transfer programs; the four-year colleges that provide baccalaureate programs in a number of subject disciplines and
a few interdisciplinary areas, along with some terminal
master's programs; and universities that provide basic baccalaureate programs along with extensive professional and
graduate programs leading to the doctorate.   In the past,
community colleges had been primarily responsible for the
education of vocationally-oriented new learners.   This condition has slowly started to change, with all three types of
institutions initiating programs to address the needs of all
new learners.   To better relate the concepts and programs
involved with the new learners, I will discuss programs peculiar to them in three parts, each related to the type of
institution mentioned above.   The types of programs may
seem similar, but the institutional setting(s) and objectives
result in differing service programs.

The Community College

The two-year colleges, because of their greater flexibility in the development of educational programs, have been
able in the last ten years to relate their activities and curricula to the needs of their respective communities.   Because of the differing audiences and the limited size of their
book collections, many of these colleges quickly capitalized
on the new technology for education in the development of
their libraries.   Rather than stress book collections, many
college libraries have become known as learning resources
centers or as instructional materials centers, always stress-
ing a total media concept for the library and its role in
disseminating information and knowledge.   While on the surface these terms may have seemed superfluous, or merely
the jargon of higher education, in practice they had genuine
significance because of the variety of materials and services
that were and are available to the client groups.   Exactly
what were some of the services that these two-year colleges
offered students, particularly the new learners?

Highly print-oriented in the past, librarians at the
two-year colleges, particularly those in new institutions and
in fairly well-to-do districts or counties, were quick to
learn from some of the more exciting and progressive advances in the high schools, particularly the use of media
and mechanized self-instructional methods. A primer for
this type of library service is Margaret Rufsvold's book,
Audio-visual School Library Service, prepared in the late
1940's.[1] This work is still valid and provides many important details that have assisted the traditional book-oriented
librarian in converting to new media materials and services.
The trends developed by the media-oriented high schools, in
conjunction with the new technology, were followed by many
community colleges as they modified their libraries to function as instructional resource centers. The immediate impact of this transition was to allow many students to proceed
at their own pace, rather than be part of a general and highly structured program. This move away from print toward
the use of different kinds of materials--visual, printed,
audio, and realia--encouraged more individualized or small-
group learning activities that new learners desperately required. Examples of media and technology that encouraged
new learners to use instructional resource centers were
films and projectors, audio cassettes and recorders/players,
instructional programs and teaching machines, and realia,
backed by individual attention by faculty and librarians. The
last example is not as out of place as it might seem because
it also involves the problems of man-machine interface, a
growing concern for librarians and educators.

The man-machine interface is crucial in the types of
services that a community college library will provide for
its new learners. The anxieties generated by the fears of
technology, coupled with their own handicaps and problems,
cause overt and latent hostility and resistance by this client
group to library service through a form of modern technology. Bruno Bettelheim made the penetrating observation that
when modern man is haunted, he is not haunted by other
men but by machines. New learners as a group often dread
technological creations; at the same time, they must rely
upon them for their education and, in some instances, their
survival. Bettelheim suggests that the answer to technology's
threat is not denying it or escaping from it, but facing its
dangers and using it "without letting it deprive us of our humanity."[2] This is basically the role of the librarian, or
should be the librarian's role, at a two-year college.

To be more specific concerning the role of the library in dealing with the new learners, an example of service to a minority group should be sufficient. Underprivileged black children of lower socio-economic status are often tracked through the school systems in the United States.[3] This invariably leads these young men and women into terminal or vocational high school programs with little or no possibility of their attending a four-year college or university. Should these young men or women decide to attend a two-year college, their learning and reading skills may often be undeveloped, and this results in a low success potential and high drop-out rate among these learners. Aware of these conditions, several colleges developed study methods and skills programs coordinated by their student services and learning resources centers. These projects involved a testing device to determine how well-prepared these black students were for college level work, and what deficiencies they might have. The role of the learning resources staff was to provide small-group instruction in the use of their materials and services, often teaching basic skills in the use of a library. This project encouraged librarians to serve as links between the academic programs and the wealth of information and materials available in the library. Furthermore, the role of many librarians became that of interpreter, particularly when some of the young blacks quickly identified with them and began to seek them out. The role of the librarian, whether as interpreter, media specialist, or study skills counselor, provided the human interface between new learners and some of the complicated media forms and associated technology necessary for these students to survive the initial college experience.

Once these black students were capable of using the library, or finding resource materials, and were able to approach and rely upon librarians, the development of their study skills quickly followed, and their success in getting through college improved dramatically. The keys in this project are: identifying study habit weaknesses and reading problems, small-group training sessions with librarians and counselors, sensitivity to the new media and technology, and reliance upon library staff as resource persons and information interpreters. Obviously, the role of the library must be one that complements the teaching program and that encourages librarians to work with new learners on as close to a one-to-one basis as possible.

The Four-Year College

The problems that new learners face at the typical four-year college tend to be more complex than at the two-year college. One of the major themes from the Carnegie Commission on Higher Education report, Reform on Campus, spoke to this issue:

> A century ago, higher education in the United States was 'modernized' to reflect the new role of science, the rapid industrial advance of the nation, the surging populism of the people. Now it needs to be more completely 'humanized' in the sense (a) of being made more accessible to more young people and (b) of being further adapted to the individual characteristics and attributes of its students. [4]

The report goes on to document a growing emphasis on the development of individual human capabilities to enhance the quality of life in all its aspects and to enhance individual and social well-being. For the student interested in a paraprofessional vocation or work role in our society, the colleges are in the midst of a change to accommodate a new significance and relevance within the curriculum. Unfortunately, too many academic libraries at four-year colleges have been caught in a traditional lock-step development program that stresses large book collections and media resources at the expense of service programs sufficiently flexible and appropriate to the needs of contemporary students, particularly new learners with well-defined career goals that include B.A. programs only. These new learners are among the first students to question the validity of materials and services provided by the traditional library, whether the materials are print or non-print or the services involve human or machine interfaces.

At this point it might seem advisable to consider a plea for assistance by a librarian at a four-year college that was experiencing a gradual but increasing decline in library use by students (irrespective of reserve book functions). The librarian in charge of this library was at a loss to explain the apathy of students--after all, she and her staff selected the best of all possible books within their allocated budgets and provided the students with audio-visual materials of the highest calibre. After some extensive discussions with students and younger faculty and a review of materials

in the college library, particularly on the new book shelves,
it was striking to see how traditional the selection program
was. Although often called uncouth and vulgar, Jack Kerouac
was the best interpreter of the "Beat Generation."[5] Surprisingly, only a few of his books were represented in the
card catalog, and those were seldom in or were in terrible
physical condition. Furthermore, materials on the applied
aspects of science and technology in our daily lives were
conspicuously absent from the library's holdings. When
queried about works by Kerouac and the lack of materials on
applied sciences, the librarian responded, "I hardly see why
a probation officer would be interested in Kerouac's works,
or why future department store managers would be interested
in biodegradable properties of synthetics!"

This example is an over-simplification of the problem,
but it is nonetheless persuasive. The career-oriented new
learner going through a four-year college program is not
only preparing himself or herself for a specific job or role
in our society; he or she is also seeking the intricate and
meaningful relationships of literature, the arts, government,
sciences, business, and so forth in our daily lives. College
libraries that fail to see this need and feel this student demand for relevance will continue to see their establishments
underpopulated and underused.

But enough of this discussion on the need for more
interplay between college libraries and the changing college
curriculum; what are some of the new approaches to these
student needs, particularly those of the new learners? The
role of women in our society is a classic example of under-
utilization of an extremely valuable resource. To address
this lack of concern on the campus, a college librarian devised a women's information service program that would be
a three-sided approach to better informing students, faculty,
and other members of the academic community on the historical role of women, the present change in the status of
women, and the future role of women. The three aspects
of the program included a collection of books and periodicals by and about the women's movement, a telephone information center for current events and ready reference devoted exclusively to this topic, and an experimental college
course taught by a female librarian that emphasized women
in various aspects of our society and the obstacles they had
to overcome in their search for recognition and success.
Exhibits, lectures, news clippings, free discussions, and
hand-outs were all part of this project. Materials were

identified that spoke to or identified the role of women in history and in contemporary society, and these were systematically secured for the library, and short annotations were prepared on most titles and included in a subject bibliography prepared for dissemination to faculty and students.   Female students were encouraged by the librarians in the women's information center to consider these materials for use in classes that had not included the role and contributions of women.   An added learning experience was evident, as female students became aware of the changes that would be forthcoming in their roles as equal members of our society, whether in a work or family setting.

Obviously, the above example demonstrates a concerted approach to the future role of women and the betterment of their present status.   Not only would print materials be secured, but films and tapes were part of the sensitivity aspects of this program that offered additional forms and alternative information resources to the traditional teaching programs within the college.   While it may be too early to predict the effect of this library program on the curriculum, it would be safe to venture--from the use made of this center--how important the impact of this service was on the growing awareness of female students and their ability to develop a positive and more integrated concept of themselves in their future work and family settings.   This interplay between academics, personal awareness, and future job and societal roles is but one example of new learners and new service potentials at four-year colleges.   One should not, however, lose sight of a basic ingredient in this example: the willingness of the institution [library] to establish and underwrite the women's information center as a viable service program!

The University

At the expense of sounding like an elite, the university setting represents the most advanced concept of higher education in our society.   However, while the academic programs of the major universities in this country may be highly regarded by academics and certain graduate students, there has been and may well continue to be an indifference toward this institutional setting by many undergraduates and graduates.   The growing size of state-supported universities, such as Ohio State, Minnesota, the University of California, and recently the State University of New York, with student populations on the main campuses in the 20,000-30,000 range, accounts for some of the indifference students feel, basically because of how they are treated by the institution.   When lecture classes begin to number in the hundreds, when students stand in lines for registration, health care, grades, and housing, and are confronted with a library system that measures itself by the number of volumes in excess of one million or the number of branches within the system, bigness becomes synonymous with mass education and indifference.   The student becomes little more than a cog in a giant machine, assigned a number at an entrance point, directed by unconcerned people into a course of action that at some future date will result in a degree if all the IBM cards are properly secured, punched, and deposited.   This concept of higher education, including the traditional pitfalls, was very poignantly reviewed by William Birenbaum in his excellent book, Overlive. [6] Unfortunately, the university and research libraries are slow to recognize this problem, and slower to take any positive action(s).

The romantic concept that many university or research librarians entertain is that the library is the one humanistic element on the university campus that offers the students individual attention, genuine concern, and personal warmth.   The concept of self-education, of being surrounded by the ideas and expressions of the greatest thinkers in the millions of tomes available in the library, seems a persuasive argument in favor of the library's role as the ideal tool for individualized education.   However, there are some realities that too many of these university librarians fail to consider, such as the relatively high demand on most research libraries for particular titles by numerous students and faculty members, the pressure on students of numerous assignments that consume enormous amounts of time, the pressure to publish that forces junior faculty to devote their time to research and investigation often more related to quantifying and organizing than reading, and the built-in difficulties of client groups negotiating large and complex library systems that number in the millions of volumes and pieces of print materials.   If these problems, then, sound so insurmountable, how do university libraries deal with new learners, and how can the highly individualistic and intelligent graduate enjoy his library experiences and find pleasure in this process?   There are, of course, no easy answers. Furthermore, the number of problems facing major university head librarians have become so acute that they are abandoning their positions at an alarming rate. [7] One technique should be discussed that addresses the problems of the

new learner in the university library experience: the use of
subject-oriented specialists or bibliographers.

The topic of subject specialists or bibliographers in
a research library has been presented and investigated by a
number of librarians, most notably Cecil K. Byrd and Eldred Smith. [8] I will not go over that ground again, but will,
instead, focus on the needs of students, whether graduates
or undergraduates, pursuing highly individualized or independent study.   Only recently have librarians begun to question their relationship to students in the process of self-
education.   Rather than conceptualize a role for interactive
relationships with these new learners, librarians have turned
to methods and procedures for the provision of services.
To interact successfully with librarians, students must relate with them as an information resource, not merely as cus-
todians of data or knowledge.   The fundamental key in the librarian's composition as information interpreter and guide
through the individualistic process of self-education is bibliographical expertise.   What this means and how it relates to
the new learner demands amplification.

Bibliographical expertise may be defined as the ability
to develop a system for the identification, organization, or
location of specific segments of recorded knowledge.   Some
of the bibliographical devices needed to approach this knowledge are abstracting journals, indexes, specialized bibliographies, and computer-related profiles. [9]   Also, the ability to
negotiate and manipulate the card or book catalog and serial
holdings list of any given library is a necessity.   For the
subject specialist, the task is to identify, within his or her
area(s) of concentration, relationships between the various
bibliographical devices in order systematically and quickly
to locate or produce the required information.   The efficient
development of such a system demonstrates the fundamental
mastery that a library specialist must possess to be considered a true professional.   Not only must the specialist
identify and possess a working knowledge of these bibliographical devices (frequently called the literature of the field); he
or she must also know their characteristics, such as their
high and low points of development over a period of time,
their changing emphases on various subject areas, and the
longevity of the most important ones.   Given such background
knowledge, the specialist is in a position to relate one work
to another, and to identify or predict what information will
be most necessary for the library and how it might be applied to solving future informational problems.

The intricate and demanding needs of the new learner frequently challenge the bibliographical expertise of the specialist. Usually, the student has not developed a system for the organization and location of knowledge peculiar to his area or field of concentration. Too often, any system devised by the new learner is a mechanistic one, restricted to one or possibly two disciplines, and predicated on a utilitarian premise tested by trial and error. As the educational requirements of the new learner inexorably move toward the interaction of many disciplines, a restricted approach to library use and research frustrates, impedes, and unsettles the student in attaining his goals. This condition provides in a favorable opportunity for successful interaction between a subject specialist and the new learner. The role of the library specialist becomes that of a teaching fellow who can, through bibliographical expertise, subject background, and library training, rapidly locate and secure needed data and information and complement the faculty in a teaching function. The final aspect of this role, that of complementing the faculty in a teaching function, deserves additional comment.

Maurice P. Marchant has long been a spokesman for the teaching role of the academic librarian:

> Current student complaints regarding the irrelevance of many course offerings is pertinent, and librarian values orient them in the direction of the students. Professors acknowledge and support self-education except as it threatens their positions or goals. By contrast, self-education enhances the librarian's role because he controls access to its means and may expect to be called upon to aid in its interpretation. [10]

The new concept of library services to the new learner at major universities involves a service role for the specialist sufficiently flexible to encourage the application of his bibliographical expertise and subject competency to complement the faculty's teaching role. This may include the specialist being required to teach courses which are primarily self-instructional or reading-oriented, where the student, under the direction of a library specialist, develops his own concepts and insights into the topic(s). Radical as it may seem, such competition with the role of the teaching faculty is an eventuality that both librarians and faculty should expect and learn to accept. Perhaps the greatest resistance to such a concept and role-relationship will come not from the teaching faculty, but from librarians and library administrators.

Some General Considerations

While the three different types of academic libraries can each address the needs of segments within the new learners' group, there are many areas of overlap and considerations common to the three of them. The three most important considerations are education and preparation of the librarians, faculty support, and administrative support and organizational flexibility within the university and research libraries. Addressing the first consideration, library education, places a new burden on the library schools. E. J. Josey and Fay M. Blake, in their excellent article, "Educating the Academic Librarian," stressed the need for library education to foster individual competence, encourage creative institutional change, and be responsive to the social needs of our society if it would prepare the superior academic librarians required to work with the new learners. [11] Professional education for librarianship has been too restricted and over-committed to practical, function-related training, or theory. Changes within the library schools must occur to accommodate a changing role for the librarian in an academic setting, particularly when the requirements of new learners are involved.

The second consideration involves faculty support. It comes as somewhat of a surprise to many librarians that faculty may be amenable to the idea of librarians performing teaching functions and involved with students in a student-tutor role-relationship. In the past, this role-relationship was considered more attainable at a community college than at four-year colleges and universities. However, the opportunities for faculty support seem to be as great in the larger universities as in the community colleges, while teaching functions for librarians at four-year colleges remain relatively static and traditional. Additional research is required to determine why four-year colleges are lagging behind in this process of equating librarians with the teaching faculty.

The issues of certification, advanced degrees, and previous teaching credentials may be important factors in whether faculty at four-year colleges will accept a new role for librarians as partners in the teaching process. My per-

sonal opinion is that library administrators and librarians
themselves, particularly those with retreating personalities
or personal insecurities, resist this new role-relationship
because of the changes involved and the new demands and
measurement devices that will be used to evaluate their performance, organizationally and personally.   Faculty can be
convinced that librarians are capable of performing legitimate teaching functions and that they have a role in the educational experience of students, especially a group such as
the new learners.   Furthermore, the three segments within
this group of learners frequently cause faculty great concern
because of the additional teaching loads, both in terms of
added time and course content, placed upon them.   With
teaching positions almost at a zero growth rate or even on
the decline at some institutions, faculty and campus administrators welcome any help from librarians that will increase
the effectiveness of the academic program and reduce faculty
workload.   This is a powerful bargaining point that too few
library administrators have employed.   This last statement
leads into the third consideration: administrative support
and organizational flexibility.

While this essay has been devoted to the development
of new library services to new learners, a new concept of
academic library administration must also emerge.   The library's administrative structure and organization should include genuine support for staff and programs devoted to the
new learners.   This involves a form of participatory management, especially in decision-making and problem-solving situations where this staff's talents must be introduced to encourage and accomplish democratic practices in administrative behavior.   In colleges and universities, because of an
increasing pressure for participation and a growing sense of
professionalism, there is an urgent need for administrators
to abandon outmoded managerial concepts based upon strict
bureaucratic relationships and to function more as statesmen
and linking-pins.[12]   The role of librarians closely associated
with faculty in the teaching process only serves to encourage
a concept of administration quite similar to that employed
by academic teaching departments, where the chairperson of
the department is more a spokesperson and representative
than a manager or absolute decision-maker.   Present library administrative and organizational structure rests on
the mistaken assumption that managers or administrators
possess both substantive subject competence and knowledge
and skills and training in administrative behavior.   To place
such a burden on one individual is short-sighted, but to com-

pel a manager to pass judgments on a variety of matters,
especially those outside of his purview of knowledge or experience, is ludicrous. The formulation of new service concepts and programs for the new learners is something that
should originate with the operational staff, who not only must
perform those functions but whose performance must be evaluated. Unfortunately, too many library administrators are
leery of any new roles or activities that bring their staffs
in contact with the faculty on a regular basis outside of the
library, particularly in a teaching or classroom situation.
Or worse, too many library administrators have never func-
tioned in any capacity other than as a member of the administrative staff and jealously guard for themselves all contacts
with faculty. The shortcomings of both situations are obvious.

The new learner in the academic setting is causing the
academic library to reassess traditional programs and devise
new ones and new service roles to meet their unique demands. This reassessment involves the education of librarians, the use of new media and technology, a new teaching
or tutorial role for academic librarians, and a correspond-
ing need for change in the organizational structure and administrative style of academic libraries and administrators.
Initially these changes may be viewed with suspicion and
even openly resisted by both librarians and administrators.
However, as with other changes that have faced our profession, such as automation, cost-effectiveness programs, and
new methods of measurement, eventually librarians adopt the
new and work to make it better. The real strength of librarianship is its willingness to serve new client groups
such as the new learners and to make changes in libraries,
service programs and the role of practitioners.

References

1. Rufsvold, Margaret. Audio-visual School Library Service. Chicago, American Association of School Librarians, ALA, 1949.
2. Bettelheim, Bruno. The Informed Heart. New York,
   Free Press, 1961, p. 56.
3. The term "tracking" is used in education to identify a
   process whereby children are placed in terminal high
   school or vocational oriented programs by school
   counselors and administrative personnel. An evil
   associated with this process is the prejudicial and

stereotypic attitudes and misconceptions that color the decisions of these educators.

4.   Carnegie Commission on Higher Education. Reform on Campus: Changing Students, Changing Academic Programs. New York, McGraw-Hill Book Company, June 1972, p. 1.

5.   Curley, Dorothy N., and Kramer, Maurice, eds. A Library of Literary Criticism: Modern American Literature. 3 vols. 4th rev. ed. New York, Frederick Ungar Publishing Company, 1969, II, pp. 171-75.

6.   Birenbaum, William. Overlive; Power, Poverty, and the University. New York, Dell Publishing Company, 1969.

7.   McAnally, Arthur M., and Downs, Robert B. "The Changing Role of Directors of University Libraries," College & Research Libraries, 34:103-25, March 1973.

8.   Cecil K. Byrd's informative and controversial piece was "Subject Specialists in a University Library," College & Research Libraries, 27:191-93, May 1966; while Eldred Smith's article that treated this subject in a slightly more expanded context was "Academic Status for College and University Librarians--Problems and Prospects," College & Research Libraries, 31:7-13, January 1970.

9.   A very interesting approach that provides academics with both a profile and automated search services is being refined and expanded at the Center for Information Services, Research Library, University of California, Los Angeles.

10. Marchant, Maurice P. "Faculty-librarian Conflict," Library Journal, 94:2886-89, September 1969.

11. Josey, E. J., and Blake, Fay M. "Educating the Academic Librarian," Library Journal, 95:125-30, January 15, 1970.

12. Bennis, Warren G. "Post-bureaucratic Leadership," Trans-action, 6:44-61, July-August 1969.

A MORE HUMAN APPROACH TO INSTRUCTION IN THE USE OF ACADEMIC LIBRARIES

Dorothy Byron Simon

In general, our English language dictionaries define the adjective "human" as that which pertains to, or is characteristic of, Man. If one were to accept this definition as satisfactory, the human approach to instruction in the use of academic libraries would have to deal with a number of characteristics which we accept as being "only human. " In common usage, this phrase rarely refers to, or extols, human strengths. We are "only human" and therefore weak, defenseless, or unalterably limited. We are "only human, " so that too much should not be expected of us. If we are "only human, " no one should demand perfection of us. "Humanum errare est"[1]--"To err is human"[2] is an ageless, long-enduring apology for our inadequate and inappropriate responses to the immediate situation. We librarians have used our problems of "too little staff, " "inadequate budgets, " "lack of recognition, " as "only human" reasons for our lesser role in the processes of modern education.

However, we humans, as a whole, do not generally allow our self-images to be totally submerged by our faults. Our nobler aspirations are therefore called "humane"--that which is characteristic of human beings. One who is humane is characterized by concern for the distressed. Thus, our everlasting apologies for our confused purposes as library instructors, our out-dated attitudes and ideas, and our uncertain values can be unflattering to our professional self-image, unless an aura of humaneness can somehow be entwined. Perhaps by re-evaluating our purposes, our attitudes, and our values, the road to humanity, and thus, reality in library instruction, might be found.

We can begin with our purposes and aims. As educators in the use of the academic library, have we clearly

defined for ourselves our role in the education process?
Our fellow educators in the "accepted" disciplines seem not
to have to justify their existence as defensively as we do.
We find students, with minimal interests and talents in a
subject, studying with great determination to achieve the requirements demanded for a prescribed mathematics, science,
or foreign language course.

As library educators, however, we are called upon
to be positively "in tune" with the needs of our times. Our
colleges and universities were once the stepping-stones of
the mentally and financially privileged, who, having con-
formed to specific pre-requisites, were ultimately stamped,
sealed, and delivered to the waiting world of good positions,
status, and success. Today's institutions of higher learning
must serve the many groups which are now a part of the
college community. Career, liberal arts, and non-credit
programs must be dealt with. Open admissions policies
have presented the academic libraries with a great challenge.
What are the needs of the open admissions student? How
can the student remedy the weaknesses in his or her past
education? Can he or she overcome the causes of inadequate preparation for higher education? Does the student
understand the vocabulary of his or her major subject? Is
he or she especially talented in a subject, thus feeling the
need to advance beyond the prescribed syllabus? These
needs suggest an awesome role for library educators. Do
we accept it? The library educator's role should be to provide students with the tools which will allow them to be
themselves. No course is irrelevant if the student is given
the skills with which to emphasize and develop an area of a
subject for himself or herself.

Could our overwhelming task be to teach the student
self-reliance? Is it possible that, by teaching the student that
the limitations of his development are in direct relation to
the amount of time he spends in finding the knowledge needed
to complete himself, we library educators are showing the
kind of respect for the human being and his freedom to be
himself that no other discipline except perhaps art and music can show?

Ralph Waldo Emerson once wrote, "It is easy to see
that a greater self-reliance--a new respect for the divinity
in man--must work a revolution in all the offices and relations of men; in their religion; in their education; in their
pursuits; their modes of living; their associations; in their

property; in their speculative view. "[3] In our present era of science and technology we can assume that there are no limits to human knowing. One can know what one wants to know and what one is capable of knowing if one can only map a path to "knowing. "

The path to "knowing" may begin with receiving a good elementary education, or it may be blocked by receiving a poor one. The path to "knowing" may begin with a background of tried and proven middle class values, or it may be obstructed by a background of poverty and lack of opportunity. A student from either end of the spectrum whose library skills have not been developed cannot become the investigator of his or her own interests, roots, problems, and purpose. Circumstances have already determined his or her educational destiny. The circumstances of good or poor teaching, home environment, and social status are in full control.

Today's students are in rebellion against our "eternal verities. " They protest our wars, awaken our consciences, and, yes, demand responsible college administration and teaching. Young dissenters can be motivated to listen to us and respect us as valuable educators if we offer access to the resources which open the records of history. There is motivation for the black, Puerto Rican, or American Indian who searches for his history, for, as Emerson says, "the man who can find no worth in himself which corresponds to the force which built a tower or a sculptured marble god feels poor when he looks at these. "[4] There is also the middle class student who has already satisfied the not-so-subtle demands of his parents for good grades and entrance into a college of esteem. Although he may now await an enviable job in the family business or a start in an honorable profession, he still must be shown the road which could lead the way out of boredom and conformity.

Educational freedom is found in the library, the research laboratory, or other non-structured learning situations. We must teach these students about this freedom. We must show them that one's mind can digress without penalty. The only joy that can be derived from learning to use the card catalog or periodical indexes will come as a result of this desire to digress. Pamphlet files will expose students to other points of view, and newspapers on microfilm will bring the past with its attitudes and prejudices to the attention of the present. Career files will help students

to plan their own futures, and bibliographies will provide in-
depth reading on a favorite subject. In our democratic society, the individual should value the freedom to develop
himself more than anything else. If we library educators
can sell our students self-reliance and educational freedom,
this should be our purpose for being.

As teachers of our subject, the approach we use in
our presentations will reflect our attitudes and ideas about
the students we face. It is easy to recognize the indifference to library instruction shown by many of our better than
average college students. It is easy to recognize the remedial needs of many of our open admissions students. Do
we, however, recognize what is positive about our students?
When we face our students, do we recognize our responsibility to them? Do we recognize the perseverence of the
mother of three who, abandoned by her husband, seeks not
welfare but a college degree and a career? What about the
ambitions of a former dropout who, now having obtained a
high school equivalency diploma, is determined to obtain a
higher education. Former drug addicts are seeking rehabili-
tation in our classrooms. Women are advancing in new
careers. It would be arrogance on our part if we blamed
lack of response to our presentations on their backgrounds.
For these people, time is precious. They want to be taught
coherently and with relevance. Their motivation is high.
They just want to be shown the way. Perhaps, more so
than any other subject, teaching the use of the library demands that the instructor be on the same wavelength as the
class. Be aware of the positive characteristics of the students seated before you. Teach the information skills for
which there is immediate need. Do not encumber them with
abstractions, generalizations, and highly technical details.
No matter what the student's background is, we must be
able to begin at the point where the student is. For example,
if he feels discriminated against, cannot knowledge of the
usefulness of information resources help him to exert greater control over his social, educational, and economic advancement? The student's self-confidence will be enhanced
if he learns early that the limits of his knowledge in a field
are dependent upon his ability to retrieve whatever information he may require. We can teach the student to develop
a skill which can place much of his destiny in his own hands.
The student can be taught to develop a skill that will help
him to make up for the gaps in his past. He can proceed
to nurture any peculiar genius that belongs to him alone.
The syllabus, the class instructor, and one's sex or social

status cannot be the sole dictators.

When one has the responsibility to recognize and solve
a problem, one's aim is to find the solution that is related
to the issue at hand. As we stand in front of our classes,
are we convincing our students that what we are teaching
them is of personal value to them? In general, our students
will exert great effort to learn what is of immediate importance to them (i. e., a test must be passed, a career requirement must be satisfied, or a term paper must be turned
in on time). If, in reviewing his or her personal needs, the
student finds that it does not matter whether or not one knows
how to use library resources, the subject will be quietly and
quickly retired from his or her mind. However, the student
will surely take a new look at the library professor who can
convincingly present, perhaps in its purest form, a liberal,
human approach to self-education.

To outline a strict methodology for presenting this
kind of instruction is to deny the individuality of each situation which the instructor will face. Where does one begin?
Among our students will be those whose backgrounds range
from no former instruction to generally unimpressive orientation lessons from which no learning has been transferred
to practical use. I have had to "teach" students that they
were "allowed" to enter the reference section of the library.
I have had to "teach" students that they were not "bothering"
librarians when they asked for help. I have met bright students who thought library instruction would be a waste of
time until they realized that they did not know how to find
a recent article in their specialized field.

The lasting effects of learning to use the library will
depend upon the method of presentation. Let us convince
them that this discipline is an aid to helping them make the
real decisions necessary for controlling the form their lives
will take. Whether one uses a lecture method, copious
audio-visual aids, or experiments with unusual techniques
depends upon the situation at hand. The route which leads
to accomplishing one's aim is the correct route. Yet, on a
moment's notice, library teachers must be able to throw
away the script if necessary. The method used must fit the
student or group need.

As library educators, we can only convince our students of what we sincerely believe about ourselves and our
profession. If we think of ourselves as being lesser influ-

ences in their lives, we will be received as such. The
functions and purposes of our libraries and our teaching will
continue to be less than adequately understood by our students unless they are convinced that the use of our resources
is vital to their education. In this electronic age, infinite
amounts of information will be at their disposal if our approach is truly effective. If our values transcend petty lessons on how to make out a charge slip, the intricacies of
our fine systems, and so forth, our students will see us as
valuable educators, who understand them when no one else
seems to. We will be the human educators who allow free-
doms for which the structure of required courses does not
provide. We will be the human educators who encourage
them to indulge themselves in the personal areas of knowledge which must be explored before one can approach the
ultimate in personal development--finding one's self.

References

1.   Seneca. Naturales Questiones, Book IV, Sec. 2.
2.   Pope, Alexander. "An Essay on Criticism." In
      Bonamy Dobrée, ed. Pope's Collected Poems. Lon-
      don, Dent, 1956, p. 71.
3.   Emerson, Ralph Waldo. "Self-Reliance." In Howard
      Mumford Jones, ed. Emerson on Education, Selec-
      tions. New York, Teachers College Press, Colum-
      bia University, 1966.
4.   Ibid., p. 114.

THE USER ORIENTED APPROACH
TO REFERENCE SERVICES

Ann Knight Randall

The concept of putting the user and his or her needs at the center of all reference and readers services activities is gaining wider acceptance in academic libraries of all types. The reference librarian must always be cognizant of the external environment of the parent institution and its community. "Academic library" is itself a rather complex term which embraces many different types of institutions. Included within its scope are found public and private schools of higher learning at junior college, four-year college, graduate, and professional school levels. The academic reference librarian may be providing service to a homogeneous student body of less than 1,000 undergraduates, or to a student body which includes diverse groups that total more than 30 times that number. Some of the urban, state, and municipally supported institutions do, in fact, fit the latter description.

Given such a range, the requirements for space and equipment, professional and support personnel, collection size and scope, and reference service patterns are predictably quite different. The opportunity and the capacity for providing special or innovative informational services will also vary. These factors are important considerations in setting up parameters of service in the reference department or division. However, an additional factor which should influence any administrative decision is the philosophy of reference service, whether it is explicit or implicit.

Few academic libraries have articulated their service policy in any formalized way. Almost every sizable library will have a series of rules and procedures which are illustrative, in a partial way, of decisions which cover specific circumstances. But the circumstances will represent only

a small part of the total service, rather than the overall
approach of the reference division.   In the absence of policy,
the level of service will vary according to the personality
and skill of the person on duty and according to the status
and outward appearance of the person who seeks information.
Such variation is difficult to avoid.

        The primary role of the general reference librarian
might be characterized as akin to that of a foot soldier on
the front line of battle.   Upon reflection, however, this
analogy seems to convey an unfortunate impression.   Carried one step further, this analogy would connote the user
as the enemy and the library operation as a defensive endeavor.   We have sometimes been accused of this unfriendly
posture, but this is not the norm.

        What I mean to state is that the general reference li-
brarian is involved in the basic, "on-line" interface between
the user and his or her information.   Even if a question is
never asked, this basic involvement continues to take place.
The following activities are examples of this "non-communicative" involvement:

        1) The arrangement of reference resources in the
reading rooms.   Basic reference sources such as indexes
and abstracts, dictionaries and encyclopedias will be easily
accessible in most libraries.   For user convenience, they
are frequently taken out of the classification sequence and
separately displayed.   On the other hand, frequently used
and popular bibliographies, handbooks, and subject surveys
are often kept in closed stack areas.   This may be for
reasons of protective custody, as well as reference staff
convenience.   The placement of reference resources does
have an effect upon informational access.

        2) The preparation of guidebooks and orientation ma-
terials.   Most libraries will prepare a concise description
of the facilities and services for the convenience of the
user.   Unless these are frequently revised to reflect accurate information about such practical details as service
hours, holiday schedules, personnel and office locations, or
a floorplan, they do not perform the function for which they
are intended.   For this reason, many libraries have selected
inexpensive reproduction processes or have published these
materials in leaflet form.

        3) The compilation of bibliographical aids to the col-

lection. Current trends towards the interdisciplinary approach to studies mean that the subject arrangement followed
by many reference sources does not provide sufficient assistance for many inquiries. While bibliographical compilation is time-consuming for the reference staff, the cumula-
tive saving of time and energy for the user makes it worthwhile. In addition, such activity has a beneficial effect in
terms of library public relations.

4) The selection of furniture and equipment for the
use of reference materials. Factors such as physical com-
fort and attractiveness enhance the satisfaction of library pa-
trons who must use the reference reading rooms frequently
or for long periods of time. Given the heavy commitment
of academic libraries to microform editions of serials, documents, and reprinted monographic works, machines for reading and printing the micro-images are quite commonplace in
reference or readers services units. There is increasing
dependence upon the bibliographic skill of the reference librarian for identification of the specific units within the
micromedia collections. With considerable amounts of new
material being published in other non-book forms, such as
audiotext cassettes, the reference and readers services units
may require several kinds of media hardware and software.
The computer terminal has not yet become a part of this
design, but the new commitment to networks and systems
and the availability of automated retrieval programs from
services such as Psychological Abstracts and E. R. I. C.
make it a likely addition.

These non-communicative or indirect reference functions complement the level of service provided in the more
traditional order of reference services priorities. There is
no implication here that the examples represent any new
functions. Rather, it is a new way of looking at old functions, which are neither routine nor insignificant. In periods of staff shortage and insufficient budget allocations, it
is the indirect functions which are eliminated first. Yet, it
is precisely in these periods that appropriate planning to
make the total reference environment accessible to maximum
use, with minimum difficulty, pays with dividends. When
the required revision of an aid to using the library is post-
poned, the traffic to all information and reference points is
increased accordingly.

In contrast, communicative or direct reference functions represent the services which are traditionally given

top priority.   These include the following:

1) <u>Informational or directory assistance questions.</u>
This is the most basic type of user-librarian interchange.
Questions about the location of materials and facilities, as
well as the easily defined "quick" reference fact, may be
included here.   Increasingly, in academic libraries, this
basic, yet important point of encounter, is being staffed by
well-trained nonprofessionals or library assistants.   Frequently, these are part-time personnel who possess a college degree and who may be enrolled in graduate programs
in library science or other subject areas.   This is not to
suggest, however, that other personnel categories might not
be utilized in this manner.

2) <u>Reference or research questions.</u>   This type of inquiry is not easily described or defined.   Most often it will
include the use and interpretation of bibliographic sources,
such as indexes, abstracts and, of course, the card catalog.
Encyclopedias, yearbooks, and miscellaneous compendia may
include the approximate display of data, through narrative
or tables, that is required.   Some questions may involve a
lengthy probe into the resources of the library, as well as
in other collections through bibliographic listings.

3) <u>Readers' guidance.</u>   Questions which require some
judgment as to the specific source of information which is
best suited to the individual user may be placed in this category.   In the academic library this may range from reference books to supplementary, recreational reading.   Of the
three kinds of questions listed, this type requires the most
detailed knowledge of the collection.   User characteristics
which will have an effect upon the material selected include
many personal and situational variables.   In the academic
library pertinent situational variables include: course subject matter, course level, format of assignment presentation,
and time alloted for completion.   Personal variables may include physical abilities such as eyesight and mobility, prior
educational background, motivation, self-confidence, etc.
Given the fact that our campuses now include more students
with educational, physical, and emotional handicaps, this
type of user orientation is a crucial part of the professional
responsibility to provide reference and information service.

4) <u>Instruction.</u>   It is equally vital that some provision
be made for instruction in the use of the library and its resources.   This is not consistently given priority in college

and university libraries. Frequently, instruction in the use
of the library is given in piecemeal, informal fashion through
specific inquiries at reference and information desks, or as
part of a brief orientation tour. Even less frequent is
formalized instruction in the use of library resources and
research techniques. The trend, however, seems to be reversing. During some recent visits to major university libraries, it was discovered that a large number of them are
recognizing instruction as part of the professional reference
responsibility. For example, bibliographic and research
oriented courses are being offered by librarians in the
Reference Department at Yale University.

   The components of the two basic types of reference
service have been outlined above. "Non-communicative"
reference service is characterized as activity which requires
an indirect involvement with the user. On the other hand,
"communicative" or direct reference service involves the
more usual pattern of interaction at some public service
point in the library. With the exception of formal instruction, the direct service pattern is more traditionally recognized as the function of the reference department. For the
academic library, the ultimate goal of user-oriented reference service is fourfold: first, efficient provision of accurate information which is pertinent to the question and suited
to the particular needs of the user; second, concise explana-
tion of the arrangement of resources in the library and the
procedures which must be followed by each category of library users; third, provision of an environment in which the
professional assistance, the resources, and the space and
equipment are conducive to maximum utility by the library
patron; and fourth, the promotion of learning that is individualized and continual, through instruction and guidance.

   Clearly, user-oriented reference service involves
knowledge of bibliographical sources and subject matter. Of
equal importance is interpersonal communication skills and
ability to assess the needs of different individuals and groups.
The effective program of reference service requires interchange with other academic departments of instruction and
administration, by individual reference librarians. The policy
and the service attitude may be set by the reference department head, but user-oriented service, at the point of contact,
requires intimate knowledge of several problem areas, including institutional goals, departmental issues, and faculty
and administrative personalities. For example, a change in
the curriculum emphasis of a department will alter the re-

source needs of the students and faculty. It is particularly
helpful if the reference librarian with selection responsibilities in that subject attends departmental meetings or, at
least, receives minutes and announcements from the department. The reference librarian will want to anticipate changing demands whenever possible, and to decide upon the appropriate library response, in terms of materials and services. Three examples of changing focus in specific subject
areas will illustrate this point.

Departments of political and social science have been
changing over the last two decades from structural, descriptive disciplines to behavioral disciplines using quantitative
methodologies. Many techniques of experimentation and ap-
proximation have been borrowed from the physical sciences.
In some cases library reference departments have been slow
to identify data sources which either provide or describe
such information as reviews of quantitative research, public
opinion data, statistical data, or census figures. Through
lack of communication, librarians are sometimes unaware
of data sources and project reports produced or received
elsewhere on campus. Intracampus and intercampus communication is not easy on large campuses, but it is an important means of gaining the necessary information to provide
user-oriented service. Some time must be allocated for individual staff participation in campus activities, and this
should be among the priorities of the reference and readers
services departments.

Another example relates to schools of education,
which have been changing from a theoretical to a perform-
ance-based approach. Thus a much larger proportion of the
total academic program is dependent upon pre-professional
field experience. Library resources are required to provide larger numbers of students with applications of research and theory upon which practical teaching units can
be based. In addition, the opportunity to examine and experiment with various kinds of media has value. In most
cases, these will not be central concerns of the reference
staff, except that identification and location of appropriate
resources will be necessary.

Interdisciplinary programs such as Black Studies,
Latin American studies, women's studies, and environmental
studies are seeking to tap the full range of human experience through particular problem approaches. While bibliographical aids are available in these fields, a great deal of

searching through general and discipline-oriented sources is still required. For example, many departments of Black or African-American Studies emphasize three phases of the black experience: the history and civilization of peoples of African descent in the United States, in the Caribbean, and in Africa. In addition to a multi-disciplinary orientation, linguistic facility is helpful for serious research. For the most part, undergraduate teaching programs will concentrate on English language resource material. But this, too, is changing. Early participation in field study and travel programs increases the demand for non-standard source materials. Latin American, Judaic, and other ethnic studies programs build upon bilingualism, in varying degrees. Because of variations from department to department and from campus to campus, the reference librarian with assigned subject responsibility must be in close communication with the relevant academic departments and the teaching faculty.

No unified description of reference services in academic libraries is possible. Variables such as organizational structure, collection size, curriculum, available staff, and many others will have an effect upon the scope of service provided. Nevertheless, the four criteria for user-oriented reference service, previously stated, may be present in any library. The high quality reference service provided in many academic libraries may be transformed into service that is more user-oriented by adhering to certain guidelines. For the most part, such guidelines must be institutionally based, representing the needs of a particular academic library and originating from the reference department staff. But, there are some factors which will have general application.

All reference librarians require a basic knowledge in general subjects and the skill to utilize bibliographic and factual sources of information. More specialized knowledge and skills may be required in some library divisions which provide reference service. Good communication skills and excellent interpersonal relations are requisites of user-oriented service. Equally important is the philosophy of service. The "minimal-middling-maximal" service formula proposed by Samuel Rothstein serves as a good basis for self-evaluation. The outcome of the user-librarian interface is a major determinant in the success of academic library service.

Additionally, the attitudinal climate and the working

environment contribute to the service approach. The techniques of group dynamics and personnel administration have
application for all reference departments, and especially
those which are composed of five or more librarians.
There are numerous ways in which the library administration can contribute to a climate which focuses upon the needs
of current and future library users. For example, administrative support in the form of time to participate in curricu-
lum-related meetings and other such activities will increase
staff knowledge and understanding of the educational programs and goals of the college or university.

Fundamentally, academic librarians have an instructional function. They must exert every effort to become acquainted with the students and scholars who constitute the
ever-changing academic community. The reference librarian
must seek to match their needs, both stated and implied,
with the informational alternatives which the technology of
the 1970's has made possible.

EDUCATION FOR ACADEMIC LIBRARIANSHIP

Ivan L. Kaldor and Miles M. Jackson, Jr.

> It is unfortunate that in the English speaking world the <u>educated</u> librarian has in most cases been replaced by a technician and administrator. [1]

It is hardly possible to consider the educational requirements for academic librarianship without giving some space to the historical background of library education as it relates to academic librarianship. Just as any other profession, librarianship has had to develop educational programs based on the recognition of common problems related to the practices and needs of the profession as well as society.

In 1887 F. M. Crunden, in an address at the American Library Association meeting, likened library organization and service to the commercial ventures of a merchant: knowledge of goods, the customers, the community, their needs, growing and expanding interest, and advertising to promote the goods. [2] No doubt, this crude analogy is still appropriate for today's college and university libraries. Certainly, academic libraries are far different today than they were in 1667 when the first paid librarian at Harvard College served that institution's constituencies. Basically, though, academic libraries still exist to support the work of students, faculty, and administration.

The question of the qualifications and status of those working in libraries, and in academic libraries in particular, has been an ever-returning subject on the agendas of professional library meetings and in the pages of the library press. As early as in 1876, the first three issues of <u>Library Journal</u> repeatedly discussed this concern.

In 1883 Melvil Dewey had outlined his proposal to

open a School of Library Economy at Columbia College where
he served as librarian.   Leaders of the American Library
Association received the proposal with optimism, with the
exception of William F. Poole of the Chicago Public Library,
who felt that there was no training school like a well-managed
library for educating librarians.

With the help of Columbia's president and the somewhat reluctant support of the college trustees, Dewey opened
the school on January 5, 1887.   The first class was held in
a lumber room because, oddly enough, women were denied
the use of recitation rooms at Columbia College.

Distinguished librarians visited the school to lecture
on intellectual matters ("Character and Dialect in Fiction, "
"Egypt Two Thousand Years Ago, " and "Making a Cyclo-
pedia").   However, the nucleus of the course consisted of
more practical training such as accession methods, classification, cataloging, library hand, and the use of the typewriter.

The growth and spread of higher education created a
demand for trained personnel that Dewey hoped to supply.
In his talks with the faculty he urged the simplification of
library rules, methods, and general procedures to facilitate
easy access to library resources by all.   Dewey's first
course lasted three months, was extended to seven months
in the second year, and followed the regular academic year
after that.

With the increasing need for librarians came the
necessity to appoint retired professors to positions in college and university libraries.   Other candidates went through
apprenticeship or were given practical training classes conducted by larger libraries.

Carl M. White identifies four reasons for the subsequent decline of apprenticeship training in favor of the technical education movement.   Libraries were growing in number, size, and complexity.   Professional leaders recognized
that more books and more schools and colleges everywhere
presented a special challenge to librarians; they were asked
to structure a body of knowledge called library science,
on which the development, organization, and administration
of libraries would be patterned.   The modern library movement itself required new institutional functions and new order.
And it became evident in the 1880's that there was a need to

bridge the gap between classical tradition and the practical application of knowledge to the problems generated by canal building, railroad extension, natural resources utilization, and the Civil War and its social and economic aftermath.

The Industrial Revolution, the Morrill Act, and to some modest extent, even Dewey's first classes in librarianship helped to create what White calls the ferment in educational thought and practice. This ferment, in its turn, prepared the way for a new educational policy for the Nation.

William E. Henry was concerned in the early 1900's that Americans were lacking in scholarly training; in fact, many did not see the value general education would hold for librarianship. Henry commented:

> I gladly admit all the good things that can be urged
> in favor of the technical training, but in the last
> analysis they must come to recognize that the real
> librarian has always been and must ever be the
> man or woman with scholarship, broad informa-
> tion, comprehensive grasp and a seeker after in-
> formation, one by nature a helper and a director
> of others....
>
> I think it safe to say that no person need hope to
> make any considerable success in any intellectual
> pursuit who has not as a foundation at least a gen-
> erous and comprehensive education in either ex-
> perience or books or in both.
>
> It is more apparent all the time that not less than
> the equivalent of a college education can justify any
> person in taking up librarianship and even that will
> always fall short of the requirements of the posi-
> tion.   College graduation and degrees are not the
> things needed, but the culture and experience and
> comprehensive view usually resulting from college
> work are the necessary attainments.   So much
> science, so much history, so much of mathematics,
> so much of language, are not the needful accomp-
> lishments for librarianship, but the relationships
> of men and things revealed by these lines are vi-
> tal. [3]

Programs were growing in number and in kind.   In 1915 the Association of American Library Schools was or-

ganized to establish and maintain standards of instruction,
entrance requirements, and curriculum.   Charles C. Williamson, head of the Division of Economics and Sociology of The
New York Public Library, was engaged in 1919 by the Carnegie Corporation trustees to study existing library training
programs.   His report, published in 1923, is considered
the turning point in education for librarianship in the United
States.   Commenting on the significance of this document,
Gates noted:

> Prior to the Williamson report, Mr. Carnegie and
> the Carnegie Corporation had contributed to the
> training of librarians by making grants for endow-
> ment and the support of the library schools at
> Western Reserve University and Hampton Institute
> and to the schools operated by the Carnegie Insti-
> tute in Pittsburgh, the Carnegie Library of Atlanta,
> and to the New York Public Library.
>
> In criticizing the emphasis which was then being
> placed on the clerical and routine aspects of library
> work to the neglect of general education, Mr. Wil-
> liams pointed out that 'no amount of training in li-
> brary technique can make a successful librarian of
> a person who lacks a good general education.' He
> explained that two types of training are required:
> (1) thorough preparation for professional service,
> represented by a full college course providing a
> broad general education and at least one year of
> graduate study in a library school properly or-
> ganized to give professional preparation; (2) train-
> ing for clerical and routine work by completion of
> a four-year high school course followed by a course
> of instruction designed to provide an understanding
> of the mechanics and routine operations of a li-
> brary. [4]

Shortly after the Williamson report there came another stinging report that was not generally discussed in library literature.   In 1924, the newly established Board of
Education for Librarianship called on the expertise of the
American Association of Universities for advice on the education of librarians.   A special committee of the AAU found
that:

> The degrees of B. L. S. and M. L. S. are not de-
> sirable.   Degrees of A. B. or B. S. and M. A. or

> M. S. with or without qualifying phrase 'in library
> science' were to be recommended provisionally un-
> til work shall have been placed on a graduate basis.
> The Bachelor's degree should be granted only on
> the basis of usual collegiate standards, including a
> major, approximately one year, in library science
> ... Two years should be required for a master's
> degree. The first year should include vocational
> courses or equivalent in practice, and lead to a
> certificate. This certificate and a B.S. or A.B.
> should be required for admission to candidacy for
> the master's degree. [5]

According to Evans, an examination of the report
made by AAU indicates that there were intentions to pre-
scribe the route of library education. He felt that the committee intended to have: 1) a graduate program equivalent
to other fields (two years for a field with no undergraduate
foundation); 2) there could be also an undergraduate program
because, in their view, the first-year program was not of
graduate or professional caliber; 3) the first year of training
should not result in the awarding of any academic degree. [6]
There are many academic librarians and members of library
school faculties who would agree with the AAU report.

The AAU did not let its original recommendations
drop. In 1927 it issued a second report to the Board of
Education for Librarianship. This report reiterated the
committee's concern with the granting of a certificate after
a year in a two-year program. Their major point, though,
was the concern for granting a one-year master's degree
without undergraduate training in the field.

Expansion of the Carnegie Corporation's library program resulted in grants to endow and support existing library
schools. In addition, more than $3 million was earmarked
for the establishment of a graduate program at the University of Chicago. Thus, the first Ph.D. degree curriculum
was formulated in 1926 at the University of Chicago's Graduate Library School, with $426,750 to support the program
between 1925 and 1942. In many quarters it was felt that
the Graduate Library School in Chicago had an ideal curriculum for preparing librarians, particularly for university
and research work.

The great strides education for librarianship had
made in the pioneering late 1800's and through the early

decades of this century have gradually come to a halt.
Though many new programs have been established since
World War II, the philosophy and practical implementation of
these programs have basically followed the patterns set by
Columbia, Chicago, and a few other schools of prestige.
Societal, economical, technological, and educational changes
deeply affecting the country have been basically ignored by
library education.   Danger signals such as the mass defec-
tion of mostly young and disenchanted specialists to the
ASIS, the inability of the profession to project and quantify
its future trends and patterns of development, and the shal-
lowness and self-serving nature of most of the research
sponsored by the profession seem to have left librarians and
library educators by and large unruffled.

        The controversy created by the ill-fated ALA man-
power survey ("Gaver Report") and the systematic and
matter-of-fact investigation by Lester Asheim[7] have galva-
nized the library community and attracted their attention to
some vital problems of the changed socio-economic and cultural environment of the fifties and sixties.   By establishing
the various levels of work in the library occupation and defining the tasks and the education involved in each, Asheim
not only diagnosed and labeled but also gave a mandate to library education, a mandate which has never been fully recognized and implemented in the process of recruitment and
education for the profession of librarianship.   This is particularly valid in the case of selection and education of candidates for work in academic libraries.

        What is the essence of this mandate?   Emphasis on
the role of both professional and supportive staff and the introduction of the concept of library occupation as contrasted
by library profession are two significant aspects of Asheim's
report which subsequently has become an ALA statement of
policy.   The report stated:

            To meet the goals of library service, both pro-
            fessional and supportive staff are needed in li-
            braries.   Thus the library occupation is much
            broader than that segment of it which is the li-
            brary profession, but the library profession has
            responsibility for defining the training and educa-
            tion required for the preparation of personnel who
            work in libraries at any level, supportive or pro-
            fessional. [8]

In his report, Asheim delineated five levels of work
in the library occupation, three supportive and two professional. The levels are library clerk, library technical assistant, library assistant, librarian, and professional specialist. The proposal also lists 35 statements and recommendations based on Asheim's earlier paper and on criticism and
suggestions which were made to the ALA Office of Education.

The emphasis placed by Asheim on the separation of
the supportive and professional categories of library personnel has reminded library administrators and educators of a
major inconsistency they face in their daily activities. It is
generally known by library educators and managers of academic libraries that too many of the M. L. S. graduates end
up working as glorified clerks. Thus, an interest in the solution of the problems of training supportive staff is undoubtedly part of the larger picture of eliminating the misuse of
human resources.

The idea of the formal recognition of employee categories which fall between the clerical staff and the master's
degree holders is also promoted by G. T. Stevenson. In
her paper published in the ALA Bulletin in 1967, [9] Grace
Stevenson writes that there is a need to recognize that there
are position categories between clerical personnel and
master's degree librarians. Most libraries hire people who
fall within these groups. However, there are no standards
as to the education, skills, and personal characteristics required for each. Stevenson also recommends four levels of
library education: 1) for the technical and clerical assistant;
2) for the sub-professional with an A. B. degree; 3) for the
master's level; and 4) continuing education beyond the M. L. S.
degree.

Asheim's work, the ensuing discussion, and the resulting ALA resolution have supplied the profession with a
basic document which reflects a consensus as to the parameters and specifics the profession considers to be mandatory
in the pursuit of selecting, educating, and engaging individuals for professional and supportive work in libraries.

The debate over the structure, organization, and even
the philosophy of the educational process which would prepare individuals for the various roles as defined by Asheim
is still going on. Lowell A. Martin[10] notes the uncertainty
that prevails over the determination of the place of the library school in U. S. higher education. Neither is there any

clear understanding as to the curriculum content that would
guarantee the best preparation for future needs, and the
methods that would be best utilized by teachers to convey
the course content.   Martin calls for more research and
scrutiny of present practice and its implications for changes
and improvements.

We shall restrict ourselves in what follows to the examination of specific problems which directly relate to the
present status and possible future development of education
for academic librarianship.   Emphasis will be placed on
changes and trends hitherto mostly ignored or underesti-
mated by the literature--on changes that, in the long run,
might even force leaders of academic librarianship and education for this librarianship to reconsider their present approach to the selection and preparation of new college and
university library personnel, professional and supportive
alike.   Finally, it would be our hope that the consideration
of these changes might result in a shift in the general philosophy followed by managers of academic libraries in the deployment and day to day use of their most important asset--
their qualified staff.

Academia

The recent striving by academic librarians to gain
full faculty status has brought into focus many human and
professional aspects of college and university librarianship.
It has also touched off heated debate within the ranks.   The
arguments submitted by the proponents and opponents of the
new status reveal a true inventory of strengths and weaknesses.   Intellectual brilliance, candor, a gift of true leadership, wit, and self-assured dignity are being contrasted
with mediocrity, cowardly double talk, and symptoms of
schizophrenic insecurity. [11]   On the whole, however, the
debate itself, the issues raised, and the developments which
have climaxed in the adoption of the new ACRL Standards
for Faculty Status for College and University Librarians[12]
indicate that academic librarians as a group are well on
their way to breaking the spell cast upon them by a long
line of management and labor experts, educational psycholo-
gists, college administrators and faculty, and, just recently,
by professors Bundy and Wasserman. [13]   They seem to re-
ject the condescending diagnosis of being members of a
"marginal or maturing profession" whose "claims of professionalism are often a melange of the real and fanciful,

in which pious longings are often confused with reality." Indeed, very few academic librarians seem to show any concern over the transparent efforts to stereotype them. Nor do they tend to try slavishly to match the list of requirements they are supposed to meet in order to fit the mold cast for them by faculty committees of their colleges.

The soul searching, negotiations, and confrontations of the sixties and early seventies have helped academic librarians to forge a new identity within the library profession and also in many college communities. This qualitative change, in its turn, is now instrumental in bringing about a new view of the role of the academic library and its staff.

Many library schools and library educators appear oblivious to the changes the academia is undergoing. They select candidates, offer programs, and educate future academic librarians without fully considering the implications of such developments as colleges "without walls," contract study, unionization of the faculty, community colleges, three-year B. A. programs, or computer-aided instruction. Furthermore, not all seem to have realized the inevitable and direct impact the new breed of educated candidates will have on the curriculum. And many of these candidates knock on the doors of the profession with the intent of becoming academic librarians!

Thus, a brief overview of the major factors that will shape academic librarianship in the seventies would seem to be in order.

Environment

Although the bureaucratic apparatus of our colleges and universities may appear unchanged, the events of the past decade and a half have made their lasting mark on U. S. academic life. The most apparent change is in attitudes and relationships. The drawing of a sharp dividing line between administration and faculty, the development of a new employer-employee relationship, the introduction of checks and balances in terms of accountability to the campus community are just some of the more noticeable outward indicators of this new climate, which inevitably calls for an urgent re-evaluation of the management aspects of academic librarianship.14 Beneath, there is a much stronger and

deeper current of change.   Constant experimentation with
ideas and methods, individualized approach to study, a new
student-teacher relationship, and the testing of the relevance
of curricula in terms of life have become hallmarks of excellence of academic programs.

          This is the climate in which academic librarians per-
form.   It is also the environment in which students, future
M. L. S. and Ph. D. candidates, live and work.   Furthermore,
they are the ones who will return to this very same academia if they choose college and university librarianship as a
career.

          There can be no doubt that the new academia of the
seventies calls for a much more intensive, innovative, and
scholarly participation by the librarian in the intellectual
pursuits of students and faculty.   The question that remains
to be answered is: will the new generation of academic librarians be ready intellectually and emotionally to meet this
challenge?

Needs, Status, Qualifications: Catch 22

          Academic librarianship appears to be most affected
by the changing patterns in the individual, collective, and
institutional approaches to study and research.   The impact
of these changes is enhanced by a large range of background
factors which, in their turn, will have a direct influence on
the library environment.

          Before turning to a closer investigation of some of
these new developments one feels a need to reaffirm the
basic functions of the college and university.   Louis R. Wilson identified these functions as: 1) conservation of knowledge; 2) teaching; 3) research; 4) publication and interpretation of the findings of research; 5) extension and public service.[15] At a time of sudden and unexpected changes it is
indeed comforting that Wilson's list of a quarter of a century
ago still had the ring of truth and relevance.   Each of these
points may serve as a yardstick for future efforts to solve
the problems academic librarianship will be facing.   And
there can be no doubt as to the significance of the role the
academic librarian will play in the realization of these functions.

          Nevertheless, the current dissatisfaction with academ-

ic library service begs some rather basic questions.   What
are the changes which have caught the academic library off
guard and utterly unprepared?   Does academic librarianship
possess the inner strength and sensitivity needed to cope
with the library problems created by recent social, educational, professional, and technological changes?   And, finally, are academic librarians and candidates for college and
university librarianship ready to meet increased educational
and professional requirements in order to regain the unique
position and role enjoyed for centuries by academic librarianship?

In their report on a recent survey of university libraries, McAnally and Downs have offered a fairly exhaustive inventory of the most significant factors responsible for
the current change.

> Several factors beyond the obvious one of expan-
> sion of existing graduate programs and establish-
> ment of new programs have affected the university
> and its library.   A major instance is the continued
> fragmentation of traditional academic disciplines.
> New specializations continue to break off from old-
> er fields; each, of course, smaller than the origi-
> nal....
>
> Another movement of the sixties which is having a
> major impact on libraries is the emergence of in-
> terdisciplinary programs, including area studies.
> New social concerns and demands for relevance al-
> so foster the growth of interdisciplinary institutes
> and other irregular patterns outside of established
> fields....
>
> To help cope with the flood of students, teaching
> methods have turned increasingly to larger classes,
> increased use of teaching assistants for regular
> classes, and, to a lesser degree, the newer media,
> such as closed-circuit TV....16

Other sources of change mentioned by McAnally and
Downs are the information explosion, inflation, unionization,
new technology, new theories of management, and pressures
from almost all directions.

One source of pressure on the academic library is the
new breed of students.   These students are action-oriented

and are demanding improvements in library service.   One
of the respondents to the McAnally-Downs survey reported:

> Under pressure from students and faculty there
> has been a forced change in academic library pri-
> orities ... Service is more important, or holds
> more immediacy than collection building.   More
> service is wanted and in more depth ...   Reference
> to limitations of funds, space, personnel is not
> accepted as a sound reply, but only as an alibi for
> non-performance. [17]

A more concrete prognosis of forthcoming changes in
the learning environment is offered by E. J. Josey and F.
M. Blake. [18]   They predict that academic librarians will
have to give direction and help to more and more students
who now are engaged in independent study.   Textbooks, re-
served book lists, "lectures to bunched herds of assembled
hundreds" are going to vanish, to be replaced by seminars,
independent study, tutorials, and special bibliographies.

Another source of pressure for specialized and in-
depth service is the faculty.   The scope of this paper does
not permit us to detail the specifics of faculty attitudes to
libraries in general, and to library services in particular.
However, their point is clearly expressed in the description
of an ideal academic librarian as construed by a "friendly
witness" at the First Japan-United States Conference on Libraries and Information Science in Higher Education.   Speaking on behalf of library-oriented scholars, P. M. Mitchell
stated:

> Librarians have become more logisticians and less
> lovers of books in recent decades.   The scholar's
> heart is not warmed by the librarian who is effi-
> cient in the techniques of circulation or cataloging
> and is not primarily concerned with the contents
> of books and the aims of research.   For this rea-
> son the scholar is pleased when librarians who al-
> so are scholars are at the helm in a university li-
> brary, despite the anguished cries from some
> quarters that the competent scholar is incompatible
> with the competent administrator.   Perhaps this
> anguish is not without foundation, but the ideal
> synthesis of the scholar and the librarian is always
> worth striving for, and there are enough examples
> of living scholar-librarians who evoke admiration

> from their peers in both categories to prove that
> the ideal is not totally unrealistic. [19]

We all know that Mitchell is not the only one who believes in the scholar-librarian concept. As a matter of fact,
this has long been a tradition in such great centers of learning as the Sorbonne, Oxford, Budapest, Cambridge, Lenin-
grad, and Vienna. Scholars of high reputation and brilliant
mind have taken pride in organizing, developing, and managing collections for the benefit of their colleagues and the
body of bright and dedicated students; and, of course, for
themselves. Mitchell's words echo the principle, and to
some extent the feelings, described on December 23, 1780,
in the General Assembly of the Sorbonne by Jean-Baptiste
Cotton des Houssayes on the occasion of his <u>election</u> as the
librarian of that august body.

> When I reflect, indeed, on the qualifications that
> should be united in your librarian, they present
> themselves to my mind in so great a number, and
> in such a character of perfection, that I distrust
> my ability not only to enumerate, but also to trace
> a true picture of them.... Your librarian, gentle-
> men, is in some sort your official representative.
> To him is remitted the deposit of your glory....
> Thus, therefore, your librarian should be, above
> all, a learned and profound theologian; but to this
> qualification, which I shall call fundamental, should
> be united vast literary acquisitions, and exact and
> precise knowledge of all the arts and sciences,
> great facility of expression, and, lastly ...
>
> A librarian truly worthy of the name should, if I
> may be permitted the expression, have explored
> in advance every region of the empire of letters,
> to enable him afterwards to serve as a faithful
> guide to all who may desire to survey it.... Thus
> the superintendent of a library, whatever be its
> character, should be no stranger to any depart-
> ment of learning: sacred and profane literature,
> the fine arts, the exact sciences, all should be
> familiar to him. [20]

Of course, in today's world of sophistication and with
the explosion of human knowledge this prescription would be
far too ambitious, if not impossible, to follow. However,
there are ever increasing signs which indicate that academic

librarians, and first of all those in public service positions,
no longer can perform satisfactorily without education and
skills beyond those needed in most other types of libraries
(special and research libraries being an exception).   Danger
signals have surrounded us for more than a decade, but
most of us have preferred to ignore them.   Appeals by the
few who had the courage to identify the need have fallen on
deaf ears.   Leaders of library education appear to be oblivious to the problem.

The general dissatisfaction with academic library
service, the demands of students and faculty for improvements in the scope and depth of library work, the constant
complaints about the lack of communication between librarians and potential as well as actual user groups, and, last
but not least, the insults hurled at librarians by some faculty members while answering the Massman questionnaires on
faculty status, all seem to point to the same hiatus: the
lack of subject knowledge in the educational background of
the academic librarian.

Student demands and the Mitchell statement clearly
indicate that users of academic libraries wish to work in
partnership in study and research with the academic librarian.   The key to such partnership, which would solve the majority of the woes of public service in the academic library,
is better education, better preparedness in various subject
areas, and the command of one or more foreign languages.

These imperative requirements for academic library
work have been clearly outlined in the Josey-Blake paper[21]
of several years ago.   The importance of subject knowledge
had been emphasized by Louis R. Wilson and many others
for decades.

For those still in doubt one could go further back
and quote the simple but forceful words of the first advocate of libraries in America.   Dr. Thomas Bray wrote in
his Bibliothecae Americanae, in 1697, that since libraries
"give requisite helps to considerable attainment in all the
parts of necessary and useful knowledge, " it was impossible
to believe that those in charge "should be able to communicate to others, what they are not themselves first become
masters of. "[22]

Why then the apathy, the resistance, the neglect
academic library administrators and academic librarians

themselves display when the question of subject education is raised? Has it become the Catch 22 of academic librarianship? Perhaps so. Those with M. L. S. degrees seem to consider their education a terminal one, that the B. A. degree has equipped them with all the knowledge they needed for the so-called "well-rounded" education which was in the vogue during their student years. We do not wish to deny the merits of a broad liberal arts education; without it a subject specialist would be just as handicapped in the academic library situation as our M. L. S. degree holders are now without the subject knowledge. What we are advocating is a combination of the two. The coldness of many academic library administrators toward the idea of having several of their professional staff members enrolled in degree programs and working toward a second degree in a subject area is understandable; indeed, to some extent, it is forgivable. Though counterproductive, this attitude is based on the realities of life. Those who have read the McAnally-Downs paper[23] would be inclined even to sympathize with such an attitude. This is, then, the director's Catch 22.

We would prefer to consider the librarian's endeavor in continuing education a very personal business, an effort which should stem as much from individual initiative, drive, and ambition as from professionalism. The director's role would be rather that of orchestrator of interests and needs than sponsor or instigator. However, the establishment and wise administration of a system of incentives (time off, promotion, selective granting of faculty status, remuneration, etc.) remains very much his duty.

The same principles, rules, and recommendations would apply, by and large, to the study of foreign languages by public service academic librarians.

The reader may wonder why we make this distinction between the public service (reference) librarian and the rest of the staff, including the director of the library. In the following discussion of education for academic library work we shall devote some attention to this problem.

Having considered the environment, the needs, and some education-related problems of the academic library, we turn now to the investigation of possible ways and means by which schools of library science and professional library education could contribute to the solution of some crucial and very special dilemmas of academic librarianship.

Recruitment, Education, Deployment

From the hierarchy of library personnel as outlined in the ALA Statement of Policy on Library Education and Manpower, we shall concern ourselves mainly with the recruitment, education, and deployment of the following two categories:

    a)   Librarian or Specialist
    b)   Senior Librarian or Senior Specialist.

Although the ALA-Asheim scale places the library director in the "Senior Librarian" category, for all practical purposes it is desirable to consider this position as a category in itself and to devote some special attention to the education, qualifications, and selection of candidates for this post.

Supportive personnel (i.e., clerks, library technical assistants, and library associates) will be considered here only to the extent of their role in the implementation of a policy for more efficient use of professionals.

One of the premises on which this paper is based is that the public service librarian (reference-bibliographer) is the backbone of any academic-research library. Other groups of librarians (catalogers, circulation, acquisitions, serials, interlibrary loan, specialists and their supervisors) are merely "supportive" professionals in the best and noblest sense of the word. Their direct impact on the most crucial role of the library--that is, on the partnership in studies and research--is often vague, diffused, and hard to document.

Finally, it is felt that within the academic model, a further refinement of the ALA-Asheim professional classification is now long overdue. The division of the professional "librarian" category into the functional groups of (a) public service (reference-bibliographer) librarian, and (b) supportive professional librarian will prove helpful when educational and skill requirements are discussed. The separation of a "management group" from the traditional hierarchy is another refinement suggested here for the same reason (see Figure 1).

These changes will enable us to submit some ideas and recommendations concerning differentiated library edu-

```
┌─────────────────────────────────────┐
│   PROFESSIONAL CATEGORY:             │
│                                      │
│ A │ Public Service (Reference-       │
│     Bibliographer) Librarians        │
└─────────────────────────────────────┘
```

```
┌─────────────────────────────────────┐
│   SUPPORTIVE PROFESSIONAL            │
│   CATEGORY:                          │
│                                      │
│     Senior Acquisition Librarian     │
│     Senior Cataloging Librarian      │
│ B   Senior Serials Librarian         │
│     Senior Rarebook Librarian        │
│     Senior Gifts & Exchange Librarian│
│     Public Relations Librarian       │
│     Personnel Officer                │
│                    Etc.              │
└─────────────────────────────────────┘
```

```
┌─────────────────────────────────────┐
│   MANAGEMENT CATEGORY:               │
│                                      │
│     Director                         │
│ C   Head Public Services Librarian   │
│     Head Technical Processes Librarian│
└─────────────────────────────────────┘
```

Figure 1.   Functional refinement of the ALA-Asheim professional categories as applied to academic libraries.

cation[24] for the preparation of academic librarians.

Let us review now the basic education and skills which are considered by many as essential for successful professional performance at various posts in an academic library. It is understood, of course, that the degree of desirability of some parts of this education will vary along the wide spectrum of academic libraries, starting with the two-year community college libraries and ending with the graduate research libraries of some of our largest universities.

Category A.   This is the category of public service (reference-bibliographer) librarians. By their name, functions, and educational preparedness this group is clearly

identifiable as part of academia, and its members are active
and direct contributors to the academic process. They are
the only group of professionals within the academic library
which is or should be qualified, equipped, and trained to
enter into a "partnership in studies and research" with students and faculty.

In addition to the human characteristics and professional attitudes generally needed for effective communication, the
following formal educational requirements are appropriate for
a successful public service (reference-bibliographer) librarian:

a) fifth-year (graduate) degree in library and information science (e.g., M.L.S.);
b) subject competency in one of the academic disciplines; and
c) working knowledge of at least one modern foreign
language.

Some would argue that this list of requirements represents an "elitist" philosophy, and that the educational
goals mentioned are beyond the capacity and reach of the
typical entrant to the library profession. Those who have
been involved recently in the process of screening applicants
for admission to the M.L.S., sixth-year, and doctoral programs in library science know better. Indeed, the large
number of excellent applicants--many with master's or even
doctoral degrees in a subject field, with language skills,
and often with substantial life experience--suggests that we
have arrived at the finest hour of U.S. library education.
Here is a unique opportunity for academic librarianship to
upgrade its ranks.

Since the crucial role of subject competency in the
communication process between the academic librarian and the
student or faculty client is now a generally recognized fact,
it is of some interest to consider the ways in which such
competency can be acquired by candidates. Of course, the
burden of obtaining this education should rest with the individual. The fifth-year M.L.S. program is definitely not the
framework for such studies. Neither should schools of library science piously embark on patronizing efforts to sponsor, direct, or even "bookkeep" sixth-year subject studies by
former M.L.S. students. Something can be said, however,
for a well-designed fifth-year curriculum in academic librarianship which would encourage participants to use some of
their elective hours for graduate studies in a subject field

of their choice.

Hence, the two alternatives library schools might consider are:

a) selective recruitment and counseling to attract candidates with subject competency for the fifth-year program in academic librarianship; or
b) program design permitting a liberal use of elective hours for participation in graduate courses in a subject chosen by the student.

In the case of fully employed academic public service (reference-bibliographer) librarians, work for a second master's degree or its equivalent will fall in the domain of continuing education. The paramount role of a whole range of incentives, including sabbatical leave, is beyond dispute.

By strictly enforcing the admission requirements, which usually include a working knowledge of at least one modern foreign language, [25] the schools of library science could significantly influence the outcome of efforts to make this skill a standard part of education for academic librarianship.

In addition to the usual incentives, designed to encourage foreign language studies by practicing academic public service librarians, a standard salary supplement (bonus) could be introduced as a routine compensation for documented and periodically tested foreign language competency. This practice is widely accepted all over the world by such language-oriented institutions as banks and foreign trade companies and their research arms.

Finally, motivations behind any argument to extend subject degree and foreign language requirements and, no doubt, the accompanying compensation, to employee groups other than public service (reference-bibliographer) librarians should be carefully analyzed. Only requirements and compensation based on real and documented needs will have a chance to stand the test of time and the scrutiny of the college or university administration. No academic library can afford to gamble on this issue.

Category B. This is the category of supportive professionals. It includes librarians (specialists) and senior

librarians (senior specialists) in charge of such operations
as acquisitions, cataloging, serials, binding, gifts and exchange, circulation, interlibrary loan, and personnel. They
may be "managers" of these units or simply primus inter
pares specialist leaders in charge of one particular activity.
If there is any truth to the complaints that present academic
library organizations display unmistakable signs of "top
heaviness, " a creative application of the ALA-Asheim hierarchy, as suggested here, may be just the answer to such
criticism.

There are three major factors which call for a complete revision of our philosophies and practices concerning
the recruitment, education, and deployment of professional
librarians (specialists) of Category B:

a) the new technology;
b) the emergence of library and bibliographic data
    systems; and
c) the availability of trained supportive personnel.

The impact of these factors is deep and tangible.
Could any cataloging department worth its salt deny that the
availability of the National Union Catalog, MARC data files,
cataloging in source, on-line catalogs, shared cataloging,
L. C. card sets and other kits have substantially altered
their lives, work, and workloads? Can or should any acquisitions or serials department survive with Stone Age-
style records, flocks of pen pushers and pedantic card fil-
ers, while on the same college campus, the registrar's, the
admissions, alumni, and scheduling offices routinely work
with modern computer files? Two factors--upgraded and
modernized educational and skill requirements for the supportive professionals, and the emergence and availability of
new groups of workers whom Asheim classifies as clerks
(library technical assistants and library associates)--seem
to supply at least a partial answer to this dilemma.

It is not at all difficult to envisage the organization
which will emerge: small, single-purpose units of well-
trained associates, technical assistants, and clerks led by
one or two professionals. Much of their work will be reduced to the manipulation of data and documents drawn from
the pools of various international, regional, and state academic and non-academic systems. [26] They will also build
and machine-process locally generated data files for circulation control, binding, serials management, and so forth.

The education and skills needed for successful performance by any supportive professional should, of course, reflect this change in philosophy, methods, and organization. They might consist of the following:

   a) fifth-year (graduate) degree in library and information science (e.g., M.L.S.); or
   b) sixth-year specialist certificate or its equivalent in business administration and computers.

Such educational and skill requirements not only would secure an efficient, businesslike, and competent leadership in many costly operations of the academic library but would also prepare cadres for promotion to higher management positions. It is understood, again, that the marriage of full-time and part-time study and continuing education should be envisaged as the ideal vehicle by which these qualifications can be acquired.

Category C. Two or three top managers of the academic library belong in this category. In terms of the generally accepted organizational schemes, the director, the head of public services, and the head of technical services should be discussed under this heading.

We have agreed earlier that, for all practical purposes, the director should be considered as a unique category. Although opinions concerning the education of the director differ widely, [27] there are three criteria which should be met by a candidate for this position:

   a) basic library education;
   b) doctoral degree in library science or, preferably, in another area; and
   c) substantial experience in management.

The M.L.S. degree would give the director a solid background in the details of routine library work. Studies toward a doctoral degree would yield an understanding of the research process and the needs of researchers. Furthermore, the doctoral degree would lend the director an outward symbol of the status this position so sorely needs within the college-university environment.

One could argue that under these terms a candidate with a B.S.L.S. degree, a doctoral degree in law or medi-

eval history, and several years experience in the management of a publishing firm could be appointed director of a
university library. Very much so! The formal education
cited here would satisfy our criteria. As far as management skills are concerned, we would fully agree with Arnold
Weber's view about the broad applicability and transferability
of these skills. He writes:

> ... there is a significant degree of transferability
> of management skills ... the potential benefits of
> this transferability have been frequently overridden
> in the name of professionalism. There is no ana-
> lytical reason for preserving this gap between
> management and professionalism. [28]

A slight variation might be called for in the education
and skills of the managers of public services and technical
processes. Language and subject competency by the public
service librarian, and computer and data processing skills
in the case of his technical services colleague, undoubtedly
would enhance their effectiveness as managers.

The Role of the Library School

Finally, what is the role of the school of library
science in the recruitment and education of academic librarians?

The primary mission of the school is to offer a solid
and substantial fifth-year (M. L. S.) program. The objective
of the program is to equip the student with a body of basic,
generalized, and mostly theoretical knowledge called library
science. The responsibility for the subsequent practical application, implementation, and constant updating of this
knowledge rests with the individual graduate.

Any attempt to accommodate "differentiated" library
education within the one-year M. L. S. program or to tag to
it course work leading to subject competency would inevitably call for an extension of the duration of this program.
Professional, financial, and market considerations will not
permit such extension, at least within the foreseeable future.
Thus, working toward clearly defined objectives and locked
in to a one-year time-span, our M. L. S. programs can offer
and encourage only very limited specialization by type of library or activity. A shift in emphasis away from the pri-

mary objective and toward specialization would inevitably result in the fragmentation and parochialization of the program.

These restrictions notwithstanding, the library school can play an important role in the recruitment and professional education of college and university librarians.

a) _Recruitment._ Schools exercise almost exclusive control over the ports of entry to academic librarianship. By careful screening and appropriate counseling, they could recruit outstanding candidates for college and university library work. During this process they could also place a premium on such established qualification requirements as subject competency (master's degree or its equivalent) and foreign language proficiency.

b) _Curriculum._ There are many areas in a typical fifth-year program which could be strengthened for the benefit of the student-candidate for academic librarianship.   A few tentative hints concerning changes in methodology and subject content are being introduced here. Some of them would enhance the education of the public service (reference-bibliographer) librarian; others would upgrade the curricular choices of the supportive professional (cataloger, serials librarian, acquisitions librarian, etc.).

1) A general thrust could be developed throughout the curriculum to give candidates all professional and psychological "facilities" needed for the assumption of an active role in their "partnership in study and research" with the academic client.

2) Proficiency in at least one modern foreign language is among the admission requirements in many schools. The usefulness of this in the academic and research environment is undisputed. Schools could have a carefully coordinated, highly visible, and continuously monitored plan for the application of this hard-earned skill in such classes as cataloging, bibliography, history of books and libraries, international children's literature, comparative librarianship, indexing and abstracting.

3) Problems of higher education and the changing social patterns and attitudes, and their direct or indirect impact on college and university life and business, could become, by design, part of courses devoted to the social role of the library.

4) Courses in general national subject bibliography could go beyond the standard sources of the Anglo-Saxon world.

5) Bibliographic methods and search strategy could be instilled in candidates by matching students with users and guiding them through all phases of such work--in a real life situation.

6) Direct encounters between advanced students and directors and staff members of academic libraries of all types could be arranged regularly. This would provide excellent opportunities to test theoretical knowledge and ideas acquired through classwork on the best possible sounding-board--the practicing professional librarian.

7) As the professional objectives of candidates for academic librarianship gradually develop, full flexibility could be given in their access to such "specialized" classes as serials, acquisitions, government publications, library systems and cooperation, advanced cataloging, media and media applications.

In summary, we quote Virgil Massman's frank and forceful words about the education of the academic librarian and its implications:

> Obviously, the question of the appropriate academic preparation for librarians is a complex matter which deserves much more discussion. As librarians we like to cite statements about the need for 'life-long education,' for education for 'successive careers,' and for opportunities for education to keep up with a 'changing world.' Are librarians to be excluded from this phenomenon? Is the master's degree the end for librarians? Is the master's degree earned in 1950, 1960, or 1974 enough to keep up forever with the complex, changing world of librarianship?

> Yes, I had hoped that the trend toward gaining full faculty status would lead to an increasing emphasis on additional education for librarians. There is no question but that if librarians had more formal education both the profession itself and our ability to serve users would be enhanced. [29]

References

1. University of Western Australia. Report of the Library for the Year 1971.
2. Library Journal, 12:169, April 1887.
3. Henry, William E. My Own Opinions Upon Libraries and Librarianship. Freeport, N.Y., Books for Libraries Press, 1931, pp. 27, 30.
4. Gates, Jean Key. Introduction to Librarianship. New York, McGraw-Hill, 1968, pp. 115-16.
5. Association of American Universities. Journal of Proceedings and Addresses of the Annual Conference, 26:26, 1924.
6. Evans, G. Edward. "Training for Academic Librarianship: Past, Present and Future." In Herbert Goldhor, ed. Education for Librarianship (Monograph, no. 11). Urbana, Ill., University of Illinois Graduate School of Library Science, 1971, pp. 114-15.
7. Asheim, Lester E. "Education and Manpower for Librarianship," ALA Bulletin, 62:1096-1106, October 1968; and "Library Education and Manpower," American Libraries, 1:341-43, April 1970.
8. "Library Education and...," op. cit., p. 341.
9. Stevenson, Grace T. "Training for Growth--the Future for Librarians," ALA Bulletin, 61:278-86, March 1967.
10. Martin, Lowell A. "Research in Education for Librarianship," Library Trends, 6:207-8, October 1957.
11. For an annotated bibliography of papers on the academic status controversy the reader is referred to: Hulig, N. "Faculty Status--A Comprehensive Bibliography," College & Research Libraries, 34:440-62, November 1973; also, Massman, Virgil F. Faculty Status for Librarians, Metuchen, N.J., The Scarecrow Press, 1972.
12. "Standards for Faculty Status for College and University Librarians," College & Research Libraries News, 33:210-12, September 1972.
13. Bundy, Mary L., and Wasserman, Paul. "Professionalism Reconsidered," College & Research Libraries, 29:5-26, January 1968.
14. McAnally, Arthur M., and Downs, Robert B. "The Changing Role of Directors of University Libraries," College & Research Libraries, 34:103-25, March 1973; and Munn, Robert F. "The Bottomless Pit, or the Academic Library as Viewed from the Administration Building," College & Research Libraries, 29:51-

54, January 1968.

15. Wilson, Louis R. "The Library in the Graduate Program of Institutions of Higher Learning in the Southeast." In The Library in the University, Hamden, Conn., The Shoe String Press, 1967, pp. 35-36.

16. McAnally, Arthur M., and Downs, Robert B. "The Changing Role...," op. cit., pp. 105-6.

17. Miller, Robert A. Letter to Arthur McAnally, dated March 17, 1972. As cited in McAnally, Arthur M., and Downs, Robert B. "The Changing Role...," op. cit., p. 112. (Italics by us.)

18. Josey, E. J., and Blake, Fay M. "Educating the Academic Librarian," Library Journal, 95:125-26, January 15, 1970.

19. Mitchell, P. M. "The Scholar and the Library." In Buckman, Thomas R. et al., eds. University and Research Libraries in Japan and the United States, Chicago, American Library Association, 1972, p. 38.

20. Dana, John Cotton, and Kent, Henry W., eds. Literature of Libraries in the Seventeenth and Eighteenth Centuries, Metuchen, N. J., The Scarecrow Reprint Co., 1967, pp. 34-36.

21. Josey, E. J., and Blake, Fay M. "Educating the Academic...," op. cit.

22. As cited in Hoole, W. Stanley. "Of the Librarian's Education," The American Scholar, 13:110, Winter 1943.

23. McAnally, Arthur M., and Downs, Robert B. "The Changing Role...," op. cit.

24. The concept of differentiated library education was elaborated by M. P. Gastfer. At the IFLA Special Libraries Section Meeting, in Copenhagen (August 27, 1969), Gastfer presented his paper "Differentiated Library Training" which could serve as a blueprint for the organization of education for librarianship along both lines: librarianship and subject competency. The paper was printed in INSPEL, 4:65-71, July-October 1969.

25. Walch, David B. "Library Education and Foreign Language Requirements," Journal of Education for Librarianship, 11:166-81, Fall 1970.

26. For information about recent developments in library automation and machine readable bibliographic data bases the reader is referred to vols. 7 and 8 of Cuadra, Carlos A., ed. Annual Review of Information Science and Technology, Washington, D.C., American Society for Information Science, 1972 and

          1973, respectively.
27.   Morris, Leslie R.   "The Head Librarian and His Edu-
          cation: The President's Attitudes," Journal of Edu-
          cation for Librarianship, 12:162-66, Winter 1972.
28.   Weber, Arnold R.   "The Transferability of Manage-
          ment Skills," Library Quarterly, 43:385-95, October
          1973.
29.   Massman, Virgil F.   "Letter to the Editor," College
          & Research Libraries, 35:52-53, January 1974.

MAKING ACADEMIC LIBRARY FACILITIES MORE FUNCTIONAL

R. Patrick Mallory

I am making one basic assumption in the beginning of this essay that the reader has a library which is functioning in an existing college or university. At the end of the essay I shall discuss the particular situation of a newly founded institution which has no functioning academic library. While the former case may be plagued by the problems of having cast into stone structures and policies which are no longer desirable, the latter will profit from observation of the errors and pitfalls of other libraries.

The first step toward improving the functionality of academic library facilities is a matter of library administration and management. Without making any assumptions on whether change is necessary, and without referring to in-house files, develop a staff statement of the purpose and primary responsibility of the academic library. This statement should be completely devoid of references to specific tasks, staff assignments, or day-to-day functions of the staff. Since many librarians tend to be task-oriented, they may find it difficult to design an abstract statement of the primary purpose of the library. In such cases, a good start is to check the by-laws of the institution's governing board. To assist further, I suggest the following word as pivotal: students.

The maximum effort of academic libraries should be directed toward providing students with recorded information resources. Access to these resources should not be restricted on the basis of format, content, or other artificial delimitations. The resources should support and supplement the curriculum and should also provide for general enrichment and continued learning which may be unrelated to a specific curriculum.

When the statement of purpose has been completed by the library staff, it should be given to the faculty library committee for comment and advice. The library committee's endorsement of this statement should be sought so that the statement may fairly reflect the needs of the institution. Once the library staff and the library committee agree on the general statement, the institution's administration should be asked to announce and endorse a statement of purpose of the library, based upon the recommendations of the library committee and the librarians.

The next step is to develop staffing structures and attitudes which will facilitate the execution of the responsibilities implied in the statement of purpose. When developing a proposal to restructure staff, the following objectives should be stressed:

> emphasize the role of public service librarians who work on a one-to-one basis with library users;
> emphasize the value of general knowledge among public service librarians rendering professional assistance to library users;
> minimize clerical routines assigned to or assumed by professional librarians;
> utilize bibliographic control data available from consortia or commercial groups to reduce the number of professionals assigned to technical services;
> utilize user-oriented non-print formats to achieve staff support economies;
> minimize the number of staffed service points and provide continual staffing of a key service point; and maximize the use of technology where it can increase the effectiveness of library personnel.

Since each of the above points should influence the arrangement and use of the library facility, each is discussed more fully below.

One-To-One Contact with Users

The librarian should be expected to play a vital role in the student's academic experiences. While group lectures and discussions are well developed techniques for a small number of subject specialized faculty to trigger the interest and learning of a large number of students, each student perceives and understands the subject in a slightly different

way. If the student is interested enough to want to discover
more about the subject, the library should be one of the
first places to turn to for discovery of previously recorded
knowledge on the subject. Here the librarian, not necessarily a specialist in the subject being explored, can influence
the student's progress. The librarian can, on a one-to-one
basis, help the student develop his or her own research and
discovery skills, beginning at a level appropriate to the particular student. The librarian can also help the student discover and explore related subjects, and thus gain a broader
outlook.

A facility which expresses and accommodates this
function will provide features which permit and invite conferences and consultations in proximity to the library's indexes, catalogs, and reference resources.

General Service from Professionals

Professional librarians should be encouraged to continue their study of specialized subjects. Desirable as continued education and enlargement of intellectual horizons are,
care must be exercised that specialization does not narrow
or limit the functional capabilities and interests of the professional. Generalization is itself a great asset within a
public service staff, since it facilitates a high degree of in-
terchangeability among professionals serving undergraduate
students. This goal does not preclude specialized skills or
talents. For example, if one of the public service librarians has specialized skills or talents in dealing with a particular form of resources (e. g., government documents or nonprint media) that librarian should be given the responsibility
of helping other librarians on the staff to develop and maintain general working skills with such resources. Assistance
can then be given to a student who needs to use a particular resource even when the "specialist" professional is not
on duty or is otherwise occupied.

Using Clerical Support Staff to Advantage

All too frequently, academic librarians can be observed busily engaged in clerical work. I have heard students comment that when they go to the library the librarians are "all busy." This "busy" appearance creates an un-
desirable barrier which reduces the effectiveness of the pro-

fessional staff in its dealings with students.

Some librarians concentrate on clerical work because of habits they developed in library school or when working as assistants prior to entering the profession.   Others appear to be unable to explain and supervise clerical tasks assigned to supporting staff, and therefore do the work themselves.   Whatever the reason, a library will not get the best return on the money spent for professional salaries unless the professionals relinquish clerical tasks to support staff.

This factor is an important consideration when planning the interior layout of a library. If workspaces are so arranged as to make it inconvenient to assign work to support staff, many professionals are likely to continue to do clerical tasks themselves. Thus, careful planning and charting of anticipated loads, communications flow and work patterns are essential.

Shared Use of Bibliographic Control Data

By the middle of this decade most academic libraries in the United States will probably have on-line access to computer-maintained files of bibliographic control data. Used wisely, this development can revolutionize the organization and staffing of technical services operations in academic libraries; large cataloging departments, in particular, should be greatly reduced. Since the data networks will be designed to provide simplified access to authoritative bibliographic control data, the need for original cataloging by individual academic libraries, and the number of expensive staff assigned to this task, will be greatly reduced. Such a reduction, of course, will depend upon the acceptance by local cataloging supervisors of cataloging data, as is, from outside sources.

With conventional methods and attitudes, a library's cataloging department too often becomes a repository for a large number of resource items awaiting processing. Both the space and the resource items will be better utilized if the cataloging function becomes a dynamic process of matching items speedily with available data. The work area can be laid out to expedite movement of materials, and the space which is now too often assigned to "in process" storage can be reassigned to better purpose.

User-Oriented Nonprint Formats

While it is obviously necessary to be selective in collecting resources, the library should provide a variety of
media.   Some students respond more readily to one medium
than another; some topics are better presented in one medium than another.   But within the options available, a physical format should be chosen which reduces technical barriers
between the medium and the user; that is, a user-oriented
format.   Necessary hardware should be built into seminar
or group study rooms and, even more importantly, into individual study carrels, and materials in the various formats
should be shelved together on the basis of similar subject
content.   Users of academic libraries are too often thwarted
or frustrated by finding library resources stored and dis-
pensed primarily on the basis of format and only secondarily
on the basis of subject content or target audience.

Translating this concept into library planning and furnishing, the result would be a library where user-oriented
formats are all shelved (stored) in proximity with one another and arranged by a consistent subject classification
throughout the library.   There would be a mix of individual
user stations (carrels), each equipped to display one format
or another.   These carrels would be liberally distributed
throughout the shelving (storage) area so that the browser
who finds a nonprint item has the same opportunity to scan
it as the user of a book or other print item.   Also, the
user who approaches the collection through the catalog should
find entries there for all of the library's resources--regard-
less of format.

Staffed Service Points

With staff salaries and fringe benefits being the singu-
larly highest cost line(s) of an academic library's operating
budget, no facility should be planned or built which requires
a proliferation of staff for its efficient operation.   In planning an academic library (or renovating an existing facility)
one should aim for only one professional service point which
will be staffed during all opening hours.   This need not be
the first contact point inside the library's front door, since
a circulation clerk can provide answers to inquiries about
the location of restrooms, telephones, vending machines, or
particular offices, but it should be within sight of the circulation desk and the main catalog.   The primary professional

service point should be close to the basic reference collection and it is helpful if it is also near the technical processing area. It should be equipped with a telephone which can pick up on any line assigned to the public service staff or work stations. Ideally, the service point will be near and in sight of staff work stations of all public service librarians, so that during peak periods or when a difficult or involved inquiry arises, the professional staffing the service point will not feel chained to the desk but can move with the user to any part of the library to render assistance, confident that another professional can move into the primary service point.

Large libraries or those with more than one floor may require more than a single service point. Additional service points may be staffed during peak use periods, but during hours of lesser use may serve as referral points through which users can contact a professional at the primary service point or its back-up work stations. This may be accomplished by providing these secondary service points with intercoms or pick-up phones connected directly with the primary professional service point.

Since much of a public service professional's time is spent repetitively in educating users on basic techniques for making the best use of library resources, academic libraries would do well to adopt a practice common in museums: that of displaying routine audio and visual messages which can be called up by users with questions. Many of these techniques are both effective and inexpensive to install and maintain. Professional librarians' time is then freed for questions at a level beyond those which can be answered by the basic displays.

Maximized Use of Technology

Traditionally, libraries have been labor intensive institutions. It is time to plan and build library facilities which invite the use of technology where it can logically replace repetitive or physical functions of human staff or where it can provide better communication or understanding between staff members or between staff and users. Academic library planners must consider all foreseeable areas where technology may be able to do the job better than it could be done by either existing or additional staff. Technology is likely to make the greatest contribution in the per-

formance of repetitive definable tasks and in expanding human powers of memory, reach, communications, etc.

Drawing from experience of the business world, academic libraries can benefit from the use of word-processing
technology.   For administrators, word processing can reduce
the cost of production of correspondence and reports while
providing for increased precision and better appearance of
the documents.   Its use can give form letters a fresh, individualized appearance.   Some word-processing equipment
will even provide teletype-compatible output formats so that
"rush" correspondence can be sent by teletype with a formal
letter as follow-up, both keyboarded simultaneously.

Word processing equipment can be "programmed" to
remember specific formats.   This feature facilitates a reduction of staff time and effort spent in producing rigorously
formatted documents such as bibliographies or catalog cards.
By combining word processing with cassette and intercom
dictation/transcription equipment, stenographic and typing support can be pooled among non-administration staff who do
not require such support on a full-time basis, as is the case
with most of the public service staff.

Intercommunication and telecommunication equipment
can greatly enhance the performance of the staff.   If, for
example, library users in the more remote parts of the facility can pick up a handset and obtain verbal assistance,
the staff can extend the range of their service without regularly patroling all areas of the building.   If users can pick
up another handset and obtain prerecorded instructions on the
use of particular indexing or abstracting tools, they will be
encouraged to ask for further assistance when necessary.
Use of video cassettes or film loops can provide additional
unattended assistance to users.   The telephone is perhaps
the simplest of the family of telecommunications equipment,
but its potential is rarely fully exploited.   There may be a
proliferation of telephone instruments and lines, but frequently no arrangement to trace or page key staff.   A Call Director can replace a receptionist's desk set.   With this device calls can be transferred to key staff regardless of their
physical location in the facility.   Short-range personal pagers
can be beneficial in locating key staff or administrators,
who then feel less confined to a particular physical location
in the facility.   Even the administrative staff can be freed
up in this manner occasionally to go to where the users are.

The remainder of this essay considers the three functional divisions of the academic library: public services, technical services, and administrative services, with emphasis on specific features designed to make the facility more functional.   This section might be used as the basis for a "Plan of Accomplishment" statement which, together with the objectives, would make up an over-all statement of the library's program.

Technical Services

The planning should consider the potential flow of people and of materials, and should attempt to remove unnecessary barriers to the traffic flow.   For example, the location of the main public catalog will be determined by the expectation or prediction that it will receive its heaviest use from library users and from technical services personnel (primarily catalogers and acquisition searchers).   These factors dictate that the main public catalog, part of the technical services department, and the main lobby be located in proximity to each other.   To cite another example, the arrangement of the acquisitions section must consider the relative volume of materials to be handled by various specialties. The serials section can expect a large volume of mail once or twice a day.   Thus, unrestricted passage from the receiving area to the serials check-in is important.   If the serials check-in is a manual operation, it is desirable that it be located near the main card catalog so that users will have ready access to current information on the check-in file.   At the same time, it may be desirable to locate this operation in an area which can be secured after hours. Since the serials check-in function logically dictates that wrappers or address labels be kept with material until it has been checked in, a well planned serials area will provide disposal facilities for large quantities of wrappers and other waste paper.

The book order area can expect to receive larger shipments but at less frequent intervals than the serials section. The general receiving area should take into account that shipments of books frequently arrive by truck.   If the trucks can deliver directly to the library, not only will on-campus handling costs be reduced but the chance of error and of misplaced shipments will be greatly reduced.   The receiving area of the library should be planned to accommodate two or more trucks at one time.   It should also provide workspace

which is out of the weather for unpacking and organizing
shipments of books and for disposal of boxes and packing
material.

The arrangement of the acquisitions librarian's (supervisor's) work area should provide space for conferences with
sales representatives and with faculty and facilities for easy
and regular communication with the library's internal book-
keeper (or account clerk). It should facilitate communication with all library staff (area resource weaknesses, for
example, are often discovered informally via a chance comment) and supervision of acquisitions personnel.

Some academic libraries have found it helpful to
maintain an in-house mending and preparation section. While
most rebinding can be more economically done through a
commercial bindery, maintenance and mending and some
emergency major repairs can be performed in-house if adequate facilities are provided. Marking and preparing materials for the shelf can be done in the same facility, but
since volatile lacquers are frequently used on books, this
mending/preparation area should have exhausts to take the
fumes directly to the outside. The area logically will be located near the output side of the cataloging area and near
the point where the circulation section moves materials back
to the stacks. Since materials for shipment to a commercial bindery may be gathered and collated in the mending/
preparation area, a convenient flow to the shipping/receiving
area is also desirable. This area should have work surfaces
which are resistant to chemicals, glues, etc., a liberal number of electrical outlets, and a convenient sink with drain-
boards. If the use of bookpresses is anticipated, a wooden
topped counter should be planned to run along one wall.
There can also never be too many cupboards and drawers
in this type of area. As nonprint resources require some
maintenance as well as preparation for the shelves, the
equipment for the most common nonprint formats which the
library collects should be considered in the planning of this
area.

Public Services

In addition to facilitating the flow of people, communications, and materials, one more ingredient is necessary
in the public area of an academic library: the flow of information. The goal must be to create a flow of informa-

tion from storage to user; hence, the suggestion above that
there be one professional service point staffed at all times
the library is open, and that this be backed up by the public
service staff offices. These staff offices should serve a
dual purpose as workspace and as a setting for conferences
between staff and users. If the office areas are composed
of landscape modules, the offices can be modified or rear-
ranged as staff or user needs change.

The interior layout should locate frequently used tools
and resources near the central service point, and should
facilitate staff movement to these areas in order to assist
users. Such movement will be discouraged if the working
environment creates staff fatigue.

Administrative Offices

The effort to enhance the academic library as a functional facility should be carried into the administrative offices. While each administrator will have a preference in
decor, general principles of office design and layout will
apply. The administrative offices should be directly accessible from the controlled area of the library, but it is convenient if these offices can also be reached without passing
through the controlled area (i.e., directly from the lobby or
the outside). A reception area should oversee both of these
entrances to the administrative offices. Administrative offices should be designed to provide necessary privacy while
still presenting an open and inviting appearance to visitors
and library users.

The clerical support pool is logically located in the
administrative area, and the general office supply inventory
can be maintained here also. When planning these areas,
which require added security during the after-office hours
that the library is open, care must be exercised not to
create a psychological barrier between the public areas of
the library and the administrative offices.

In addition to providing workspace, files and supply
storage, and a reception area, the administrative offices
should provide a conference area with provision for use of
charts or a chalk board.

This entire area should reflect a continuation of the
effort to facilitate the flow of communication and information,

while also providing staff with comfortable, attractive work-space which can be modified as staff or library needs change.

Conclusion

This essay has attempted to suggest practical con-siderations in making an academic library facility more func-tional.   Institutions which hope to retain an existing library facility must rely upon an imaginative, energetic library staff to make that facility workable (or more efficient), and this is usually possible when the staff and administration sub-scribe to the library's statement of purpose and plan of ac-complishment.   If the library program cannot be carried out in the existing facility, the time has come to bring in a con-sultant to evaluate the library program and the existing fa-cility and to suggest modifications (of program or facility) where necessary.   A consultant can assess a specific local situation with all of its attendant variables while not being biased by local pressures, personalities, or crises.

In new institutions or institutions which are planning to construct a new library facility, the administration must work through the library director in all dealings with the architect and interior designer concerning the design, con-struction, and equipment of the new library facility.   The library director should be able to expect and receive the necessary support and information from the institutional ad-ministration, the library staff, the architect, the interior designer, and consultants to back up all decisions which will affect (and effect) the new library facility.   Visits by the librarian and the institutional administration to other academ-ic libraries which serve similar institutions are beneficial, particularly in helping to avoid repetition of mistakes.

Above all, a great deal of planning and predicting must go into the library's program statement.   But when all the best thought and design have been applied to the opti-mum functional academic library facility, the final test will still be the way in which the library staff directs and com-municates its attitudes, energy, and enthusiasm for learning.

MANAGEMENT PLANNING TO ACHIEVE
ACADEMIC LIBRARY GOALS

Jerome Yavarkovsky

Probably the outstanding emerging characteristic of academic library administration is the self-awareness of the library as a corporate enterprise with resources demanding rational management. The forces bringing this about include effectively diminishing resources, the changing nature of academic librarianship, the changing perception of working relationships and their influence on work effectiveness and satisfaction, the changing attitude toward organizations' responsibilities to their employees, and the recognition of the enormously valuable resource that a large library has in its professionals and skilled staff.

The academic library has recently been confronted with enormous growth in the volume of publication; increasing fragmentation of disciplines into narrow areas of specialization; and the growth of multidisciplinary programs that organize specializations in new ways. These factors present two major problems for the academic librarian. One is a continually diminishing ability to acquire all the materials needed in all the disciplines served by the typical academic research library. The other is a diminishing ability to organize and make materials accessible in an environment of constantly changing intellectual orientation. Also, the evolution of the library in the academic environment from a passive repository of research materials to an active participant in the educational process, whether through reserve course readings or the provision of multi-media instructional facilities, has changed the concept of the library's role in learning. It has brought about a need to coordinate the direction of academic library service with the evolution of teaching techniques and disciplines and has created new and additional demands. Finally, the library is becoming more and more aware that it has, in fact, two populations to

serve; that its obligations extend not merely to its public
and its governing body, but also, and equally importantly,
to its staff members.   The emerging reaction to this growing realization that the library's resources are decidedly fi-
nite--indeed, ever diminishing relative to the growth in opportunities, needs, and costs--is one of recognizing that
conscious choices must be made among alternatives and that
these choices are best made in an informed environment,
so that they most effectively satisfy the constituencies they
are meant to serve.

     To some extent, what is happening in librarianship
is comparable to what has taken place in commercial and industrial environments over the past 20 years.   However,
while the commercial enterprise is motivated to maximize
profits, the library wishes to maximize service--the library's
often intangible return on its investment or expenditures.
Where the risks of commercial enterprise are risks to the
profitability of their operations, the risks to the library are
those of lost service opportunities, less effective service
for the dollars spent, wasted or misdirected resources, and
diminished access to resources.

     If industry is motivated to pursue rationally its rea-
son for being--profits--academic libraries are similarly motivated to determine rationally their course in satisfying
their principal goal--service.   The route to this rational approach to resource allocation which is being chosen more
frequently today is advance planning.   Planning is not a pan-
acea, and it is not a technique for solving problems.   Rather,
it is a process, differently applied in its details in each setting, of defining the purpose of the enterprise, establishing
goals consistent with that purpose, articulating a strategy to
achieve the goals, and developing procedures to carry out
the strategy.   Hence, it does not solve problems, but rather
obviates them to some extent by delineating a course of action.   When problems do arise, planning helps to put them
in the perspective of the overall movement of the enterprise
toward its objectives.   Certainly, problems are solved or
reduced or more readily addressed through analysis, articu-
lation of assumptions, assessment of alternatives, and other
aspects of planning.   However, the emphasis in planning is
on decision, commitment, and action directed toward the
purpose of the enterprise rather than its problems.

     It is important that this kind of planning be compre-
hensive and pervasive, encompassing all the activities of the

library, rather than focusing on isolated activities or incremental changes in activity. Planning is not new in libraries, but it has generally been used in conjunction with new facilities or services rather than as an ongoing process to determine the continuing direction and operation of the library. Hence, as important as planning is for the new reference service or circulation system or microform facilities, nevertheless, the fundamental library activities and expenditures cannot be omitted from the overall planning effort. The greatest potential return for rational decision-making rests in such areas as collection development, cataloging, order and materials processing, and stack operations, because these are some of the functions where the greatest costs are incurred. The refinement of collection policy and improvement in cataloging, order processing, serials check-in, or searching procedures are among the areas which might be overlooked in library planning that emphasizes new or added services or facilities. All of the library's work should be regularly reviewed and evaluated to ensure that it is contributing to ongoing service objectives and doing so economically and efficiently.

This type of overall review and evaluation program is essential to the planning effort, and suggests that coordination and monitoring of performance in relation to plans is appropriately directed to two levels of attention--unit operations and individual performance. At the unit level, it is the responsibility of the library administration to review and evaluate performance against targets established during planning. As it relates to individuals, the planning effort is ideally linked to a general program of performance evaluation and staff development.

Unit Operations

The element of coordinating and evaluating the progress of plans that takes place at the organization unit level is one which is an inherent responsibility of the management of the library. The planning structure must permit management to make resource allocation and priority decisions, set performance targets, develop strategies, and monitor performance.[1, 2] Whatever the source of plans, whether at the highest administrative levels where the concerns and decisions are comprehensive, or at the most detailed level of the library organization where specific task- and staff-oriented planning take place, communication must

be sufficiently thorough to permit intelligent decisions.   If
there is not enough information to make a decision, it is appropriate to establish fact-finding groups to investigate particular issues or courses of action and include their reports
in the planning communications.   The planning structure,
then, must comprise the senior administration of the library
and be arranged so that communications will take place
among all staff levels.

Because a major element of the planning process is
the development of measurable or observable performance
targets, the principal coordinative and monitoring activity is
concerned with measuring performance against these targets
and adjusting resources or schedules if conditions change or
if some of the planning objectives themselves change.   Ex-
pressing targets in terms of budgets, time, units of production, or specific activities allows periodic review and evaluation of the accomplishment of plans.   A reporting structure
which provides informative or evaluative reports for comparative or decision-making purposes without burdening or
interfering with operations is a key to the review process.
The planning activity, when it reaches the level of detail
where specific tasks are defined, must include reports based
on selected events or time periods during the progress of
the plans.   These reports will provide opportunities to make
adjustments if necessary as the work proceeds, and offer
opportunities to assess the activity underway in terms of its
progress toward some end point or in terms of some observable, if not measurable, accomplishment units.

The Management Approach

Fundamental to planning is the management approach
itself.   Several institutions which have moved toward comprehensive planning have taken steps to examine the academic
library as an organizational system, understand its operating
relationships and decision-making structure, and make
changes to improve its effectiveness.   At the Columbia University Libraries these changes have taken the form of
structural adjustments in the operating organization and reporting relationships. [3,4]   At the Cornell University Libraries
changes have been made in the decision-making structure, [5]
and a planning mechanism has been established to incorporate
a maximum number of staff members in the planning process.
Finally, through the efforts of the Association of Research
Libraries' Office of University Library Management Studies,

a number of libraries have thoroughly examined their operations in order to identify areas of potential management improvement. [6] The assumption in all of these cases is that
improving the management process will bring about improved
service and operations--a reasonable expectation as long as
the techniques for coordination, control, and reporting do
not overwhelm the ends they are meant to achieve.

Staff Participation

        A feature that has characterized all of these efforts
has been the significant amount of staff involvement in the
analysis and decision-making underlying the recommendations
and changes made. In several cases there is a continuing
commitment to a high level of staff participation in the administrative process. This may not be an essential ingredient in planning itself, since effective planning can be confined to the highest levels of the library administration;
however, staff contributions to planning are valuable, especially at the detailed level, because they offer the experience and competence of individuals who often have more
thorough familiarity with the library's procedural operations
than the senior administration has. The perceptions of the
library's administration are supplemented by additional ideas
for determining and accomplishing the library's mission. In
addition, if the conclusions of research into the behavior of
individuals and groups in organizations are correct, then a
combination of mutually supportive attitudes and an environment in which staff and administration jointly develop their
objectives will be salutary to the professional health and ac-
complishments of the library. Thus, beyond the substantive
contributions of the staff to planning, their participation can
be expected to foster support and individual commitment to
the accomplishment of the plans. Since it is ultimately the
staff who will be responsible for performing the tasks which
make up the operating plans, this commitment is highly desirable both in terms of the success of the work and the
personal satisfaction of the staff.

        In general, the planning process is as important as
the plans it produces. [7] The interaction of senior and lower
level staff which takes place, the stimulus to creativity, and
the participation of individuals who often do not have opportunities to contribute to the development of the library outside of their specific responsibilities tend to make the substantial investment of staff time worthwhile for several rea-

sons.   There is a broadening of the individual's perspective
and understanding of his role in the overall mission of the
library.   This tends to add to the satisfaction derived from
his specific duties a more concrete sense of contributing to
a larger purpose and a better understanding of the nature of
that contribution.   The opportunity to work on plans with
staff members with whom there is normally limited or no
contact, at all levels and from other sections of the library,
often creates a feeling of community and reduces mythologi-
cal attitudes toward senior administrators.   Finally, as
noted earlier, staff participation in determining the direction
and specific goals of the library creates a personal involvement in defining the purpose of one's work and consequently
develops a higher level of commitment and support for that
purpose.   These arguments for widespread staff participation
in planning are made in the conviction that a better plan is
created, the plan's likelihood of success is enhanced, and
the degree of staff satisfaction is increased.   Although the
ultimate responsibility for ensuring the accomplishment of
plans rests with the administration of the library, that accomplishment is a composite of the efforts of administration
and staff.   It seems reasonable to expect, then, that the
collective talents and experience of a large number of diverse
professional and, where appropriate, supporting staff members will provide a larger pool of ideas and a superior
product than will a small number of senior administrators.

Individual Performance

If the commitment to planning is accompanied by a
commitment to satisfying the personal and professional needs
of the staff in the context of achieving library goals, then
the monitoring of plans should be integrated with individual
performance evaluation.   In effect, it is a logical extension
of the chain of objectives which begins with the broadly
stated purpose of the library, continues through the more
specific goals of each organizational component, and ends
with the detailed objectives of each staff member.   If the
planning activity permeates the structure of the library,
guiding it through the day-to-day work to the achievement of
the library's goals, then it is properly pursued in an environment where those goals are well understood and brought
to a level of detail which is directly relatable to each individual's work and, where possible, to his professional
growth.   Not everyone has clearly defined career goals in
terms of specific positions or even increased competencies.

Nevertheless, where there may be even general aspirations to career advancement or expansion of personal scope, the planning and evaluation process provides an opportunity for these to develop and be realized. Recent changes in organizational attitudes suggest that the library's responsibility goes beyond the obvious principles of financial compensation for work performed to some assurance that each staff member has the maximum opportunity for personal growth consistent with the service objectives of the library. This implies the need for a mechanism to inform staff members of the quality of their performance relative to their own and unit objectives--one which will acknowledge their strengths and identify areas of potential improvement. Hence, individual performance appraisal should take place not only in relation to library plans, but as part of a comprehensive program of professional and career development in a climate where library purpose and individual goals converge.

Planning, with its emphasis on determining a course of action and monitoring its pursuit through relatively straightforward procedures, is likely to be an expensive and difficult process to implement. The comprehensiveness of the kind of planning described here, involving a considerable amount of staff and administrative time and modes of behavior which are foreign to most libraries (as they are to most other organizations), requires a commitment to a new way of thinking. However, because of its anticipatory and rational decision-making, more effective coordination and control of resources, concern with performance, and sensitivity to individual aspirations in the context of library goals, its cost is justified.

References

1.   Kemper, Robert E. "Library Planning: The Challenge of Change." In Melvin Voigt, ed., Advances in Librarianship. Vol. 1. New York, Academic Press, 1970.

2.   Steiner, George A. Top Management Planning. New York, Macmillan, 1969.

3.   Booz, Allen and Hamilton, Inc. Organization and Staffing of the Libraries of Columbia University: A Case Study. Westport, Conn., Redgrave Information Resources, 1973.

4.   Columbia University Libraries. The Administrative Organization of the Libraries of Columbia University:

A Detailed Description.   New York, Columbia University Libraries, 1973.

5.   McGrath, William E.   Development of a Long-Range
Strategic Plan for a University Library.   The Cornell
Experience: Chronicle and Evaluation of the First
Year's Effort.   Ithaca, N. Y., Cornell University Li-
braries, February 1973.

6.   Webster, Duane, assisted by Frankie, Suzanne.   Library Management Review and Analysis Program: A
Handbook for Guiding Change and Improvement in Research Library Management.   Vols. 1 and 2.   Washington, Association of Research Libraries, 1973.

7.   Ackoff, Russell Lincoln.   A Concept of Corporate Planning.   New York, Wiley-Interscience, 1969.

THE NEED FOR MULTIMEDIA
IN SERVING STUDENTS

Harry Robinson, Jr.

To improve quality and to extend higher education to more students, institutions are investing increasingly in media and in multimedia systems. Out of necessity more and more libraries are beginning to take a harder look at including more nonprint materials in their collections. The inclusion of these multimedia systems could not have come at a more opportune time because today's college students are of the multi-image generation. The advent of the newer technology also carries implications for the newer patterns of learning and instruction in colleges and universities and directly affects libraries and learning centers.

The multimedia concept is thought of by some people as a coupling of library and audiovisual facilities and services. Most proponents of the concept, however, consider it more than just a combining of the traditional idea of the library with the modern notion of audiovisual; the concept embraces thoughts of unity and totality--of integrated learning resources, facilities, and services.

The employment of multimedia systems has become necessary to meet the diverse needs and interests of changing student bodies. The age of greater use of multimedia is brought on by many factors, several of which are listed and discussed below.

Change in Our Society

Change is the "constant" of our emerging society. Higher education must help people prepare to change in at least two major ways. Students must be provided with flexible intellectual tools which facilitate a truly analytic ap-

proach to problems and their solution. Likewise, students
must have full opportunity to gain an understanding of trends
which will help in the anticipation of future changes. It is
critical to select and buy problem-oriented materials with
these goals in mind.

Knowledge Explosion

The so-called knowledge explosion and the development of the knowledge industry places a heavier load on college teachers and students than at any other time in history.
Faculty expectations of students are rising.

Four years is still the standard period for earning
the college degree. Although course work such as trigo-
nometry, analytic geometry, and calculus is being pushed
into high school--and a basic college degree in such fields
as architecture or engineering often takes five years--more
students are being required to learn more in the same four-
year period. As a result of these increased demands, more
students must borrow money or obtain scholarship aid to
attend college. Less time can be taken for outside work or
extra activities--and none for so-called remedial or deficiency
courses in mathematics, English composition, oral communication, or study skills. Programmed materials and independent study centers provide ambitious students with the opportunity, through self-study, to make up deficiencies or
move ahead more rapidly in course work.

Different approaches to independent study, such as
those at Monteith College of Wayne State University, God-
dard College, the University of Colorado, and many others,
change the conceptual framework for organization and dispo-
sition of learning resources. Professors can determine
which skills and knowledge do not demand their personal ex-
planatory efforts and which concepts, ideas, and understandings may require their interaction with the students--so that
the time of both will be used optimally. In moving from
what Jerome Bruner called the "expository" mode of teaching to the "hypothetical," more problem-centered mode, the
professor can free himself from routine exposition and the
mere imparting of facts. Learning resources staffs must be
organized to help in this analytic process.

Change in Population Factors

Change other than numbers takes place constantly in our population. We move continually--from rural to urban to suburban and possibly, in the future, back to the central city. Migration trends show people moving to the North, the West, and the Southwest. Any one college or university will have students from diverse educational and cultural backgrounds. A broadly conceived "learning resources" program can be a base for developing some common understandings.

Our population now includes an increasing proportion of youth and senior citizens. A smaller proportion of the population now works to support them. Productive workers need better total educational experiences to be more efficient and to produce more, in order to support and educate the youth and older citizens.

Changing Technology

Changing technology and increasing knowledge require a constant upgrading and re-education of the total work force. Such diverse workers as doctors of medicine, teachers of physics or biochemistry, oil refinery technicians, and firemen need regular, continuing re-education. Learning resources of all types must, therefore, be kept up-to-date, and internal technical processes must be speeded up to make new materials available immediately. Computer-based retrieval of stored micro-miniature materials is presently "around the corner," but must be tested, analyzed, and planned for use in future decades. It may be limited to specialized libraries or especially large libraries, but it will be used in higher education. Television, of course, can provide "immediacy from afar" if needed for educational upgrading or retraining. Local campuses need to have facilities to pick up and relay such learning materials on campus, and also to provide duplication facilities to store video-tape materials for later study analysis.

Increased Leisure Time

Leisure time for all citizens is rapidly increasing. The profitable use of leisure time is a problem of major concern to our entire society, and the outlook of the person

faced with additional leisure time is strongly conditioned by
his educational background.   Added leisure time is characteristic of all economic levels in our society and is created
by many factors.   For example, automation of production
lowers the numbers of workers needed to produce food and
goods.   In addition to forcing retraining, it also makes possible productive earlier retirement from active employment.
An increasing number of persons work in service industries
rather than in direct productive industries.   Welfare sub-
sidies of less-productive workers give them leisure time as
well.   Our society needs a continuing, careful evaluation of
all forms of work, and of the training and retraining needed
for each.   This continuing evaluation will create a need for
additions and changes in the learning resources available in
the college or university resources center.

Changes in the Work Force and Working Hours

In the past few years there have been changing patterns in the work force and in service industries.   Since
World War II women have entered the work force in large
numbers.   Shopping habits have changed, and many stores
and service industries now stay open nights and on week-
ends.   To some extent this has increased the attendance of
part-time students at colleges and universities.   It has also
placed pressure on colleges and universities to expand their
service schedules.   In the future, learning resources centers may have to open six or seven days a week, and
around the clock.[1]

Improved Transportation

Improved transportation, primarily the automobile,
has increased the proportion of college students who are
regular commuters to the campus.   Simultaneously, the
number of students in residence halls has not grown in proportion to the total attendance in colleges and universities.
For both types of students there has been some attempt to
provide learning resources where they live, or to provide
check-out opportunities for portable equipment and materials.
Commuters to Chicago Junior College and San Francisco
State College, for example, have had some instruction by
open-circuit TV.   Resident students at the University of
Michigan have language or audio laboratories in the residence halls.   Michigan State University sends instructional

TV courses into residence halls. Of course, for years many residence halls have included small, selected library collections, but the abundance of paperbacks has led to extensive expansion of such collections. Learning resource programs, more and more, have expanded to provide a wide variety of materials for use where the students are, rather than forcing them to come to a central location. For commuter students small study stations have been set up on a few campuses; these are sometimes known as offices, carrels, or "Q" spaces.

Expansion of Services of Higher Education

Demands of modern day society have led to rapid expansion of services by institutions of higher education. Adult education for many professional groups is an important change for professional schools and colleges. Extension services provide continuing cultural, professional, and upgrading forms of community service.

Another important factor that has forced libraries to become more than depositories for the printed word is the requirement that various curricula be developed from a competency-based teaching approach. This approach requires libraries and learning centers to play the integral part with which they have always been credited, whether they fulfilled that responsibility or not. Those who employ this approach are more concerned with the end than the means of learning, but competency-based teaching provides for many means for achieving stated instructional and learning objectives, and the library or learning center must be in a position to make these means possible; that is, it must provide a variety of learning and instructional resources. The use of a transparency might assist a learner in achieving a stated objective. On the other hand, a taped lecture of the Centennial Lecture Series might provide the learner with the kind of speech he needs to analyze to achieve a stated objective in Public Speaking 200.

There is no longer any real doubt about the value of multimedia systems for students who come from culturally different and academically deprived backgrounds. Colleges and universities which admit such students, if they are determined to graduate the same kind of product that comes from the middle class group, will have to develop their libraries and learning centers as multimedia centers. Learn-

ers who are considered as high risks usually come with a
background that has prepared them to deal more successfully
with concrete and visual objects.   They, too, are a part of
the television or visual generation.   Students from an academically deprived background need more remedial instruction than most of the other learners.   Much of this can be accomplished through multimedia--cassette tapes, filmstrips,
videotapes, and so forth, [2] which if made readily accessible,
can reinforce the student.   Programmed learning packages
in basic skills are classic examples.

The Commission on Instructional Technology has appropriately summarized the situation:

> ... learning in our schools and colleges is in-
> creasingly impeded by such troubles as the grow-
> ing gap between education's income and needs, and
> the shortage of good teachers in the right places.
> Formal education is not responsive enough: the
> organization of schools and colleges takes too little
> account of even what is now known about the pro-
> cess of human learning, particularly of the range
> of individual differences among students.   This
> condition makes schools particularly unresponsive
> to the needs of disadvantaged and minority-group
> children.   Moreover, formal education is in an
> important sense outmoded--students learn outside
> schools in ways which differ radically from the
> ways they learn inside school.   Educational insti-
> tutions make scant use of the potent means of com-
> munication that modern society finds indispensable
> and that occupy so much of young people's out-of-
> school time. [3]

The utilization of multimedia resources in education
can aid in the equalization of education.   The Commission
on Instructional Technology declares:

> Equal access to rich learning environments is not
> possible without some recourse to technology.
> Through television or film nearly every school in
> America can have the luxury of seeing Sir Lawrence
> Olivier play Othello.   When the telecommunications
> network envisaged by the Interuniversity Communi-
> cations Council (EDUCOM) is operational, the stu-
> dents and faculty of a small rural college can have
> direct access to the greatest libraries of the

country. At the present time, via the National
Library of Medicine's Medical Literature Analysis
and Retrieval System (MEDLARS), doctors in Denver can obtain as much bibliographic information
on recent medical literature as can doctors working
in the hospital across the street from the computer
center in Bethesda, Maryland. [4]

The changes in emphasis have led to the re-naming of
positions once held by librarians or audiovisual specialists,
or to the creation of new positions, such as dean of learning
resources, assistant vice president for instructional resources, or educational development officers. The creation
of such positions is doing more than just merging the traditional library with the equipment-oriented audiovisual specialists. These persons have been charged with the responsibility of implementing significant improvements in learning
and instruction. They insure appropriate participation, support, and involvement in the entire learning and teaching
processes on the campus.

Libraries or learning centers must respond to these
growing needs, or other units will be created to do what they
should be doing. Already, some institutions have given up
trying to persuade libraries to become more responsive to
the needs of the more diversified student bodies. Some administrators seem to be convinced that the traditional library is not willing to change as the patterns of learning and
instruction change. The establishment already of learning
resources centers separate from the traditional library is
confirmation of this. Libraries must be prepared to meet
the challenges of changing higher education or they can expect other units to answer the call.

The call to librarians and educators, to provide a
learning environment in which print, sound and imagery are
merged in a single facility, was sounded clearly by the
Carnegie Commission on Higher Education in its recent report, The Fourth Revolution:

> ... nonprint information, illustrations and instruc-
> tional software components should be maintained
> as part of a unified informational-instructional re-
> source that is cataloged and stored in ways that
> facilitate convenient retrieval as needed by stu-
> dents and faculty members. [5]

References

1.   Finn, James D. "A Revolutionary Season," Phi Delta
     Kappan, 45:348-54, April 1964.
2.   Finn, James D., Perrin, Donald G., and Campion,
     Lee E. "Studies in the Growth of Instructional Tech-
     nology, I: Audio-Visual Instrumentation for Instruct-
     ing in the Public Schools, 1930-60--A Basis for Take-
     Off, " Occasional Paper no. 6, Technological Develop-
     ment Project of the National Education Association,
     Washington, D. C., Department of Audio-Visual In-
     structor, National Education Association, 1962.
3.   U. S. Commission on Instructional Technology. To Im-
     prove Learning, Report to the President and Congress
     by the Commission on Instructional Technology.
     Washington, D. C., U. S. G. P. O., 1970, p. 6.
4.   Ibid., p. 33.
5.   Carnegie Commission on Higher Education. The Fourth
     Revolution: Instructional Technology in Higher Edu-
     cation. New York: McGraw-Hill, 1972, p. 34.

Part IV

PATTERNS OF LIBRARY INFORMATION SYSTEMS,
NETWORKS, AND CONSORTIA PROVIDING
INFORMATION AND LIBRARY SERVICES
TO ACADEMIC LIBRARY USERS

THE 3R'S SYSTEM AND THE
ACADEMIC LIBRARY COMMUNITY
IN NEW YORK STATE

Nina T. Cohen

As one of the first directors in New York State's
3R's program, I understood what Lura Currier[1] meant when
she said, "If only libraries of the Seventies could implement
the vision of the Thirties." Ms. Currier was referring to
the vision that stimulated the development of the country's
public library systems and such programs as the Center for
Research Libraries, the Pacific Northwest Bibliographic
Center, the Union Library Catalog of Pennsylvania, and national cooperative plans like the Farmington Plan. New York
State's 3R's program is another of the products of visionary
planning for the solution of real problems.

Late in the 1950's academic institutions had begun to
feel the pressure of increased enrollments; predictions were
that the increased student populations would continue to push
at the limits of available library resources. At the same
time, industry was embarking on basic scientific research
funded by U.S. Government grants in the aerospace industry
and the National Institutes of Health. The pressure on established academic and public libraries was clearly more than
either their existing funding or staffing was prepared to
meet. Solutions to these problems seemed to point toward
cooperation, a sharing of whatever wealth might be identified.

New York State responded by planning a system of libraries that would respond to research needs as its public
libraries had already responded to popular needs. It seemed
logical to extend the use of existing research library resources to all who might have need for them. It seemed intelligent to do it economically by developing cooperative research library systems.

239

In 1961, the Report of the Commissioner of Education's Committee on Reference and Research Library Resources[2] recommended the establishment of a series of regional library systems called Reference and Research Library Resources (3R's) Systems. The sixties saw the emergence of new institutions of higher learning and the reorganization of the State University of New York (SUNY) into universities, colleges, and community colleges. The increased demands on scholarly collections were not being met adequately. But by 1965, the new systems had still not been funded. After a Governor's Library Conference at which the library community reiterated the need for 3R's, the New York Legislature agreed to fund the systems on a pilot project basis. Nineteen sixty-six saw the founding of nine 3R's systems and the establishment within the Division of Library Development[3] of the Bureau of Academic and Research Libraries.

The membership of the systems varied, but each included the public library system or systems within its geographical boundaries, at least one large college or university library, several libraries affiliated with private and public colleges and community colleges, plus whatever historical, industrial, and other special libraries were eligible in each of the nine regions. Each system established a board of trustees, most of whose members were directors or users of member libraries. As the systems qualified for charters from the New York State Board of Regents,[4] they became eligible for the pilot project funds that had been allocated ($25,000 annually for each system). The funds, called "establishment grants," were outright grants which were administered autonomously by each of the systems.

The Commissioner's Committee Report had also recommended that the Division of Library Development establish a coordinating body that would loosely administer the systems' activities, identify projects that would be more appropriately initiated on a statewide basis, and become the center for the study of solutions to problems in academic and research libraries. The pilot project funding also established the Bureau of Academic and Research Libraries.[5]

By 1967, all of the 3R's systems were chartered and had been staffed with professional librarians as directors. There followed considerable activity, involved primarily with identifying the needs of member libraries. Most systems moved in the direction of planning for interlibrary loan, delivery services, union catalogs, and union lists of serials.

The Programs

It was logical that the systems developed as they did. The original document[6] upon which the 3R's systems were modeled had recommended the following "sample" programs:

A. **To Make Better Use of Existing Resources**

1. Union catalogs or finding lists
2. Duplicate exchange and distribution
3. Central storage of little used materials and central disposal of obsolete materials
4. Bibliographic centers
5. Public relations programs to interpret existing resources and services
6. Mechanical devices to supplement existing bibliographical tools
7. Improved communications systems

B. **To Build More Adequate Resources**

1. Coordinated acquisitions programs for certain categories of materials or subject areas (e. g., foreign languages)
2. Supplementary academic libraries (New York City)
3. Cooperative microtext collections
4. Cooperative periodical and newspaper collections

C. **To Provide Better Reader Services**

1. Increase public access to research materials through contract reimbursement to service agency
2. Accelerated access to materials through delivery service and modern transmission systems
3. Photographing and copying services
4. Research on user needs and research library methods

D. **To Assist Librarians to Assist Readers**

1. Field advisory service to academic and special libraries
2. In-service training for research librarians

3. Subject oriented bibliographic workshops
4. Centralized purchasing and processing of
    materials
5. Shared use of certain types of equipment

By 1973, 3R's systems had all embarked on programs
that "make better use of existing resources." The interlibrary loan programs, for example, developed both on a
statewide and regional level, provide 90 percent of the materials requested by participating libraries from resources
within the state.

On a statewide level the New York State Interlibrary
Loan system (NYSILL) has identified specific research libraries as resource centers. It has been agreed that specific subject requests be referred to the appropriate resource
library. The resource library is reimbursed for both
searching and supplying the requested material.

The model has been repeated on a regional level
wherever possible. For the academic library user, materials in the great research libraries of New York State
(e.g., Cornell, New York Public, Engineering Societies) become available within ten days of the request. For libraries,
the impact is reflected in the simplification of the search
procedure. Interlibrary loan departments submit one request. The search through the various levels of possible
sources of supply is done automatically until the material is
supplied or reported as not to be found in the system.

There are other examples of improved use of existing resources. The New York State Union List of Serials[7]
has the capacity to spin off regional lists as well as to use
regional lists to contribute to statewide listings. A current
cooperative effort, spearheaded by the State University of
New York in cooperation with the New York State Education
Department, will provide the state with a shared cataloging
system similar to that of the Ohio College Library Center
(OCLC). Eventually, the New York State Education Department will provide interface with already established computer
projects in the state, e.g., The New York Public Library's.

Building "more adequate resources" has been among
the most difficult aspects of 3R's planning. The reasons
are varied, but such projects as coordinated acquisitions
programs are subject to the stress of local needs and continued competition among academic institutions. Some pro-

grams have, nevertheless, been implemented. The Capital
District Council[8] has negotiated legal agreements to assure
continued purchase of all indexed journals. The South Central System[9] has purchased new material on a contract
agreement negotiated among several members. METRO[10]
has outlined a program called SHARES, that sets criteria
for establishing cooperative acquisitions programs. Many of
the 3R's systems are concentrating on programs that identify
expensive purchases for regional purchase. "Alert systems, "
which identify expensive purchases already made, are being
developed as well. Research has been conducted that will
lead to a definition of "expensive" as well as a basis for regional sharing. As all these efforts evolve into operating
systems, there will be systematic cooperative acquisitions.
It is naive, however, to assume that effective cooperative
acquisitions will take place on a large scale among the academic institutions in New York State until they have agreed
on their curricula and research programs.

     All of the systems have done basic preparatory work
in relation to readers' services and assistance to librarians.
An example of such programs is the patent-copying service
available in the Rochester and Western New York regions.
Library users purchase coupons and request a copy of a
U.S. patent by number. The patent is copied from the de-
pository set at the Buffalo and Erie County Public Library.
Patents are mailed on the same day the requests are received. Region-wide use is made of the only patent set
available between Cleveland, Ohio, and Albany, New York.
The service is now used heavily by industry and the legal
profession.

Guidelines

     A number of guidelines developed as the 3R's systems
proceeded to develop meaningful programs. Early, it became clear that the systems were to be coordinating entities, not operating libraries. This stress on coordinative
action removed the threat that 3R's systems might duplicate
already existing library operations. This guideline permitted
the systems the freedom to identify excellent existing services and prepare contractual agreements that would enlarge
the existing services to serve the entire region. As coordinating agencies, the 3R's systems were no longer seen as a
super-library structure that might threaten the autonomy of
the participating libraries. Interlibrary loan programs were

the first to build on the new relationships that were established.

The potential for competition for resources among member libraries was further eliminated by the guideline that no member library was to receive a direct grant-in-aid. If a contract was negotiated with a member library, it was to reflect work done for the benefit of the 3R's region. Through these kinds of arrangements, Cornell University provided bibliographic data from its card catalogs, the Buffalo Historical Society collated and filmed a rare run of local newspapers, and The New York Public Library provided a reference service for other research libraries.

As the systems tried to establish open, direct access to all libraries for anyone who might need to use them, another guideline prepared the way. No member library was to provide service exclusively through the use of other cooperating libraries. All libraries, upon joining the systems, agreed to provide adequately for the normal and anticipated needs of their own users. Research and academic library users could look forward to the day that they might use the most appropriate library resources in a region rather than be limited to the library with which they were affiliated.

All 3R's systems were expected to establish delivery and communications systems among member libraries. By 1970, the systems had established some form of delivery service ranging from use of United Parcel Service to contracts with public library system delivery facilities. Throughout New York State almost all libraries have a predictable free delivery service to and from other libraries. The delivery network will be extended to inter-system service as part of a statewide program in the near future.

Aside from these (and other) stated guidelines, [11] there were the implicit requirements for the systems. It was assumed that the systems would do basic research leading to the development of better operations between cooperating units. Many studies have been executed. An example of the importance of research are studies conducted by two of the systems which led to widely divergent recommendations. The Western New York Library Resources Council concluded, after a feasibility study, [12] that a union catalog should not be developed because it was possible to guess with a high degree of accuracy where any title could be located within the region. Conversely, the Capital District Council found

that collections in that region were unpredictable, and therefore required the use of the union catalog. The practical
value of research becomes immediately apparent. Less
clear, but equally valuable, is the evidence that regions
must respond to local idiosyncrasies. There is no all-en-
compassing "excellent" model.

Funding

The activity described above has been accomplished
on budgets from the original pilot project funding. The systems are still funded from the State Purposes Budget, the
current figures (1973) being $85,000 annually for each sys-
tem. Some of the 3R's systems have been recipients of
grants from private foundations, and a few have received
grants through HEW (Health, Education, and Welfare).

As originally conceived, funding was to be based on
a formula that would allocate both to the state coordinating
agency and the regional systems specified amounts based on
the number of part-time and full-time students within each
region, plus specified numbers of dollars for each professional (as defined in the U.S. Census) citizen of the region.[13]
Under the original funding recommendations the cost of the
total program was projected at $12.5 million annually. In
a state supporting 215 institutions of higher education, 22
public library systems (incorporating more than 700 public
libraries), and an estimated 1,000 special libraries, $12.5
million of additional support does not represent a staggering
expenditure.

For those who feel that the 3R's systems have not
produced results commensurate with the expectations, a
simple comparison of projected costs with actual expenditures might provide the reasons: under the original plan,
no system was to receive less than $250,000 annually; to
date, no system has had more than $85,000 in any one year.

Problems

In a 1972 Library Journal symposium on cooperation,[14]
a number of contributors agreed that there had been very
little progress toward cooperation in academic libraries.
None of the contributors discussed the emerging 3R's programs, although the NYSILL system was described. The

LJ article correctly identified the inherent problems in co-operative programs. It might be useful to restate the basic ambivalences generated by cooperation for academic libraries.

A director of a large research library is confronted with all or some of the following conditions:

1) the library must, in some way, be reimbursed for the added obligations involved in contributing to a network;

2) the library must not penalize its primary users by opening access to its resources to non-affiliated users;

3) the library must remain autonomous yet permit others to design ways of improving service;

4) the quality of work must remain high despite the added pressure on staff;

5) the library must be able to justify sharing its resources at the same time as it details its need for additional budget support;

6) the library must receive clear benefits from other contributing libraries.

In the 1970's, the cost and nature of "trade-offs" will be even more closely watched by academic libraries than they have been in the past.

A serious problem confronting cooperatives is the difficulty inherent in explaining the sophisticated levels of service to which cooperatives address themselves. Such programs as systems design, computer networks, and cost-saving by centralized record production are not easily understood by legislators. Developing political support for such projects is very different from advocating the free use of books by every citizen. Once libraries move out of the "apple pie-motherhood" level of appeal, they find themselves competing for funds with projects that have higher priorities. The "right" of access to research materials may not be significantly appealing when measured against the "right" to drive on excellent highways and roads.

Assuming libraries can sell cooperative services and systems, there is the further problem of explaining just how we are saving money while we ask legislatures for money. The fundamental fact is that academic and research libraries continue to be under-funded by their own administrations. Only additional support will provide a basis for improved

services.   Cooperative systems may provide the most
equitable and economical form of additional financial support.   But it should not be assumed that the additional support is not required.

A less striking, but possibly important, problem confronts implementation of regional or national systems, especially if the experiences gained from public library system development are to be used as a model.   As the public
library systems developed, work had been accomplished
through contact with professional librarians and governing
boards of trustees who had been educated concerning the nature of library services.   The 3R's systems had another dimension in the academic community, i. e., the institutional
administrative structures.   Many system directors found
themselves able to appeal successfully to academic librarians, but unable to proceed through the hierarchy of higher
education's decision-makers.

Direction for the Future

The library literature is replete with articles about
the problems of academic libraries, but seldom points the
direction to successful use of consortia, networks, and cooperatives.   There are some lessons in the experience of
3R's system development that should be examined closely
toward this end.

1.   There must be a clear definition of "territory. "
The cooperative programs that have worked in the past (Farmington Plan, LC cataloging, Denver Bibliographic Center)
have had as their goals easily definable operational results;
those results have been clearly directed toward benefits to
participating libraries, not to the library's users.   This is
not to imply that the user is considered unimportant.
Rather, it stresses the feeling that individual libraries remain the best judge of how to provide the best service to
their own users.

2.   There must be no confusion over funding.   For
the most part, consortia and networks provide improved services.   Improvement of those services by an individual library or a consortium of libraries must be recognized as
involving increased costs.   The difference is not in total
cost but the degree to which the benefits can be enjoyed by
more libraries.   Where libraries are taking on added re-

sponsibilities of service to a larger community, they must
be adequately reimbursed.

3.   Planning is a fundamental and necessary part of
the development.   The new systems generated from cooperative activity are likely to be more complex than those now
functioning in most libraries.   They will, of necessity, be
expensive if they are to meet the layers of need represented
by the membership.   Unless there is a clear and predetermined picture of costs and benefits, it is unlikely that responsible members of the cooperatives will risk their repu-
tations or their budgets.   The planning processes that measure current costs and benefits as well as projected ones
will become increasingly important in the work of academic
consortia.

4.   There should be a coordinated system.   The Bureau of Academic and Research Libraries serves a unique
function in New York State.   It is a "home" for research libraries and represents their needs to funding agencies and
the public.   Beyond that, the bureau encourages, coordi-
nates, and supplements the work of the regional systems.

Among college and university libraries, where there
is a strong tradition of competition and individualism, there
is a persistent resistance to cooperation and coordinated action.   By taking a leadership role among these libraries,
the 3R's program has demonstrated that it is possible to
work toward mutually beneficial operations without altering
the individual qualities of any of the contributors.

As libraries move toward automated systems, it becomes imperative that they move systematically through coordinated programs.   During 1973 and 1974 the National
Commission on Libraries and Information Science has been
presenting this view in the first draft of its "White Paper."

5.   Finally, the networks must be perceived as developing, changing, dynamic.   There seems to be a fear
that new library operations growing out of joint decisions
will form a bureaucracy that will hinder the development of
individual programs.   There is nothing inherent in cooperation that precludes individual activity.   It is important that
regional (or national) systems "hang loose, " always ready
to respond to newly perceived needs, methods, and ideas.
At the same time, academic libraries must recognize that
their tradition of working alone with the resources available

to them has not significantly changed the service patterns or improved them. The great strides possible in the seventies will emerge after dynamic investigation of universal library service problems. The traditional "loner" of the library world will have to "hang loose, " too.

References

1. Director of the Pacific Northwest Bibliographic Center in Seattle, Washington.
2. Commissioner of Education's Committee on Reference and Research Library Resources. Report of the Commissioner of Education's Committee on Reference and Research Library Resources. Albany, The University of the State of New York, The State Education Department, The New York State Library, 1961.
3. A part of the New York State Education Department.
4. The chartering and certification body for educational and professional institutions in New York State.
5. Within the Division of Library Development.
6. Commissioner of Education's Committee on Reference and Research Library Resources, op. cit.
7. New York State Union List of Serials. 2 vols. Prepared under the direction of the New York State Library. New York, CCM Information Corp., 1970.
8. Located in the Albany, New York, area.
9. Encompassing the region including Cornell University and SUNY at Binghamton.
10. New York City's 3R's Council: New York Metropolitan Reference and Research Library Agency, Inc.
11. The guidelines comprise an internal document of the 3R's program.
12. O'Neill, Edward T. A Survey of Library Resources in Western New York. Buffalo, N.Y., Western New York Library Resources Council, 1971.
13. For specific information about suggested funding, see Addendum IV of the Report of the Advisory Committee on Planning for the Academic Libraries of New York State. Albany, The University of the State of New York, The State Education Department, 1973.
14. "Cooperation: A Library Journal Mini-Symposium, " Library Journal, 96:1767-75, May 15, 1972.

THE OHIO COLLEGE LIBRARY CENTER:
A User-Oriented System

Frederick G. Kilgour

New educational programs in Ohio colleges following World War II stimulated interest among Ohio's academic presidents in the establishment of an organization that eventually came into being as the Ohio College Library Center. The late Président Howard F. Lowry of the College of Wooster had inaugurated an independent study program in the late 1940's, and he realized that the library of the College of Wooster could not possibly build a collection to support entirely the new educational program. President Lowry clearly saw that new educational practices would be greatly facilitated if the resources of all Ohio colleges and universities could be made available to the faculty and students of each.

President Lowry persuaded his colleagues in the Ohio College Association, established in 1867, to form a subcommittee to investigate techniques for making the resources of Ohio college and university libraries available throughout the state, and at the same time lower library costs through cooperation. Concurrently, in 1951, the librarians of the College of Wooster, Denison University, Kenyon College, Ohio Wesleyan University, and the University of Akron began to meet to consider such library cooperation programs as revising an existing list of serials in Ohio academic libraries, cooperating in maintaining serials files, and developing a cooperative bibliographic center and a central acquisitions center. This group of librarians became a formal joint committee of the Ohio College Association and the College and University Section of the Ohio Library Association. Subsequently, the Ohio College Association (OCA) established the Librarians' Committee on Library Cooperation. The Librarian's Committee was particularly active during the first half of the 1960's, and in 1966 recommended to the Ohio

College Association the establishment of the Ohio College
Library Center. The OCA approved the recommendation and
established an implementation committee that brought OCLC
into being as a not-for-profit corporation on July 6, 1967.

At that time, institutions qualified to be members of
the Ohio College Library Center were academic institutions
in Ohio that paid an annual assessment fee to the center.
In the first year of the center's existence, 54 of a potential
66 members paid assessments. The member institutions
constitute OCLC, and their representatives elect a board of
trustees from their body.

During the discussions that led to the establishment
of OCLC, the participants assumed that at some time in the
future membership in the center would be enlarged to include nonacademic libraries, and in January 1973, the OCLC
charter was amended to accomplish such an expansion. In
the autumn of 1973, nearly a dozen public and school library
systems had joined OCLC or were seriously considering doing so.

In the spring of 1973, the OCLC membership voted
to extend services outside of Ohio on a continuing basis. In
the autumn of 1973, there were seven regions with which
the center had concluded agreements to supply on-line services from Columbus, and by the end of the year, nearly
200 institutions ranging from Maine to Texas were participating.

The center has two principal objectives: 1) making
available the resources of participating libraries to individual users of those libraries; and 2) reducing the rate of rise
of per-unit costs in participating libraries while increasing
the availability of resources. Both of these objectives are
possible because OCLC is a centralized, computerized, cooperative organization. Individual libraries, even when computerized, cannot achieve either of these objectives. [1]

The center succeeds in making library resources
available throughout the participating group of libraries by
having an on-line union catalog. This catalog automatically
comes into being as books are cataloged on the system, and
in the autumn of 1973, barely two years after the inception
of the on-line operation, the on-line union catalog contained
over a million and a quarter location listings. Although no
quantitative study has been made of the increase in avail-

ability of resources, it is clear from the experience of libraries that the availability of materials is increasing. Indeed, several libraries are paying for terminals located in their reference departments to facilitate searching of the library's collection and the location of wanted items outside the library.

Various libraries that are making efficient use of the on-line shared cataloging system have demonstrated that it can be cost beneficial. One large library has dropped eight positions from its budget while increasing the number of titles cataloged from 25,000 to 39,000. Another small library is realizing a net savings in dollars that equals the amount of money paid to the center.

William J. Baumol and Matityahu Marcus[2] have recently shown that in the two decades following 1950 the cost per student in academic libraries rose at more than five percent per year compounded, while the increase in the wholesale price index was at an annual rate of less than one percent. The authors point out that inflation and growth in student bodies cannot explain the difference in the annual rise of more than four percent.

It is obvious that this excessive increase of four percent annually in per-unit costs in libraries is driving academic libraries in the direction of either financial or educational and research bankruptcy. However, there is every reason to think that centralized computerized cooperatives, such as the Ohio College Library Center, will be able to increase staff productivity in libraries and bring the rate of rise of per-unit costs more into line with those in the general economy, even while increasing the availability of resources.

The Ohio College Library Center has been designed as a comprehensive library system that is primarily oriented toward users and consists of six subsystems: 1) on-line union catalog and shared cataloging; 2) serials control; 3) acquisitions subsystem; 4) interlibrary loan module; 5) remote catalog access and circulation control; and 6) on-line access for users by subject and title.

The on-line union catalog and shared cataloging subsystem is already operational, and as already mentioned, the on-line union catalog contained over 1.25 million location listings in the fall of 1973. During September 1973, participating libraries cataloged daily an average of 3,100 copies of titles with catalog card production reaching as high as 27,000 for a single day.   In the autumn of 1973, the center's staff was programming an on-line serials control system and an acquisitions system.   When these two systems go into operation, the basic processing activities will have been computerized.   Although OCLC is primarily user-oriented, it was necessary to activate these three subsystems first to provide the data base for the computerization of user subsystems.

The last three subsystems listed above are directly oriented to the user.   The interlibrary loan subsystem will enable libraries to communicate with each other to negotiate interlibrary loans.   The remote catalog access and circulation control system will enable users to learn rapidly, without having to go to the library, whether or not the local library has a desired book, and whether or not it is immediately available.   Remote access by author and title and by title already exists, but the last subsystem will make it possible for users to search the computerized data base by subject.   When the subject approach has been activated, the OCLC system will have become a comprehensive library system for users, although there will still be many modules to be added to the system that will enhance its ability to make materials available.

OCLC has designed its computer system so as to make the interaction between the user and the system as easy as possible.   Many on-line "packages" supplied by manufacturers require an excessive amount of interaction between the user at a terminal and the computer.   Such interaction can be frustrating, distracting, and exasperating, for it sometimes requires more time to exchange greetings and courtesies with the computer than to acquire the desired information.

The center has also facilitated the use of the system by diminishing the effect of error in the user's knowledge of a reference being sought.   Search keys entered into the system contain only six characters, whether they be author-title keys, or title keys.   An author-title key consists of the first three letters of the author entry and the first three letters of the first non-English article word of the title, while a title key contains the first three letters of the first non-English article word of the title and the first letter of the next three words.   Only a relatively small amount of accurate information about a reference is required to retrieve it.

Similarly, this use of but few characters facilitates retrieval of complex entries. For example, the publication having the title <u>Agency Training Centers for Government Employees</u> bears the following author entry: "U.S. Civil Service Commission. Bureau of Training. Division of Centers." It is a rare library user who knows fully such detailed author entries. However, in the OCLC system he need enter only "US, AGE."

From the foregoing description of the Ohio College Library Center, it is obvious that the center is mimicking neither the objectives nor the techniques of classical academic libraries. Moreover, it has designed and is implementing subsystems to be the basis of future development of a new librarianship. In particular, the system has been designed to accommodate the personalization of libraries in the future. Classical libraries are unable to respond to individual users as individuals. In other words, a classical library cannot classify and subject index its collection and produce its catalogs to respond to the requirement of each individual using the library. However, future computerization may well achieve this end, and present computerization already does so to some extent. For example, selective dissemination of information based on profiles consisting of the specific needs of specific individuals is a type of personalization of information services achievable by computerization. Also, the OCLC system does not contain any files that remotely resemble catalogs. Rather, when a request is put to the system, the system responds to the user by building a small catalog that may contain from one to n entries and in effect states that if the entry is in the system it is contained within the little personalized catalog.

The new librarianship should also make every effort to furnish a library user with information when and where he or she needs it. The OCLC system achieves this goal to some extent with its on-line union catalog, which makes it unnecessary to write to some distant card catalog to determine the location of an item. Similarly, the system provides catalogers with cataloging information when and where it is needed, without having to conduct searches in multiple locations or to order it from a distant source.

The technical knowledge of the present time is adequate to design and implement a user-oriented system that will increase the personalization of the library and, at the same time, deliver information to the individual user when

and where he or she needs it. It is particularly exciting to
contemplate the interfacing of two-way cable television systems with library systems. Hardware already exists whereby it is possible for an individual participating in a two-way
cable television system to request from his or her own television set programs and, hence, data from the CATV system. Interfacing the CATV head-end computer with an
OCLC-like system (a non-trivial task) will make it possible
for library users of the future to access bibliographic information, and ultimately textual information, from libraries.
It may well be that academic librarians of the future will
be bragging about how few users come into the library.

References

1.   Kilgour, Frederick G. "Computer-Based Systems, a
     New Dimension to Library Cooperation," College &
     Research Libraries, 34:139-43, March 1973.
2.   Baumol, William J., and Marcus, Matityahu. Eco-
     nomics of Academic Libraries. Washington, D.C.,
     American Council on Education, 1973.

NELINET, NASIC, AND THE
ACADEMIC LIBRARY USER

Ronald F. Miller and David M. Wax

        To assess the dimensions of the impact of a complex
program of library and information service on users is risky
business indeed. Operating assumptions about information
value and utility, user behavior, the behavior of economic
factors, technology change, and the degree to which people
and institutions can move together in common cause are subject to erratic buffets from forces mysterious and legion.
The essence of successful response to these and other un-
certainties is to develop organizational flexibility to face
change, viewing the manifestations of such change as a landscape of opportunities rather than of barriers. A certain
boyish amazement and delight is often the best response one
can make to change in the face of its apparent destructive-
ness. It buys thinking time to prepare a more creative response.

        The New England Board of Higher Education has un-
dertaken to sponsor two major programs which are intended
to have positive and long-lasting impact upon libraries, upon
the services which they provide, and upon the constituencies
which they are intended to serve.

        In this essay, the constituency of the academic li-
brary is regarded as post-secondary level students, teaching
and research faculty, administrators, and other users for
whom special arrangements have been formalized. The
latter category of user includes off-campus individuals as
well as private and public institutions.

        The real impact of the services under development
by the New England Library Information Network (NELINET)
and the Northeast Academic Science Information Center
(NASIC) to this constituency remains, for the most part, as

a horizon yet to be reached. Although the intentions of both
programs are reasonably clear and honorable, the assumptions upon which they are based are open to continuous revision. The intentions, or objectives, of each program are
described below, and are then synthesized in a scenario of
a system of services as they may appear to the constituency.

NELINET

Since 1967, when the New England Board of Higher
Education began to develop the New England Library Information Network as a means of sharing the bibliographic resources of academic libraries in the six-state region, the
specific impact of the network upon the users of the founding
libraries was projected to be increased access to library resources by means of staff or user consultation of a union
catalog of member holdings. Produced as a by-product of
catalog card and label production, the catalog has been constructed in machine-readable form almost exclusively from
records supplied through the MARC Tape Distribution Service by the Library of Congress. These records, representing about 90,000 volumes held by 28 libraries, have remained invisible as a union catalog, since access to them
has been through Library of Congress card order number,
input by means of paper tape or punched card. Because a
participating library received cards and labels, local access
to the bibliographic information representing a relatively
small quantity of its current accessions is through conventional catalog access points: main entry, added entry, subject headings, and call number. In this environment the measurable impact which could be directly felt by users was
minimal, except perhaps that some books were ready for the
user faster.

A service derived from cataloging--accession list
production for one or multiple libraries--was used by a few
members. Although other services were posited in several
versions since the NELINET service design was first proposed by the designers (Inforonics, Incorporated, Maynard,
Massachusetts), a change in the means selected to attain
the service goals of NELINET has effectively deferred this
realization until other pre-conditions could be met. This
change was begun in the spring of 1972, when the network
members agreed to cast their lot and their future with the
Ohio College Library Center. This decision was made primarily because it appeared that NELINET goals could be

met earlier and with less dependency upon external financial
support for research and development.

The research and development components of both
systems were strikingly similar. The means, timing, and
costs for their realization were quite different. (The services being developed by OCLC are described elsewhere in
this book, and the reader is referred to that essay.) At
this point in NELINET's development it is unclear as to
which OCLC services will be provided to New England libraries beyond shared cataloging and on-line union catalog
access. It is the intention of NELINET, as an organization,
to define those user services which are needed but which
will not be provided by OCLC, and to develop the means
whereby such services will be provided. Within that context, some of the assumptions noted briefly above need further explication.

Some Assumptions

An assumption within which NELINET operates about
the utility and value of information to the user is that
printed information will remain the primary professional resource for the academic library's constituency at least
through 1990. This view includes the various packages and
formats in which printed information may occur beyond paper books and journals. The value of information will continue to be judged solely by the user within the boundary
circumscribed by the material made available to him or her
and the ease with which the user is able to obtain it.

We have, therefore, made further assumptions about
the interaction of the user and information resources:

1. that the availability of the widest possible array
    of information-bearing resources should be open
    to the user;
2. that information is more likely to be sought if it
    is relatively convenient to locate and use;
3. that, in terms of effort, time, and money, the
    cost of access to information on the part of the
    user should not exceed the cost of ignoring it al-
    together;
4. that the library remains the major institutional
    and personal source to obtain most of the infor-
    mation which a member of the user community

needs to perform his or her academic and research work.

Assumptions about library services include:

1. that members of the academic library's user constituency have access to the collections under the
   administrative control of the library, as well as
   interlibrary loan services;
2. although there is not yet uniformity of procedure
   on this point, the assumption is made that service policy is generally expanding to provide items
   to undergraduates through interlibrary loan and on-
   site use arrangements among groups of libraries;
3. that interlibrary loan and searching of machine-
   readable bibliographic data bases for retrospective and current-awareness output are services
   which are developing as non-overhead services,
   i. e. that users will pay for some or all of the
   costs associated with their provision.

Assumptions about networking and telecommunications
are:

1. that the utility of rapid interlibrary communications of bibliographic data by means of computer-
   mediated networks is a demonstrated reality;
2. that geographically contiguous libraries are developing services which are supplemental to dis-
   tance-independent networks, e. g. document and
   people transfer systems;
3. that the cost of both computing and telecommunications technology is declining absolutely, even
   more so if such costs are shared by participating
   institutions;
4. that because of technological change, networks
   will be designed and organized so that new technology can be integrated with recent technology
   without the necessity for starting a new system
   from scratch.

   Given these assumptions about information packaging,
utility, user-behavior, libraries, and technology, NELINET
has taken the role of a synthesizer of library information
services devoted to making effective use of resources which
are available from a multiplicity of service centers. A
summary of active and proposed NELINET services and their

impact upon the user appears at the conclusion of this essay.

First, however, a description of the program of the Northeast Academic Science Information Center is in order.

NASIC

The Northeast Academic Science Information Center (NASIC) is also a program of the New England Board of Higher Education and represents an attempt to apply the concept of brokering computer-based information services on a multi-state basis. Through promotion and marketing of services, and through training of Information Service Librarians on the campuses of academic institutions, NASIC aims to create, tap, and serve the substantial market of researchers in the Northeast who are in need of information resident in machine-readable data bases. Through aggregation of user demand and negotiation of bulk purchase contracts with multiple suppliers, NASIC intends to serve the research community of the Northeast at a reasonable cost while assuring its own continued viability as a self-supporting organization. Through utilization of available computing capacity in the Northeast and existing communications networks in the region, NASIC aims to become an efficient, self-supporting supplier of low-cost services appropriate to the needs of the region's research community. These goals and the efficiencies and economies which they imply are the basis for the decision by the Office of Science Information Service of the National Science Foundation to underwrite the development of NASIC, and for the support of this cooperative effort by many of the principal universities of the Northeast.

The Functions of NASIC

As of this writing the program is less than nine months along and is still in its formative stages. It is intended that NASIC will direct its efforts toward the fulfillment of six basic tasks:

1. to perform a continuing market analysis of both the user population and computer-based data services;
2. to promote and market computer-based information services from existing processors;
3. to train library personnel to provide competent

        interface with users;

4. to negotiate contracts with suppliers at bulk discount rates;

5. to supply information services directly to individual users; and

6. to participate in the development of an efficient
bibliographic and document delivery network.

Each of these functions is tied directly to the long-term viability of NASIC as an organization and to the information
brokerage concept as a realistic means of providing information services from existing sources.

      The activity involving the determination and evalua-
tion of the market for computer-based information services
underscores the basic principle underlying the NASIC approach to the provision of information services.   NASIC is
devoting a significant amount of its resources to an assessment of the Northeastern United States.   To determine the
nature and extent of the market, NASIC utilizes many of the
techniques common to product introduction in the industrial
and commercial environment.   This analysis will enable
NASIC to ascertain demand for particular information services and will help in formulating cost allocation formulae
necessary to assure NASIC's self-support.

      In addition to the determination of the existing and
potential market for computer-based information services,
NASIC will identify new users through active advertising and
promotion.   Various methods and media--campus newspapers,
bulletin boards, and department meetings, to name just a
few--will be evaluated for effectiveness.   Recognizing that
word-of-mouth is probably the least expensive and most effective means of publicizing the utility of information services, NASIC will concentrate on developing a core of satisfied users on each campus which undertakes to participate
in NASIC services.

      An important aspect of the NASIC concept is that
computer-based information services constitute a logical extension of the information services and products traditionally
provided by the college and university library.   Within the
library of each major research institution in the region,
one or more staff members will be trained to function as
Information Service Librarians (ISL's).   With the understanding of the principles underlying the search techniques for each
data base, with awareness of the content of the broad range

of available data bases, and with the skills to develop and
code effective search profiles, the ISL's will function as the
interface between the supplier and users of information services so that the user can obtain the best possible services
from existing information processing services.

It will be the first function of the ISL to assist the
researcher in the definition of his or her specific information requirement.   Second, the ISL will have the responsibility
to select the most appropriate processing source for the information required by the user.   This decision involves not
only the determination of appropriate data bases, but also an
awareness of the search algorithms employed at the various
information centers processing that data base.   Third, the
ISL will develop search profiles that will yield optimum recall of citations and abstracts needed by the user, minimizing irrelevant and unnecessary references.   Fourth, the ISL
will review search output for relevance and completeness
judgments.   This review will also serve as the basis for determining the desirability of modifying the search profile
in the case of continuing current awareness services.   Finally, the ISL or a colleague in the library staff will assist in
arrangements for document delivery related to the search
output.

While the traditional role of the library is thus not
modified by the introduction of computer-based information
services--a computer printed list of bibliographic citations
and abstracts is not significantly different from a typed list--
the manner and means by which services are provided by
the library to the user will be changed.   For this reason,
an important component of the NASIC program will be the
orientation of the academic library community to the utility
of computer-based information services and the training of
library personnel to enable them to acquire the knowledge
and skills necessary to function as effective Information Service Librarians.

Another important aspect of NASIC's brokerage role
will be the aggregation of demand from a multiplicity of users dispersed over a large geographic region.   The economies of scale in the provision of such services are substantial, and only through aggregation of demand can the real
costs of these services be kept at reasonable--and market-
able--rates.   The true costs of providing these services on
a single campus, particularly in small or medium sized universities, are very high--in most cases prohibitive.   Through

regional aggregation of demand, the cost components--includ-
ing hardware, data bases, technical staff input, and administrative and management resources--can be prorated over a
large number of searchers, with the add-on to any individual
search kept relatively low.

Further economics of scale and competition can be
generated through the negotiation of contracts with a range
of suppliers at discount rates.   Because of the existence of
competitive suppliers for many of the relevant services and
because most of these suppliers have capacity to provide
significantly greater quantities of services at only marginal
increases in real costs, the discounts resulting from aggregation of demand should in many cases be sufficient to cover
the entirety of the NASIC overhead costs.   Finally, NASIC's
activities as a broker and aggregator of demand will enable
NASIC to provide the research community of the Northeast
with a much greater variety of services than would otherwise
be available.

The basic assumption underlying this brokerage experiment is that it is inconceivable that a large number of
universities in the Northeast would be willing to underwrite
on their own the provision of a broad range of computer-
based information services.   It is even less likely that any
of the small or medium sized institutions would be able to
offer even minimal services.   And if one or more institutions
did make such marginal services available, it would be impossible for them to provide the great variety that NASIC as
a broker and aggregator of demand could offer to all of the
researchers throughout the entire region.

The provision of bibliographic and abstract services
at a reasonable cost, while in itself a worthy goal, does not
constitute the sole objective of NASIC.   The user often requires services beyond a listing of citations and a collection
of abstracts.   In many cases, document delivery is an essential component of total service to the user.   Through its
close ties to the academic libraries of the region, NASIC
will work toward the development of systems for delivery
of the necessary hard copy to the user, whether it take the
form of reprints, photocopies, microfiche, or monographs.
NASIC's link to the computer-based library support system of
the New England Library Information Network (NELINET) and
the ultimate utilization of that system for serials control,
interlibrary loan, and circulation control will play a significant role in the development of a document location and de-

livery capability.

NASIC also recognizes that there is a broad range of potential information services that are not now available anywhere, and it is likely that NASIC will become a direct supplier of such services should a market for them be identified. Activities in this area would include the development by the New England Board of Higher Education of data bases that have national or regional utility. Such products may include an alerting service to keep segments of the research community of the Northeast up-to-date on new developments related to information in their particular fields of interest.

Finally, NASIC sees as one of its primary functions the utilization of existing resources within the region as a basis for efficient delivery of information services. Reference has already been made to potential use of the NELINET system to assist in an economical document location and delivery capability. It is also planned that the New England Regional Computing Program (NERComP) communications network will be used for a portion of the process for computer-based information services. Should the NERComP network prove effective, it is possible that the network might expand to include the entire Northeast region. Furthermore, if demand for information from one or more data bases warrants it, NASIC may begin to "spin tapes" on its own, utilizing existing hardware and technical resources within the region to do the processing, and tapping the NERComP network for message routing and electronic delivery. As NASIC moves into an operational mode, it is likely that other existing resources will be identified and added to the efficiency of the system.

NASIC: The User's Perspective

From the point of view of the user, NASIC must provide fast and economical access to a body of information that is of use to him or her. Thus, to meet its objectives NASIC will be able to provide information from a broad range of data bases and to deliver information products that are timely, complete, and relevant, at a price that will make the purchase of this service desirable.

It is the operating plan of NASIC that the user perceive these computer-based information services as the logical extension of the information services presently provided

by the university library. When he or she is in need of information, the user will arrange to discuss his or her particular requirements with the Information Services Librarian
(ISL) resident at his or her own institution. Should the specific subject area be outside the range of competence of the
local ISL(s) or should the user be located at an institution
too small to employ a trained ISL, the user can be directed
to an information specialist at the NASIC offices or to an
ISL at another university in the region who has special competence and knowledge in the specific discipline in question.

The ISL, after discussing the research problem with
the user, will utilize the knowledge he or she has acquired
about the various data bases and search techniques available
to determine the most appropriate means of providing the
necessary services. A search profile will be developed and
coded by the ISL and the search ordered under the auspices
of NASIC. The mode (on-line or off-line) to be used in developing the profile and ordering the search will depend on
a number of factors including the availability of processing
alternatives, the time requirements of the user, and the
price the user is willing to pay. Within a period of time
ranging from a few minutes to a week or more, the output
will arrive at the desk of the ISL, who will review it with
the user for relevance and completeness. At the same time,
the user will be informed as to the options for obtaining
hard copy of those documents which are of particular value.

In most cases the user will pay for these services
by charging them to his or her personal or grant account at
the university. In some instances, departments might allocate funds for acquiring these services in their budgets, as
support to the research of department members. In other
situations, the college or university might choose to make
these services available to all faculty members and students
either free or on a token charge basis, with a portion of
the service costs provided from general library or academic
budgets. The user will also be aware of the fact that the
availability of this kind of information service was the result of a cooperative effort of his or her own institution and
similar institutions operating under the auspices and guidance
of NASIC in his or her behalf.

Summary

Many of the effects of the NELINET and NASIC pro-

grams upon the academic library user are conjectural, since
no user study has yet been undertaken to identify and measure
them.   It is also too early to undertake such a study, since
network libraries are not yet fully exploiting available services.   Some of the expected effects are summarized below:

1. The user should perceive more public service
    staff available to him or her to aid in the use of
    collections and in the use of computer terminals
    for data base browsing.

2. The pressure to charge users, either directly or
    indirectly, for services which the library gov-
    ernance structure defines as beyond the standard
    core services will result in "pay-for-information
    environments. "

3. The user will be able to find new accessions
    through on-line bibliographic tools faster than in
    many manual systems.

4. The user will be able to compile his or her own
    mini-catalog of items arranged by author and sub-
    ject for convenient browsing by cathode-ray tube
    terminal or printed list.

5. The user will be able to locate materials both in
    his or her local library or any other library tied
    into the network and begin the process of reser-
    vation or delivery of such materials to his or
    her home or office.

6. The user will, with the help of trained library
    staff, be able to access multiple discipline-
    oriented data bases, to be continuously up-to-
    date in current printed media.   This service will
    be similar to current SDI and retrospective
    searching systems, but the user may elect to
    negotiate his or her own search profile.   The lo-
    cation of needed items will be found through the
    network union catalog, or other services pro-
    vided by government or commercial vendors.

7. The reliance of the user upon the telephone for
    providing bibliographic and library services will
    increase, as in the case of the Ohio State Uni-
    versity's remote catalog.   The operative model

is the airline reservation system, supplemented
by document delivery systems.

8. Finally, if user services are not curtailed from
their current levels, due to high people and materials costs, energy conservation, and institutional priorities, strides in reversing current
trends will have been made.

For these events to occur, there must be a strong desire on
the part of librarians, governmental agencies, users, and
administrators to make them happen. The controlling factor
will be the cost acceptability to the institution and the user.

We must constantly collect and review evidence which
may force us to change our assumptions. Should evidence
fly in the face of our cherished personal beliefs of what a
library should be, we should be willing to change, to lead.

To paraphrase a notion current a few years back:
"We should seek to identify the inevitable, and claim it as
our own." Despite the logical contradiction inherent in this
process, it is only in that fashion that we can influence the
ineluctable, rather than be run over by it.

THE COOPERATIVE COLLEGE
LIBRARY CENTER, INC.:
An Historical Perspective

Hillis Dwight Davis

The Cooperative College Library Center is located in
Atlanta, Georgia, at 159 Forrest Avenue, N. E., Suite 602
of the United Methodist Center Building. The prospectus
states that it is the only consortium in the United States
specifically designed and implemented by predominately black
colleges to accelerate the growth and development of black
college libraries. The center was officially established on
August 1, 1969, and began operation in late October of that
year. The Cooperative College Library Center is a non-
profit, tax-exempt corporation governed by a board of
trustees. The board consists of a representative of each
member college, usually the president. This body sets
center policy. The director of the center is an ex-officio
member of the board. There is also an advisory committee
to the center, made up of the chief librarians of member
colleges, the primary function of which is to advise the director on technical matters.

The original objectives of the center were:

1.) to stimulate the improvement of library facilities and services;
2.) to coordinate cooperative acquisitions, interlibrary loan, and the reproduction of materials;
3.) to aid in the training and development of library
personnel;
4.) to promote programs for the expanded use of library resources;
5.) to assist member college libraries in the selection of materials; and
6.) to purchase, catalog, and process library materials.

The original objectives are all attainable. However,
I, as director, feel that the center was established mainly
to serve as an academic technical processing center, to save
both money and staff for its members so that more books
and services could be provided with the money available.
All colleges, especially small colleges, are experiencing financial hardships. They are all required to save money
wherever possible while the cost of providing a good education continues to rise. A good library is an important element of a good education. However, there has been a tremendous increase in the overall cost of library management. [1]

Historical Background

Dr. Earl J. McGrath, executive officer of the Institute of Higher Education, first conceived the idea that such
a center be established for Negro colleges. In his book
The Predominantly Negro Colleges and Universities in Transition, which was published in 1965 by the Bureau of Publications, Teachers College, Columbia University, the entire
area of black higher education was examined. Dr. Warren
J. Haas, then director of libraries at the University of Pennsylvania, who was responsible for the chapter on libraries,
points out that:

> The demand for higher education generally, and
> among Negroes specifically, and an increased per-
> centage of attendance in the appropriate age group,
> will in the years ahead expand the average insti-
> tutional size and thus make better use of the li-
> brary facilities. A more direct approach, however,
> would be to improve the efficiency of present pur-
> chasing and cataloging practices. The creation
> and operation of a college service center to act as
> the purchasing and cataloging agent for a number
> of small colleges in a given region would effect
> material savings and increase efficiency. A com-
> prehensive but uncomplicated plan for such a ser-
> vice center could be prepared with little difficulty
> by drawing on the experience of any of the several
> existing technical service centers in public library
> systems. Reasonably accurate estimates of oper-
> ating cost and of potential savings could be pro-
> jected for libraries of varying sizes. With this
> information in hand, the merits of the service

center concept could be presented to college administrators and librarians in a geographical region.

The success of such a project would hinge on the care with which its goals were defined and on the skill with which the system was designed and presented to prospective users. Individual libraries, whether Negro or not, could send to the center a check list of books indicating desired titles. They would then receive fully catalogued and processed volumes ready to be put into their collections, together with full sets of cards for their catalogues. Financed on the basis of a combination of subscription fees and service charges, the center would submit monthly itemized bills to the colleges. At the outset, private colleges would doubtless be the principal users of such a center, but the efficiency and economy of its service might eventually overcome the restrictive purchasing procedures in public institutions and open the way to contracts with them.

Large research libraries have already recognized the need for cooperative cataloguing and coordinated collecting. The staff of small libraries no less need to be relieved of the burdens of many operating routines to enable them to get on with the educational aspects of librarianship. A service agency of the type proposed would give small libraries the operating advantages of large ones. As volumes dictated, data processing or copying equipment could produce catalogue cards in volume at low unit costs as a byproduct of the order routine. Maximum discount rates could be obtained on purchases, billing procedures could be automated, and the time consuming, essentially clerical, routines of technical activities would be largely eliminated from individual libraries. Thus the staff would be freed for the more important work of reference service, collection development, and student instruction. In the long run, this increased emphasis on the professional aspects of librarianship would attract more promising and much needed young people to the profession than any other steps these libraries could presently take. [2]

The concept of cooperative technical processing for
black academic institutions was given added impetus in The
Negro and Higher Education in the South, a statement by the
Commission on Higher Educational Opportunity in the South.
The statement was prepared by Dr. James M. Godard, project director, and Dr. Lionel H. Newsome, then associate
director of the Southern Regional Educational Board, and
was presented at the annual meeting of the Southern Regional
Educational Board on August 29, 1967, at White Sulphur
Springs, West Virginia. Several suggestions were offered
in an attempt to promote interinstitutional cooperation as one
of the most efficient and economical means for broadening
and strengthening higher educational opportunities at black
colleges. One of the recommendations stated that:

> A pilot project be undertaken to test the value of
> a cluster of Negro institutions establishing a joint
> center for the purchasing and cataloging of library
> resources for purposes of economy and the opti-
> mum use of library personnel. [3]

The Jessie Smith Noyes Foundation made a grant of
$2,000 to Stillman College, Tuscaloosa, Alabama, in No-
vember 1967 to begin exploring the possibilities of establishing such a cooperative library program. Dr. Charles C.
Turner, then academic dean at Stillman College, was instrumental in securing foundation support for the project. He
was also responsible for bringing together the presidents
and librarians of six black colleges for the initial discussion
of library problems and possible solutions. The six original colleges were Miles, Oakwood, Stillman, Talladega, Tuskegee (all in Alabama), and Tougaloo (in Mississippi).
These colleges held a series of meetings to discuss mutual
problems.

During the early part of 1967, several black college
presidents requested that the National Council of Churches
establish an agency to promote cooperative programs for
black colleges which would be almost impossible to execute
unilaterally. The United Board for College Development
was established as the body to meet this request. Early in
1968, Dr. Turner left his position of dean at Stillman College to assume the position of director of the United Board
for College Development. His office was supported originally by a Ford Foundation grant and later by churches and
private grants. Dr. Turner located his agency in Atlanta,
because of that city's close proximity to black colleges.

One of the first ventures undertaken by the United Board for College Development was continued support of the concept of a cooperative library project. Dr. Turner secured the consultant services of Dr. Maurice Tauber, Melville Dewey Professor of Library Science at Columbia University, and Dr. Warren J. Haas. They recommended that a feasibility study be made of the technical services departments of the original six colleges. The United Board commissioned Dr. Annette Hoage Phinazee, then a professor in the School of Library Service at Atlanta University, as the principal investigator and Casper LeRoy Jordan, supervisor of technical processes, Nioga Library System, Niagara Falls, New York, as associate investigator. The selection, acquisition, cataloging, classification, card production, and processing of materials were all investigated at the six colleges.

The study revealed that the technical processing cost ranged from a low of $1.89 to a high of $6.66 per title. It was the opinion of the investigators that none of the six libraries studied was capable of processing 12,000 to 20,000 volumes annually without a significant expansion of both the library staff (professional and nonprofessional) and the physical facilities in the technical processing area. They also felt that additional equipment would have to be acquired by each library to make the 20,000 volumes a possibility, and that the technical processing cost should be reduced substantially.[4] Based on their findings, a manual cooperative technical processing center was recommended as the most feasible alternative for efficient, effective, and economical reasons. The investigators further felt that a staff of 11 full-time and four part-time workers would be sufficient to technically process 90,000 volumes per year at a cost of $1.05 per volume.[5] Listed below are the staff requirements as stated in the study:

Director (1)
Cataloger (1)
Bibliographer (1)
Chief Clerk (1)
Multilith Operator (1)
Typists (3)
Secretary-Bookkeeper (1)
Delivery Driver or Mail Clerk (1)
Pages (4) Part-time
File Clerk (1).[6]

The following are the recommendations of the feasibility study for the establishment of the center.

Recommendations

A single processing center for the selection, ordering, cataloging, and processing for these six libraries is recommended for the following reasons:

1.   Other studies show that there is a great deal of duplication of cataloging going on in libraries, with a negligible amount of unique cataloging being done.   There is evidence to support drawing this same conclusion about the six libraries in this study.   Their institutions are offering similar courses and they are buying many of the same titles.   Thus it appears that five to six times more cataloging is being done in the libraries than need be.

2.   No significant differences in cataloging practices were found.   All of the librarians buy LC cards and they can get them for most of their holdings.

3.   A center would cost less to operate than it would cost to expand facilities in the individual libraries and titles could be processed more cheaply.

4.   Professional personnel which is now involved in technical services in these libraries would have more time to make policies, plan and improve services, effect joint efforts with faculties to increase the use of library resources, provide more guidance in the use of the libraries, and actually get involved in the teaching or substantive aspect of the academic program. [7]

The study states that there are many problems that should be worked out prior to the establishment of the center. It was their feeling that in order to achieve the maximum economies and efficiencies, the librarians would have to agree on uniformity in as many areas as possible.   Listed below are their recommendations in this regard.

a.   Selection of materials by the center is recom-

mended. It was approved by all six libraries.
Additional selections could also be made by member librarians.

b. Ordering by the center is desirable. The librarians agreed to this, but one did not approve
of having the center acquire state and United Na-
tions documents; two disapproved of the purchase
of periodicals, newspapers, federal documents,
and phonorecords; three did not consent to have
films, filmstrips, and microtexts acquired by the
center.

c. Cataloging practices of the present colleges
could be standardized, though there would be problems involved. To some extent existing differences
in cataloging practice may reflect differences in
the experience and ability of catalogers. If there
were only one cataloging center, there would be
the opportunity to encourage a uniformly high level
of cataloging content through the employment of the
most highly qualified professional to perform the
function. A uniform cataloging code would have to
be adopted. This is a must; any system proceeding without it invites disaster.

All of the librarians indicated that they would like
to have the center make cross references. However, only five wanted simplified serials cataloging and wanted serials cataloged as monographs
when possible. Recataloging is desired at Miles
and Stillman. Miles and Stillman are the only
schools interested in exploring the possibilities of
substituting a book catalog for the card catalog.

d. Classification according to the LC system is
recommended, although Miles is the only college
now using it. If the remaining five schools would
consent to adopt this system, many of the problems of classification would be solved. However,
working with two systems at the center would not
present insurmountable odds. Stillman, Talladega,
and Tuskegee indicated that they would be willing
to adopt the LC classification; Oakwood wrote 'perhaps, ' and Tougaloo wrote 'no. ' Five libraries,
including Oakwood, expressed a willingness to
adopt the LC numbers on the cards without modi-

fication. Any reclassification should be directed
toward a reconstituted collection. Materials acquired by the center will add much to the educational potential of these colleges and revitalize
their collections.

Tougaloo would reclassify the entire collection if
LC were adopted; Miles plans to convert approximately 30 percent of the collection; Oakwood, Stillman, and Talladega would change added copies and
volumes; Stillman would also reclassify the literature collection. Tuskegee's reclassification 'would
depend on available staff.'

e. Physical preparation of materials at the center
would not be large enough in volume to justify acquiring electronic data processing equipment; however, records should be set up which can be converted with a minimum of effort and money.

f. Communication must be maintained between the
member libraries and the center if it is to be effective.

g. Delivery of materials to the member libraries
should be swift and economical. Studies of the use
of mail, a center-owned truck, and commercial
trucking service should be investigated.

h. Bills should be sent directly to the member libraries for materials purchased by them. [8]

To qualify for membership in the center the six colleges agreed:

1. to expend 80 percent of the book funds through
   the center;
2. to remain in the center for at least three years,
   and to give one year's advance notice of intentions to withdraw; and
3. to adopt the LC classification system.

Establishment of the Center

The United Board for College Development secured a
grant of $233,000 from the Carnegie Corporation, payable in

three annual installments, for the establishment of the Cooperative College Library Center. The first installment of
$134, 000 was made through the National Council of Churches
in the spring of 1969, and the center was officially established on July 1, 1969. In early spring of that year, I was
appointed director of the center, and it was decided jointly
by Dr. Turner; Dr. Luther H. Foster, president of Tuskegee Institute and chairman of the board; Butler T. Hender-
son, then assistant director of the United Board; and me to
locate the office in Atlanta, Georgia. On August 1, 1969, I
assumed my new position, and the center was officially incorporated by the State of Georgia on September 2, 1969,
with Attorney Isabelle Gates Webster serving as legal coun-
sel. Casper L. Jordan was retained as consultant to the
center for the first year, and Dr. Annette H. Phinazee assumed the position of associate director in charge of cataloging on September 15, 1969. Mrs. Mildred W. Jackson
was appointed secretary to the director on September 15,
and Mrs. Arneize F. Ramseur was appointed bibliographer
effective November 16, 1969. Six additional staff members
were added on January 1, 1970.

    Earlier that same year the United Board secured a
grant from the Jessie Smith Noyes Foundation to conduct a
workshop on "Conversion of Classification Systems and Improvement of Library Technical Assistants in Negro Colleges. " Twenty-five predominately black colleges were invited to attend, and each was allowed to send three participants (head librarian, cataloger, and library technical assistant). The workshop was conducted in the center from October 16 to 24, 1969. There were approximately 80 participants. It is reported that this workshop was one of the
first of its kind ever conducted for black college librarians.
I feel that the project did much to dispel the fears of converting to the Library of Congress classification.

    The center held its formal opening on October 28,
1969, when the first book was processed. The presidents
and librarians of member colleges and representatives from
educational agencies and foundations were present for this
occasion. The book Born to Rebel, by Dr. Benjamin E.
Mays, was the first title processed through the
center.   .

    I spent a great deal of time during the first six
months visiting the processing centers of the Atlanta Public

Library System, the Atlanta Public School System, and the DeKalb Public Library System. A large amount of time also was spent in locating, evaluating, and purchasing the necessary equipment, furniture, and supplies. In addition, most of the member college libraries were visited. Actual processing began in early 1970.

On July 1, 1970, 12 additional colleges were added, namely: Bennett College, Greensboro, North Carolina; Bishop College, Dallas, Texas; Claflin College, Orangeburg, South Carolina; Clark College, Atlanta, Georgia; Dillard University, New Orleans, Louisiana; Florida Memorial College, Miami, Florida; LeMoyne-Owen College, Memphis, Tennessee; Morris Brown College, Atlanta, Georgia; Morris College, Sumter, South Carolina[9]; Paul Quinn, Waco, Texas; Rust College, Holly Springs, Mississippi; and Virginia Union University, Richmond, Virginia.

In the fall of 1971, the 19th college was admitted: Mary Holmes College, West Point, Mississippi.

On July 1, 1972, three additional colleges were added: Fisk University, Nashville, Tennessee; Kittrell College, Kittrell, North Carolina; and Paine College, Augusta, Georgia.

At the beginning of fiscal year 1973-74 six additional colleges became members. These are: Huston-Tillotson College, Austin, Texas; Jarvis Christian College, Hawkins, Texas; Texas College, Tyler, Texas; Tusculum College, Greeneville, Tennessee; Virginia State College, Petersburg, Virginia; and Wiley College, Marshall, Texas.

At the present time, there are 27 active members. The feasibility study recommended a maximum of 25 institutions for a completely manual operation. However, we have changed to a completely automated system (to be discussed later), and I feel that the center can perhaps handle a few more colleges.

Center Operations

The staff at the present time is composed of the director, a professional cataloger, seven clerical workers, and four student pages. This is two less than the number of full-time staff members recommended in the feasibility

study. Initially, there was a bibliographer, as recommended
by the feasibility study, to assist the member librarians with
book selection, but it was quite evident from the outset that
this was an area of cooperation that the librarians resisted.
When the bibliographer resigned for personal reasons, the
position was filled quite satisfactorily with a clerical worker.

At the beginning, as director, I attempted to follow
the suggested work flow chart as given in the study. However, it became quite apparent that this flow chart had too
many unnecessary steps. An assembly line operation was
implemented similar to those employed at the DeKalb Public
Library Technical Processing Center.

The reasons why commercial firms and technical processing centers for public library systems and public school
systems had been successful in cooperative technical processing became apparent: 1. Acquisitions were limited to
a certain copyright time-span; and 2. Multiple copies for
several branches were ordered, received, and processed at
the same time.

The center staff immediately recognized that some
method of synchronizing acquisitions would have to be implemented. Consequently, the members were put on an ordering schedule to maximize duplication. Dr. Dougherty states
that:

> ... Currently, most titles ordered through the
> Center are unique titles: moreover, many of the
> titles ordered were published before the Center
> was established. If the Center could concentrate
> its resources on handling multiple copies of new
> titles rather than dissipating them on single copies
> of older materials, the goal projected by the Di-
> rector might be attainable. [10]

The Cooperative College Library Center was established, as the feasibility study indicates, to:

1. Increase the purchasing power of the dollar
   through quantity purchasing.
2. Decrease the overall cost of technical processing
   at each college. It was estimated that the processing cost at the individual colleges ranged
   from $1.89 to $6.66 per title, with an average
   cost of $4.39 per title. The study concluded

that through the establishment of a technical processing center, the cost of technical processing
could be reduced to $1.05 per volume.

3. Minimize the need for additional staff (both clerical and professional) and in time replace the
existing technical processing staffs at the individual colleges.

In a completely manual operation it was mandatory
that a staff of nine technically process approximately 50,000
volumes.   Table I is a chart of the work-flow that was finally adopted.   It is reasonably self-explanatory, but several
areas may be amplified.   Initially, CCLC placed two copies
of the multiple purchase order form in the union file with
any available catalog copy.   This step increased the existing
filing time by approximately 30 hours per week.   A minimum
of 70 hours per week was spent filing proof slips, catalog
copy, and multiple order forms.   We were able under the
manual operation to decrease filing time to less than 20
hours per week.   Initially, there was very little duplication
of orders in the ordering procedure.   However, through our
efforts at coordinating ordering this figure was increased
appreciably.   As a result, CCLC was able to decrease the
amount of typing and thereby increase output.   If CCLC received three or more copies of a title, the center would produce one set of cards and type the added entries on this set
together with the charging materials.   This set was revised,
and all other complete sets were generated from it.   This
innovation saved on typing, revising, and the type of worker
that could be used for final checking of material.   The average turn-around time for a book with available catalog copy
was from 10 to 14 days.

Cost

The feasibility study said that a technical processing
center could process 60,000 titles and 90,000 volumes at a
cost of $1.05 per volume.   I now feel that both of these
figures are wrong.   The Colorado Center began its operation by giving its cost as $3.10 per volume.[11]   At a later
date the Colorado Center implemented a new price structure
by cataloging class.[12]   This new fee schedule reflects an
overall increase in centralized technical processing cost.
However, there are definite savings to be realized from
centralized processing.

TABLE I

CHART OF WORK-FLOW
FOR MANUAL OPERATION

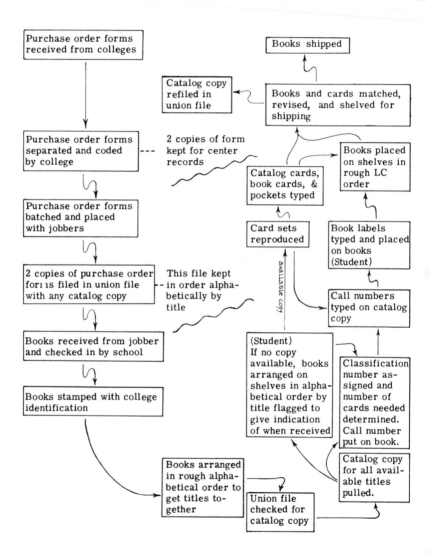

Growth

The Cooperative College Library Center has had continuous growth over the past four years. Table II demonstrates this fact. I believe that the present staff can process approximately 70,000 volumes using the OCLC system for card catalog production. We have now reached the approximate size (in terms of the number of volumes processed) of one of the major universities. Consequently, we must conclude that the Cooperative College Library Center can effect a net savings for our members. However, we feel that our technical processing fee must be increased to a minimum of $2.25 per volume. We also feel that a manual technical processing center would be almost impossible for academic institutions because of the many variables in institutional acquisition programs.

The Ohio College Library Center

The costs of running college and university libraries continue to skyrocket. It is said that staff salaries consume approximately 60 percent of a library's total budget. There has been an increase of approximately 200 percent in the number of books published for college libraries over the past several decades, and a tremendous increase in the cost of these materials.

It is reported that automation and mechanization have contributed to an increase in the productivity per man hour in manufacturing and that libraries have continued to lag behind in this regard.[13] It appears that the Ohio College Library Center will fill this void.

On July 1, 1971, the Office of Education made a grant available for the demonstration of the possible implications of the OCLC system for the member colleges of the Cooperative College Library Center.[14] The funding was for an 18-month period. CCLC negotiated a contract with OCLC at the conclusion of the experimental period.

Table III is a chart of the work-flow using the OCLC for remote-access catalog card production via a terminal. Five of the 19 required steps in the manual system have been eliminated. To date CCLC has been able to find bibliographic data in the data base for approximately 85 percent of the titles purchased by our members on the first call up. Since

TABLE II

GROWTH OF CCLC FROM ITS BEGINNING

Year	Staff Full-Time	Student Help	No. of Vols. Ordered	No. of Vols. Received	No. of Vols. Processed	Member- ship
1969-70	9	5	8,338	6,185	3,828	6
1970-71	9	5	30,555	26,610	26,492	18
1971-72	9	4	41,650	31,636	35,311*	19
1972-73	9	4	50,517	42,939	42,958	21
	9	4	131,060	107,370	108,589	21

*Includes approximately 5,000 volumes which were counted when processed, but were not ordered through the acquisition system and were not counted as volumes ordered or received.

TABLE III

CHART OF WORK-FLOW
USING THE OCLC TERMINAL

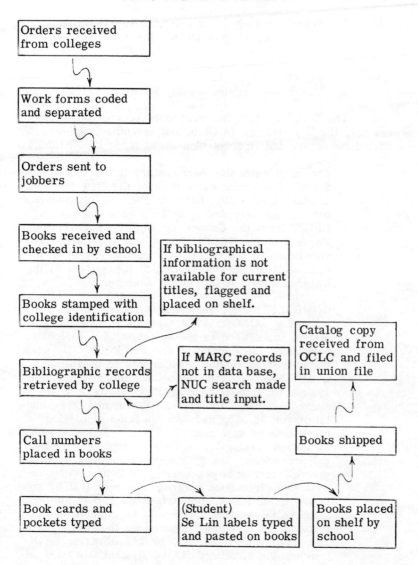

most of our members are undergraduate liberal arts colleges, we should notice an increase in our hits, up to approximately 95 percent on first call up, as a result of the shared cataloging concept. The reasons for this are:

1. Several colleges and universities are recataloging, converting, or just putting the shelflist files into the data base.
2. New colleges and new networks are affiliating with the OCLC system.
3. There are regular weekly MARC additions.

The OCLC system has proved to be cost beneficial not only for the colleges in Ohio, but for other regions. Listed below are the findings of a study made by NELINET.

> The most extensive examination of the system was a test of its transferability that the New England Library Information Network (NELINET) conducted between January and June 1972 on a grant to NELINET from the Council on Library Resources. Phase I of the NELINET test was a computerized simulation of the OCLC system and Phase II, an evaluation and demonstration of the system at the Baker Library at Dartmouth College.
>
> COMPRESS, Inc., the firm that carried out a simulation for OCLC in 1969 designed to produce information to be used in the selection of a computer, performed the simulation for NELINET. Because the shared cataloging system was in operation, COMPRESS was able to validate the model of the system by comparing computed results with observed results. COMPRESS performed this simulation for 35, 75, and 249 libraries employing three sets of systems: 1) shared cataloging only; 2) shared cataloging, serials control, and technical processing; and 3) shared cataloging, serials control, technical processing, remote catalog access and circulation control, and retrieval by subject. COMPRESS summarized its report stating, 'The OCLC system appears to be capable of performing the functions required by the NELINET consortium, be it 35, 75, or 249 libraries.' Of course, the simulated 'OCLC System' included additional units of equipment; the present configuration could not possibly handle all five subsystems

for 249 libraries. However, the COMPRESS report warned that 'simulations for NELINET were
configured to represent an equal distribution of
messages on each route on the network. When
faced with the environment of the real world, of
determining which libraries will share a common
route, this will be the most significant factor in
the performance of the system, as currently conceived. '

Phase II of the NELINET test was a demonstration
of the use of a terminal at Dartmouth College where
records were kept of costs before and after on-line
cataloging began. Dartmouth found full cataloging
including card production costs to be $. 37 per
title if cataloging information was in the OCLC
data base; this cost excludes the cost of the OCLC
system and includes only costs incurred at the
Baker Library. Cataloging costs for titles not in
the OCLC data base was $ 3. 02. Dartmouth was
able to reduce its cataloging staff through attrition
subsequent to implementation of the OCLC system
by seven full-time positions and three full-time
equivalent part-time positions. Dartmouth concluded
that if it were to pay full OCLC fees, 'with a savings of over $16, 000 in rental charges for MT /ST
and MCRS, with little loss in efficiency, plus the
tremendous staff savings we can readily meet the
projected costs and still show a budgetary decrease. '15

There are definite cost benefits for small colleges
participating in the OCLC system. However, I suspect that
these benefits will not be as dramatic as at Dartmouth initially because of the small size of both the collections and
staff. Small colleges should be able to reduce the professional /nonprofessional mix of technical service staff. This
in turn should appreciably reduce the technical processing
costs at these institutions.

Conclusion

Library costs are expected to continue spiraling up-
ward for the next several decades. It has been predicted
that it will take an annual increase in the library's budget
of at least ten percent for them to maintain the present level

of annual additions to their libraries. If this is true, computerization will have to perform many library functions. It
is quite apparent to me that the Ohio College Library Center
offers the best solution to most library problems.

References

1. "College Library Costs Skyrocket Since '49; Report
    Predicts Major Increases in Future, " The Chronicle
    of Higher Education, August 27, 1973, p. 3.
2. McGrath, Earl J. The Predominantly Negro Colleges
    and Universities in Transition. New York, Teachers
    College, Columbia University, 1965, pp. 133-34.
3. Southern Regional Education Board. The Negro and
    Higher Education in the South; A Statement by the
    Commission on Higher Educational Opportunity in the
    South. Atlanta, Georgia, Southern Regional Educa-
    tion Board, 1967, p. 39.
4. Phinazee, Annette Hoage, and Jordan, Casper LeRoy.
    A Feasibility Study for Centralized Library Purchas-
    ing and Technical Processing for Six Predominantly
    Negro Colleges in Alabama and Mississippi. Atlanta,
    Georgia, United Board for College Development, 1968,
    pp. 22-24.
5. Ibid., p. 25.
6. Ibid., pp. 26-27.
7. Ibid., p. 24.
8. Ibid., pp. 27-29.
9. Dropped by CCLC.
10. Dougherty, Richard M. An Evaluation of the Coopera-
    tive College Library Center. Atlanta, Georgia, Au-
    thor, 1972, p. 7.
11. Leonard, Lawrence E., et al. Colorado Academic Li-
    braries Book Processing Center. Phase I and II.
    Boulder, Colorado, University of Colorado, 1968,
    p. 76.
12. Dougherty, Richard M., and Maier, Joan M. Cen-
    tralized Processing for Academic Libraries. The Fi-
    nal Report (Phase III, January 1-June 30, 1969) of
    the Colorado Academic Libraries Book Processing
    Center: The First Six Months of Operation. Metuch-
    en, N.J., Scarecrow, 1971, pp. 64-65.
13. Kennedy, John P. The Feasibility of Establishing an
    OCLC-Type Center in the Southeast; Final Report.
    Atlanta, Georgia, Author, 1973, p. 1.
14. Kilgour, Frederick G., and Davis, Hillis D. The De-

velopment of a Computerized Regional Library System: Final Report. Columbus, Ohio, OCLC, 1973, p. 1.

15. Ibid., pp. 32-34.

UTILIZING PUBLIC AND SPECIAL LIBRARIES
TO SERVE POST-SECONDARY EDUCATION

Vivian D. Hewitt

During the past 20 years there have been vast changes
in higher education in the United States. In the late sixties
it was subject to questioning, restlessness, and rebellion.
Students searching for a different kind of learning beyond
secondary school launched new kinds of experimental educational experiences. Relevance became the watchword.

Students from previously neglected minorities began
to be admitted in significant numbers to American colleges
and universities. Some of them used the campus as a base
for "outreach" work in minority communities. Others demanded and got changes in their instruction including a series
of new curricula based on ethnic studies.

By the beginning of the seventies, a number of forces
acting in concert upon institutions succeeded in opening up
the system of higher education. Procedures for instruction
and curriculum sacrosanct for years were now open to question. Ethnic studies, inner city tutoring, and other experimental programs became part and parcel of the established
institutional pattern. Now, in the significant seventies, the
people of the United States are beginning to grow familiar
with new ways of securing baccalaureate and advanced de-
grees--ways which are novel in this country but ancient and
familiar in other parts of the world.

The University of London, established in 1836 to conduct examinations and to confer degrees, has been granting
external degrees for over a hundred years to students who
do not need to put foot inside the university. Currently
there is the Open University, also in Great Britain, which is
specifically designed for adults, particularly those employed
full-time. No academic bars to admission were set by OU,

though in filling the first 25, 000 first-year places available in 1971 from among 40, 817 applicants seeking to take 62, 147 courses, some balancing occurred in terms of occupation, geographic distribution, clarity of purpose, and course desired.[1] These two examples of the external degree in England, as well as others, have caused U.S. educators to consider profoundly their own plans and possibilities.

The external degree has come suddenly and powerfully to the attention of the academic community. It is one of the most fashionable of all topics for discussion in the intellectual world today; newspapers have devoted columns to it, magazines have carried numerous articles about it, new colleges to provide for it have been created, and foundation grants have been made in support of it. The external degree is an emotional subject, condemned by some, praised by others. The term itself has come to have countless meanings. Alan Pifer, the president of the Carnegie Corporation, said that "the external degree--one that can be earned by a student outside of the normal institutional framework--is an idea whose time seems to have come in this country."[2] There is a whole new set of ground rules as to how degrees are awarded, who should get them, and what kind of studies should be recognized as valid. Nontraditional study is not just study outside the regular disciplines, but an attitude which

> puts the student first and the institution second, concentrates more on the former's need than the latter's convenience, encourages diversity of individual opportunity rather than uniform prescription, and deemphasizes time, space, and even course requirements in favor of competence, and where applicable, performance.[3]

Evidence of the growing importance in the United States of informal, less highly structured learning experiences can be found in the following comparison: in 1960 the education core (elementary, secondary, undergraduate, and graduate private and public schools) had an enrollment of 48.4 million, or 63 percent of those engaged in all forms of education. In 1970 the enrollment rose to 63.8 million, but the proportion of the total represented by the core dropped to 51 percent. Comparable data for the education periphery (industrial, organizational, neighborhood, and other programs) show a 1960 enrollment of 28.3 million, or 37 percent of the total. [4]

As the number of persons undertaking some form of informal but organized learning begins to exceed those within the traditional programs, books, libraries, and librarians take on even greater importance, and access to them must be provided in new and varied ways.

Traditionally, public libraries have been stimulated to develop new modes of services to their users when social changes have made clear the gap between the client and the library. The public library has accepted its role as a learning center for more than a century, although passively in many instances. But technological advances and social change combine presently to make new the meaning of the phrase, "a community learning center."

People want to learn, to continue to learn in the voluntary sense of "lifetime learning," unhampered by the requirement of the single-track, laddered educational system so long prevalent in this country. Many persons want to be able to choose their educational paths more freely and with flexibility, and to continue education at any point more easily.

The range of possibilities for the public library in its shaping of services to special publics is great. Libraries have a decisive role to play in supporting the learning society. For one thing, they are unique in having no educational bias. They can serve as a catalyst for all learning resources in the community--schools, colleges, industrial laboratories, talents of local residents, and so forth. Public libraries can no longer be enclaves in an alien community. They are "in the unique position of becoming course counselor, materials resource person, and instructional go-between for those students who want an unstructured higher educational experience." [5]

Independent study is now evolving in many forms and formats. The forms that challenge the public library to this new role are those that rely on exemption examination-- based on earlier study, reading, or life experience--and on competency examination after a program of independent study to confer credit equivalence. Such forms of independent study, once availability through the public library is known, will no doubt also be pursued by adults who merely wish to learn and who have no plan for, nor reason to pursue, degree programs. In short, learning materials, organized in a study center and attractive in their presentation, can and will stimulate adults to use the public library as a learning center for independent study.

Most libraries and librarians have had no exposure to independent study programs which would give them the incentive to carry them out in their libraries. Cognizant of this fact, The Office of Library Independent Study and Guidance Projects, headed by José Orlando Toro, director, an activity of the College Entrance Examination Board, has come up with A Design for Learning in the Public Library: a Program for Adult Independent Study--a Unique Plan for Extending the Learning Resources of Libraries. 6 Sponsored by four national agencies, public and private--the Council on Library Resources, the National Endowment for the Humanities, the Bureau of Libraries and Learning Resources (U.S. Office of Education), and CEEB--several public libraries geographically distributed throughout the United States and varying in size were selected and are currently participating in the pilot project experiment. Among them are: the Dallas Public Library; Miami-Dade Public Library System; Saint Louis Public Library; Denver Public Library; San Diego Public Library; Portland Public Library (Maine); and the Worcester Public Library and Central Massachusetts Regional Library System.

To help launch its Independent Study Project, the Dallas Public Library issued an eye-catching booklet by the same title which details the essential information on its cover:

> ISP is a program of self-education for purposes of self-enrichment and/or preparation for College-Level Examinations for credit.

> There are no classes, no teachers in classrooms, no time limits, no pressures of competing in a group, and no homework assignments.

> Independent study services and materials are available at no cost. 7

Enticed to open the booklet and to explore further, one learns that at each of the five participating branch libraries in the program can be found:

> CLEP brochures: CLEP May Be For You;

Description of the General Examination; and Description of the Subject Examinations; and Bulletin of Information for Candidates.

Study Guides and Reading Lists: each guide corresponds with a subject examination to help you prepare for that test.

Workshops are held at the participating branches on a regular basis.

Special tutoring is available for independent students upon request.

Guidance and help from librarians at the branches are available during the hours the branches are open. [8]

The booklet lists the study materials available, describes in detail the College-Level Examination Program (CLEP), names the participating institutions, and concludes by addressing some very succinct statements to employers about what CLEP could help them achieve:

CLEP's basic philosophy rests on the observation that there are well-qualified and mature adults without college degrees whose equivalent college-level achievements have not been properly recognized. Within any company there may be such individuals working in low-level positions, demonstrating responsibility and loyalty to their employers, who have more to contribute. By virtue of their experience and past training, they might be as well qualified for a better position and for further educational development as a new college graduate brought into the company by outside recruitment.

Employers have an opportunity to tap this source of talent by utilizing the Independent Study Project's materials and by recognizing CLEP credits.

CLEP can help a company to:

Tap a source of talent that may have been previously ignored.

Develop a potential pool of well-educated employees
within the company's ranks to meet future needs.

Utilize its best human resources in communities
where local shortages of professional personnel
exist.

Secure greater benefits and lower costs from com-
pany-subsidized tuition payments.

Improve and establish good company-employee relations. [9]

The Dallas Public Library's efforts show sensitive
judgment and understanding of the role of the library in as-
sisting many learners willing to try independent study.

The success of the Independent Study Project, a two-
year pilot program (1971-73) in the Dallas Public Library,
has been documented in an attractive report:

... students had earned 850 aggregate hours of
college credit through ISP and CLEP examinations.
Defined in years of credit, ISP students had earned
a total of 28 years of college credit. This represents $18,000 to $60,000 worth of college credit
which otherwise would have been out of the financial or available-time reach of the students.

Yet the ISP program ... cannot be measured in
hour or dollar values. It is impossible to measure
the self-satisfaction, the self-confidence, pride, the
increased enthusiasm for the world and for life,
earned by those ISP students. And the rewards in
realizing they had done it on their own.

The project brought new opportunities, new horizons, new concepts, new information. All essential to the continued growth of man's greatest as-
set--the human mind. [10]

Similarly, Denver Public Library's project, called
"On Your Own," which is still in the developmental stage,
is based on the concept of the independent learner and his
or her needs. Denver's first project under OYO was CLEP,
the College-Level Examination Program. DPL began to
work with participating institutions early in 1972 and launched

the program in December 1972. Because so many inquiries
were received about different independent learning situations,
it was decided to expand the program to make it more inclusive.

The On Your Own Newsletter, beginning with the June
1973 issue, will cover "all programs, activities, and events
that fall under the 'On Your Own' umbrella title. CLEP is
included."[11] Other programs included to date are: the
Great Books Program, the Right To Read Program, and
TIME*LIVE (formerly Catalytic Synchronisms).

In addition to the programs referred to already,
others are being designed or in operation, among them the
Regents External Degree of the New York State Education
Department, Empire State College of the State University of
New York, the University Without Walls, Syracuse University Research Corporation's Five-County Project (also in
New York State), Minnesota Metropolitan State College, and
the two new statewide plans being projected by the university
and college systems in California.[12]

The availability of such national programs as CLEP
and of evolving statewide programs provides great encourage-
ment for public libraries to provide the support of materials,
guidance, and stimulation which are its special talents.   In
truth, the public library is literally a college around the
corner.   Originally conceived by Benjamin Franklin to be
the primary community resource for individual intellectual
growth, it is a free institution where the individual has open
access to great quantities of information.

Another kind of library resource available in limited
degree to the independent learner is the special library,
created for and serving a definite group of users.   Special
librarians work for commercial, industrial, governmental,
or non-profit institutions, such as research organizations,
banks, manufacturing companies, newspapers, local, state
and federal government agencies, hospitals, insurance companies, museums, very specialized departments of public
or university libraries, and so forth.   In general the collections and services are not open to the public, but are
limited to the staff of the organization in which the library
is located.   Increasingly, though, as some companies become public relations-oriented and assume a more positive
social responsibility role, their library collections are being
made available to outsiders on some kind of limited basis

or through interlibrary loan.

Some of the aerospace and other special libraries in the southern California area, for example, have made a special after-hours effort to serve students who are sometimes restricted in the materials available to them, especially if they are in a location served only by a small public library or are without access to a major network.

Since librarians themselves are an educational resource, trained to know all the educational possibilities, where to go first, and next, they become, in many communities--whether public, school, college, or special librarians --a network of referral and exchange information. [13]

Within their own organizations, special libraries are contributing to the external degree concept with a great deal of relevancy. Time magazine has had in operation a program which allows its employees to take adult education courses in any subject and for which the company pays most of the fees. As a result, employees of various educational levels can grow in the knowledge and enjoyment of the field of their interest. In a communication-oriented library, such as Time's, there are vast holdings in the general reference area plus many specialized materials from which the employee-user can find assistance for the courses which he or she is taking.

Large corporations such as General Motors and General Electric encourage their employees to attend management seminars. Materials for their assignments and idea-provoking bibliographies are often willingly provided by their own special libraries. These executives (top or middle-management) are continuing the learning process to make them grow in their jobs, long beyond the earned degree stage.

In an electronics firm in the Southwest, an interesting educational experiment has been successfully tried, with the plant employees gaining additional instruction in courses of their selection by closed-circuit TV. In an increasingly sophisticated technology, they need to know the latest in skilled and semi-skilled techniques. This takes them beyond the basic technical institute courses they needed to obtain their positions in the first place. The Sci-Tech library of the firm can assist with reading lists, literature searches, acquisition of textbooks for the courses, and routing of the latest periodical articles.

Union organizations sponsor outstanding educational
programs and institutes. The AAUW, with its impressive
Detroit headquarters and many local chapters, has always
contributed toward and encouraged the continuing education
of its members. The labor collections (with many other related subjects in their special libraries) have continued to
add to the American worker's varied background, which has
placed him or her in a leading position among the laboring
classes throughout the world.

Chase Manhattan Bank and other large banks have initiated training programs for high school graduates (often
with emphasis on the disadvantaged groups)--an on-the-job
training approach. Their libraries can contribute to the edu-
cative and training process by helping familiarize the participants thoroughly with the subject field (e.g., banking, fi-
nance). All of these people are using components of the independent study concept--not degree seeking in a formal
sense but seeking knowledge for their own individual enrichment and eventual contribution to solving the social problems of the country.

In this context, there is the area of reclaimed woman-
power (after children have grown, going back to work) whose
re-entry into the work force is a monumental contribution.
The process of "going back to work" requires brushing up,
and often they come to a business collection of a special or
public library for this purpose of re-learning. These various examples illustrate the degree to which the independent
learner is an increasing force in American education. The
library, whatever its categorization, will be called upon to
participate actively in this welcome revolution. Educators
are becoming more active in the process of social change;
libraries should be too. It is essential that librarians become active rather than passive participants in the whole
program of education, that they become partners with educators and with all the citizens that they serve in their communities and who potentially would be users of library resources. Public and special librarians--in truth, any kind of
librarian--would heartily concur.

References

1.   Gould, Samuel B., chairman, Commission on Nontra-
     ditional Study. Diversity by Design. San Francisco,
     Jossey-Bass, 1973.

2. Pifer, Alan. "Is It Time for an External Degree?"
    College Board Review, 78, Winter 1970-71.
3. Ibid.
4. Knowledge Industry Report. Vol. 3, No. 22, April 15,
    1970.
5. Doiron, Peter M. "Open University," Library Journal,
    September 15, 1973, p. 2527.
6. College Entrance Examination Board. A Design for
    Learning in the Public Library: A Program for Adult
    Independent Study. New York, College Entrance Ex-
    amination Board, 1973.
7. Dallas Public Library. Independent Study Project.
    Dallas, Dallas Public Library, April 1972.
8. Ibid., p. 1.
9. Ibid., p. 7.
10. Dallas Public Library. Independent Study Project.
    Dallas, Dallas Public Library, 1973, p. 1.
11. Denver Public Library. "On Your Own." Newsletter,
    June 1973.
12. Houle, Cyril O. The External Degree. San Francisco,
    Jossey-Bass, 1973.
13. Waldron, Helen J. "The Business of Running a Special
    Library," Special Libraries, 62: 63-70, February 1971.

PATTERNS TOWARD A USER-CENTERED
ACADEMIC LIBRARY

Robert S. Taylor

There are several possible scenarios for academic libraries toward the end of this century. The first one may run something like this. Academic libraries will remain pretty much as they are, warehouses with frills--victims of the powerlessness of librarians, of indecision by academic administrators, and of the conservatism of academic faculties. In general, these libraries will not be particularly affected by internal automation of processes. As a result of this and a failure to comprehend their communities, they will, depending on individual staff and institutional personality, become rather pleasant, even necessary, havens in a sea of change and brassiness. But they will be havens for only a few. The majority of users will become increasingly frustrated and will turn (have already turned?) to other sources for their information and cultural needs.

In the second scenario, academic libraries, through networking and internal automation, will make significant savings in costs for processing. However, these savings will only mean that there will be fewer library personnel, because savings in personnel will be eaten up by the need to pay computer and communication costs. Even though the library staff in this case may wish to provide better personal services, they will not be able to, and the library will more and more resemble a very efficient warehouse. True, the user will probably receive much better service than he or she does now, but it will be highly impersonal in the sense that there will be little human interaction. This may be, for the user, an improvement over present libraries, but it will meet a smaller and smaller part of his or her total cultural and information needs. This does not deny the desirability of the efficient warehouse. It will certainly be better than the inefficient warehouses we now have. How-

ever, many, if not most, academic libraries will stop at
this stage, because internal efficiency is their only goal.
The point is that this is not enough--and it never has been.

In the third scenario, the user becomes the center of
the institution--not the packages, not the systems, but the
individuals in the community that is served.   In this case
the academic library will become a true switching center, a
community center in which the dynamic process of negotiating and connecting users to people, materials, and media is
the heart of the enterprise.   This may happen both inside
and outside the building called "a library."   It will become
a "library without walls."

The first two scenarios really do not need explication.
They are either in existence now, as in the first case, or
emerging, as in the second.   Consequently, this essay will
examine the third possibility and attempt to ascertain and
discuss: a) what this "library" might look like, i. e. what
it will do; b) how to get from here to there; and c) some
necessary changes in thinking and assumptions.

Possibly the best descriptive model for this can be
found in Ivan Illich's metaphor of the "convivial institution, "
which in his spectrum is a "left-wing institution" and "tend[s]
to be networks which facilitate client-initiated communication or cooperation. "[1]   In contrast, at the other end of the
institutional spectrum, in Illich's frame of reference "on the
right, " are "social agencies which specialize in the manipulation of their clients, " such as school systems.   On the
right, "what counts is that education is assumed to be the
result of an institutional process managed by the educator. "
It should be noted that this is a spectrum and that there are
many stations between the extremes.

Libraries, by the way, are one of the few informational institutions that have retained this sense of "conviviality. "   There have been, however, certain constraining influences.   There has been, for example, an inability to respond to user--i. e., student--needs in situations other than
research and the purely instructional.   Consequently, students tend to associate the library with the manipulative side
of the educational process.   The reserve book, overdue
fines, door checks, and other forms of control--however
necessary they may be--strengthen this association.   There
has been little realization or willingness to recognize that
much of a student's education takes place in the context sur-

rounding the formal educational process.   There is a whole
"blooming" world on the campus outside the library.   It may
be, however, that the academic library is the only traditional agency geared to work in this context, if librarians (and
faculty and administrators) will allow it to do so.

   A second constraint is that librarians have a relatively low level of expectation as to what they can do, indeed
and more subtly debilitating, as to what they are allowed to
do.   This essay is not, by the way, concerned with the self-
deprecating and tired image of little old ladies in shirtwaists
and sneakers.   We must forget this narcissistic sort of self-
pity and concentrate on something else, something more positive.

   What kinds of users have libraries traditionally served?

   1.   There are the educated and the self-educated,
   those who take a delight in books and reading.   These
   are the linguistically literate, probably a very small
   proportion of the population.   And these have been
   able to take advantage of the library as a convivial
   institution.   But these happy few are turning increasingly to the paperback book and other media, as inexpensive forms, in both money and energy, to meet
   their needs.

   2.   There is the student or the researcher, who en-
   ters the door because he or she must in order to
   achieve some specific goal.   However, the sophisticated researcher finds it far easier to develop his or
   her own information channels than to use library resources.

   3.   There is the person who comes in from the cold--
   a student looking for space to study, a tramp looking
   for warmth and yesterday's newspaper, and the curi-
   ous who just want to browse and taste, not knowing
   what they want until they find it.   This, by the way,
   is an audience worth cultivating a little more, because they too have a sense of the library's conviviality.

   No one person, of course, is any one of these types
all the time.   Each person at different times is a different
type of user.   It is worth noting, however, that, although
the research user is a very small proportion of even the
academic population, the academic library is designed es-

pecially for him or her. Library structure reflects this
bias--its catalogs, its efficiencies, its packages, its bias for
print, for literacy. These elements have very little to do
with the idea of conviviality, and, because library resources
and budgets are committed in this direction, they tend to
work against the convivial.

A third constraint lies in the institutional setting of
higher education and the rigidities that have grown around it
in the past half-century, although, as we will note later,
this may be breaking down. In this context, the role of the
library is predetermined. Academic faculties see the library only as a supporting service for their courses and their research. Indeed, librarians themselves in seeking faculty
status may in fact be strengthening this pattern and losing
what may be uniquely their strength--that is, their neutrality,
"conviviality, " and ombudsman potential--in the triangular
and sometimes adversarial positions of students, faculty,
and administration.

Despite these constraints, several threads are beginning to be apparent which, if the library profession is willing and able to develop them, may provide the kernel around
which a new kind of institution can emerge. The first of
these is the result of the educational changes growing out of
the student pressures of the sixties. These go under a
variety of names: university without walls, open university,
campus free colleges, educational voucher schemes. Though
these are possibly only surface phenomena, they bear the
seed for change, even if they become institutionalized and
co-opted by the educational establishment. It is not that
these forms will replace present education, but rather they
will present the student with many more options from which
to choose.

At the same time, these options present the academic
library with challenges and a new set of opportunities.
There is a widened variety of audiences and needs and a
unique opportunity for the academic library to develop counseling and consultative capabilities. The relevant point here
is that it places more of the control over his or her educational progress in the hands of the client, with concomitant
growth in need for consultation and advice which is both
neutral and not institutionally bound. That is to say, it begins to make education more like the ideal library--client-
based rather than directed toward externally decided goals.
As Marvin Adelson has pointed out in his essay "Education:

At the Crossroads of Decision":

> The changeability of the environment and the enor-
> mous, growing mass of knowledge are leading to a
> shift away from attempting to learn what is known
> in anticipation of its possible later value, toward
> learning the means of finding out what one has to
> know when the need arises. This means learning
> to use the information process... [2]

The academic library--indeed, other libraries also, especially the public library--has a real and fundamental nonware-
house role to play in this process, if the profession cares
to take the responsibility.

A second thread stems from the work of the past two
decades in communication, organization theory, and the dif-
fusion of innovation. It runs something like this. Like any
organization, a university is a series of networks for the
movement of both formal and informal messages. There are
at least three major categories of networks or information
systems on a campus. There are the management information systems, providing data and information necessary to
make decisions about the total enterprise. Except for its
managerial usefulness, this has little to do with libraries,
although one might suspect that, were librarians better able
to define and evaluate their own data, better input from the
library might well be significant for institutional decision-
making. The second system is the instructional information
system, and this is the prerequisite of the faculty. Though
the academic library participates in the process in a peripheral way--providing books and reading materials--its function
is purely one of service, with substantive contributions dependent on individuals. Again, one might suspect that, given
better library data and more insight into the educational process, librarians could provide materials of interest, if not
significance, to academic planning.

The third general type of campus information system
has to do with the cultural surroundings of the educational
process. It is here that the academic library could make
its finest contribution, because at present the needs are so
diffuse and so diverse as to beg organization without manipulation. The messages in this third network serve a variety
of roles and, indeed, may show a spectrum parallel to that
of Illich's, from "manipulative" on the right to "convivial"
on the left. It is interesting to note that the use by Illich

of the concept of <u>institutions</u> on a spectrum may indeed be a sort of shorthand for communication networks and message types.

For the academic library, if the organizational model is examined, it suggests that there are many roles, other than the traditional one of book and package custodian, which could be considered. Such roles will usually assume a change from concern only with long-term memory and its messages, where the library presently operates, to one of both long- and short-term memory. In the latter case the user himself or herself, moves toward the center of the system, because short-term messages are generated, directed, and controlled by users. This essay suggests that by making a more conscious move in this direction, the academic library would begin to place the user rather than the package in a critical role in the system. It would, because of proximity, tend to show relationships and association between long- and short-term messages.

The varieties of information and communication networks that live within and surround an academic institution are truly tremendous. To cite just a very few: the events announcement system; the poetry, ceramics, computer, chess, and other networks; the newspaper network, ranging from daily tabloid to weekly mimeograph sheet; the disciplinary networks which also provide significant contact with the outside environment. We exclude management information systems as well as the purely instructional activities, which, though we might like to think otherwise, are probably not the major information inputs for students. There is as yet no taxonomy of these networks which could provide a sense of their structure, their role, their interfaces, or their messages. The extensive variety and overlap and, in many cases, their ineffectiveness are a result of two factors. The first is overload--the explosion of inexpensive channels for message dissemination from bulletin board to mimeograph machine to video cassette. Such messages may serve no other purpose than to support the ego of the sender, but they are messages in the system. Secondly, there has been a vacuum on academic campuses--indeed, in society as a whole--that does not allow for organizing and servicing short-term, rapidly changing messages. Of course, newspapers play a role, but yesterday's deadline does not allow for today's change. Television and radio serve some role, but as nonrecorded (for the user) media they provide no way the user can refer to the information for confirmation or

specifics. The interactive computer network, though its potential is high, can only be effective for the few.

There is a need for an institution like the academic
library, with its capabilities in the organization of information, its sense of public service, its neutrality, and its cen-
trality and long hours of availability, to become both a campus information center and a community center. The layers
and diversity of information disseminating agencies on a
large campus betray a naivete and ignorance about the dissemination, organization, communication, and use of information in all its forms. This also illustrates the unwilling-
ness on the part of faculty and university administrations to
view the library as anything but a warehouse for books, and
the hesitation by academic librarians to dilute the concern
for books and to move into an uncharted sea of ephemeral
information.

In this move toward a user-centered institution, there
is a subtle but significant problem. There is the danger of
becoming a "manipulative" institution as one takes up the
tasks of counseling and advising, and of disseminating a
broader spectrum of messages. In a sense libraries have
avoided being "manipulative" in the past, because in many
cases they have not been much of anything but purveyors of
packages. By this means they have essentially avoided the
issue. It has been safer to deal with packages than people.
(It is easier to chart the moon than to solve social problems.) This has the asset, to be sure, of neutrality in
academe--and that may, indeed, be a significant asset. But,
because it is a passive neutrality, it has also meant powerlessness on the campus. If the library is to become a truly
interactive and community agency on the campus, it will require a very special talent on the part of librarians and a
very special style on the part of the library to avoid becoming "manipulative. "

References

1.   This section partially derived from Ivan Illich. De-
      schooling Society. New York, Harper & Row, 1971,
      pp. 52-71.
2.   Adelson, Marvin. "Education: At the Crossroads of
      Decision. " In Information Technology, Some Critical
      Implications for Decision Makers. New York, The
      Conference Board, 1972, p. 112.

EPILOGUE

THE ACADEMIC LIBRARY IN THE YEAR 2000

E. J. Josey

I will not pretend that I am very certain about what the academic library might be in the year 2000. It is only 26 years away. The year 1987 is one-half of the way from now to the 21st century; will we have drastic changes in academic library service? Dean Taylor in the foregoing essay believes that by the end of the century "Academic libraries will remain pretty much as they are...." He may well be correct in his prognostication. One of the contributors to this volume of essays, H. Vail Deale, believes that the 21st century will bring forth the library-college concept. His view is shared by Richard W. Hostrop:

> There will be an increasing demand for research for there are strong winds of change indicating that before the year 2000, the entire antiquated structure of credits, majors, and degrees, may be a shambles. No two students will move along exactly the same educational track. Destandardization will be the norm. With destandardization, and its concomitant diversity, there will be no choice but for the college library to be transformed into a learning center--having diverse multi-media learning materials and services available which are unheard of today. Critical self-study through research and evaluation will result in accountable structures to meet the complex learning needs of a diverse society in the 21st century. The trend is for the academic library to become a 'library-college.'[1]

While there are a number of librarians excited about the library-college concept, the large majority have adopted a wait-and-see attitude, noting that there has been much discussion of possibilities and the mentioning of a few institu-

tions that are experimenting, but they quickly point to the
fact that faculty and librarian roles are not "blurring" and
that the library is not becoming the college and the college
is not becoming the library as library-college proponents
contend.   And, of course, university librarians by and large
say, never!   It is clear that college and university libraries
and learning-media centers have entered a period of major
reassessment of their aims and methods; however, the evidence to date is too fragmentary to predict conclusively that
the library-college will be the academic library of the 21st
century.   In spite of the fragmentary evidence, who should
dare predict that the library-college will not be the library-
learning environment of the 21st century?   This leads to the
question: is it possible to predict accurately?

     With reference to prediction in general, Fred Charles
Iklé tells us that there are some common errors in predicting.   He indicates that "if we want to make 'guiding predictions' rather than entertain, accuracy is no longer irrelevant,
even though it may be difficult to judge."   He counsels that
as "the first step in 'guiding predictions' we have to infer
from past observations to future ones...."[2]

     At the 77th annual meeting of the American Academy
of Political and Social Science, the academy's theme was
"The Future Society: Aspects of America in the Year 2000."
Anthony J. Wiener read a paper that dealt with "The Future
of Economic Activity, " and his comments regarding speculat-
ing, prediction, and planning for the future, in my opinion,
are pointers that academic librarians may very well wish to
use in future planning.

>   The purpose of speculating about the relatively dis-
>   tant future is not to predict.   A crystal ball is
>   impossible.   The future does not exist: it pre-
>   sents us with no data; it is indeterminate in crucial
>   respects.   In the naive forecasting model, one
>   'looks at' the future using some methodology.   On
>   the basis of what is 'found, ' expectations are
>   formed and decisions made, that either accommo-
>   date or change the future.
>
>   There is a more realistic procedure: long range
>   planning.   The basic concept for long range plan-
>   ning is the present viewed in retrospect.   The
>   most important consequence of developing alterna-
>   tive expectations about the distant future is a better

perspective on current trends and tendencies. Current decisions, intended to intervene in these
trends, can be made to effect both near and long
term improvements. Moreover, it is clear that
expectations are based, necessarily, on trends that
connect the past with the present. Trends--and
therefore history--play central roles in long range
planning.

One must expect many surprises to occur over
several decades. A simple continuation of current
trends would be, in itself, extremely surprising.
Yet, any scenario containing particularized, specific
surprises would be even less plausible. Therefore,
the design case for long range planning must be the
surprise-free projection--although, no projection is
really surprise-free. It would be most surprising
if there were to be no surprises. Long range
planning must deal with the questions: 1) what are
the long range tendencies which, in the absence of
surprises, will continue and 2) what are the major
alternative scenarios?[3]

The foregoing recommendation regarding planning for
the future in order to forecast what academic libraries will
be like in the year 2000 seems to me the best approach to
utilize. Therefore, I will cite some of the current trends
in academic libraries and indicate some of the planning now
being undertaken that may aid us in determining some of the
major alternative scenarios in college and university libraries
in the 21st century.

The American Academy's Commission on the Year
2000 was created as a result of a grant from the Carnegie
Corporation. Its chairman, Daniel Bell, contends that "the
future is not an overarching leap into the distance; it begins
in the present." Professor Bell also contends that "there
are four sources of change in society, and they can be
charted with differential ease." One of these sources of
change which relates inextricably to libraries is technology.[4]

As we examine the current state of technology in libraries, we note that technology is dramatically changing
college and university libraries in 1974 and will continue to
have a greater impact which will provide possibilities for
on-line programs of information storage and retrieval and
other invaluable services that will substantially change aca-

demic library service in the future.   Frederick G. Kilgour's
essay relating to on-line services from the Ohio College Library Center and Ronald F. Miller and David M. Wax's essay on NELINET and NASIC support Professor Bell's dictum
that "the future is not an overarching leap into the distance;
it begins in the present. "

There are a number of programs of a technological
nature in academic libraries around the country that are
worthy of mention, for while the technological scenario is
not replicated at most of America's college and university libraries in 1974, because of developments and long-range
planning currently underway, technology will certainly alter
the strategies that will be employed in academic libraries to
gain and provide access to information.   One or two para-
graphs from the most recent annual reports of four academic
libraries will attest to this fact.

The director of libraries at Stanford University,
David C. Weber, states in the Stanford University Libraries
Annual Report 1972-73 that

> BALLOTS (an acronym for the project of Biblio-
> graphic Automation of Large Library Operations
> using a Time-sharing System) is moving ahead suc-
> cessfully, thanks to the pioneering work in library
> automation by the BALLOTS staff.   Efforts that
> date back to 1967 resulted in the implementation in
> fall 1972 of a first subsystem using bibliographic
> data from the Library of Congress machine-read-
> able tapes to generate catalog cards, purchase
> orders, and spine lables.   In April 1973 the second
> module added an on-line file showing the status of
> all new books from the time an order is placed
> until they are cataloged and shelved, thus elimi-
> nating much of the filing and searching formerly
> done manually.   In June the catalog file module
> was added in the form of an on-line union catalog
> of all books processed through BALLOTS.   This
> file will grow and eventually replace the present
> card catalog.   It can presently be searched by
> author, title word, call number, and subject head-
> ing, or parts thereof, with the result that books
> can be discovered much more readily than with the
> manual file.   In August 1973 a module was being
> readied for fall implementation to support input of
> original cataloging data and to handle almost all of

the remaining catalog processing.

Ben C. Bowman, in the University of Rochester Libraries Annual Report for 1972-73, called upon the university to continue investment in computer technology when he declared:

> The utilization of computer, telecommunication, and micrographic technology is providing academic libraries with promising and increasingly effective means for reversing cost trends long associated with labor-intensive practices and procedures. But further application of these technologies has much more significance than cost effectiveness. It has radical, if not profound, implications for what and how much of recorded and current information libraries acquire, how they acquire it, and how they organize it promptly and responsively for use. Therefore, in order to respond to requirements of the changing present and future, this University's libraries, like academic libraries generally, need to continue their investments in computer-oriented and micrographic technologies as these affect both local as well as inter-library systems and resources. They need to develop radically new library skills and additional managerial sophistication enabling them to analyze, measure, and evaluate needs and responses. And they need to enrich local collections so that resources for creative learning and research commensurate with the University's aspirations are available.

In the Report of the University Librarian to the Senate, University of British Columbia for 1972-73, Basil Stuart-Stubbs writes:

> These days reference service is not confined to the use of the printed word. Machine readable data bases are being exploited to search for citations and to make users aware of library resources in their areas of interest. During the past year, all library divisions and branches have offered to compile 'interest profiles' for groups of faculty members and graduate students, and for individuals. Each month, these profiles are run against the records of books catalogued by the Library, and personalized listings of materials are produced.

By the end of August, seventy-two such profiles
had been constructed, and new profiles were being
added at the rate of a dozen a month.

At the Woodward Library, a terminal was connected to the U.S. National Library of Medicine's
MEDLINE system, which permits on-line searches
of the literature of the health and many of the life
sciences. This service has proved particularly
effective in handling questions in clinical medicine,
and most inquiries to the system come from health
science personnel in the Lower Mainland who are
not associated with the University. The installation is supported by a grant from the Woodward
Foundation.

The Science Division continues to offer a similar
off-line service for other sciences, through the
National Science Library of Canada's CAN/SDI system. Currently forty-seven profiles, representing
about three hundred individual users, are being
used to search the system's data bases. The National Science Library is planning to set up an on-
line system in its next stage of development.

Warren N. Boes in his final report as director of libraries at Syracuse University for the year 1972-73 made
the following comments relative to automation development
at Syracuse University:

With the move into the Bird Library, it became
possible to have terminals available to every major subject area and floor in the library. As a
result, more of the processing responsibilities
were shifted to the floors, along with staff who
came from the processing divisions. Without the
automation capability, the increased workload of
the Bird Library could not have been handled.

Some problems in automation did exist. The first
and most frustrating was that the cabling had not
been completed when we moved, thus delaying full
implementation of all the active automation modes.
Another frustration was that a theory, based upon
research as written in the library literature, that
new and current material was the most likely to
be circulated, was proven not to be true. Al-

though we had been placing book cards for automated circulation purposes in our books for the
last three years, it was a shocking discovery, although a pleasurable one, to find that such material represented only 8% of our total circulation.
Most of our circulation was proceeding from the
other major parts of the collections. This means
we must work much harder to produce more book
cards for the retrospective collection in order to
fully activate the total circulation mode.

It was gratifying during the year to learn of a
growing interest in our system on the part of others. Although our automation programs have not
been well publicized, we've learned of interest on
the part of SUNY-Central, the California State University System, and others. It is our belief that
the system now running in the libraries at Syracuse will have momentous impact upon the organization and processing activities in major libraries
across the country as it becomes more understood.

The current trends in library automation reported
above are related to long-range planning, and, as Anthony J.
Weiner has suggested, these current developments in library
automation will affect the future. Planning to utilize and
harness the new technology is underway in the country.
One excellent example of planning is the work of the Joint
SUNY/SED Task Force on Library Data Centers in New York
State. The Task Force on Library Data Centers was appointed jointly by the State Education Department and the
State University of New York in September 1972. The goal
of this task force has been defined as:

> to promote the development and to advise in the
> implementation and operation of a statewide biblio-
> graphic computer network which will improve ser-
> vices to users of libraries within the State through
> on-line access to various data bases for the pur-
> poses of shared cataloging, circulation control and
> interlibrary lending, serials control, union lists,
> information retrieval, acquisitions and other simi-
> lar services. [5]

The foregoing goal statement of the task force and its
progress report list a range of activities that are being
planned for the libraries in New York State. One of its am-

bitious projects is retrospective data conversion.

It is proposed to build a large, computer data
base to serve as the foundation for a New York
State Library Network. The increase in cost and
number of items published has resulted in an increased demand for sharing resources. Sharing
is possible only to the extent that information concerning availability of items is known. A multi-
faceted effort by the State Library, SUNY, NYPL,
and the Library of Congress is proposed. The
addition of retrospective records to a data base
is costly. Much of this cost is incurred entering
catalog data, rather than holdings data. Recognizing that there is a high rate of overlap amongst
many libraries in the State, it is proposed to sub-
sidize the conversion of records for several of the
largest libraries and provide a mechanism through
which local libraries can add ownership information
and unique data to a master file at their own cost.

SUNY and the State Education Department have developed complementary proposals for retrospective
library catalog data conversion. The SUNY project proposes an investment of $420,000 for re-
search and development and hardware acquisition
in the first year. Under this proposal, it is expected that after one year, one million records per
year could be converted online at a cost of $520,000
per year using a team of 30 operators, plus supervisors. This file will be maintained as a byproduct
of participation in shared cataloging systems. [6]

The planning and coordination of programs to harness
technology for the libraries of the State of New York will
ensure that the academic libraries of the State will be able
to benefit from the new technology for the next century.
The programs at the four universities reported above and
the statewide planning undertaken in New York in regard to
the application of the computer and related technology to library processes are by no means all of the automation programs in academic libraries in the country, for there are
programs at the University of Minnesota, the University of
Chicago, University of Pennsylvania, Harvard University,
Bucknell University, and, of course, the famous Project In-
trex at the Massachusetts Institute of Technology. All of
these programs at individual institutions and the statewide
planning effort will benefit all academic libraries of the future.

Another current trend in university libraries is the utilization of management and planning techniques. The Council on Library Resources has taken a leadership role in the establishment of an Office of University Library Management Studies at the Association of Research Libraries. This office has worked with member libraries in its Management Review and Analysis Program (MRAP). In addition, the new office publishes ARL Management Supplement and Occasional Papers which provide useful data in this field.

The Council on Library Resources has funded a research and development unit at the Joint University Libraries, Nashville, Tennessee, which has served Vanderbilt University, Scarritt College, and George Peabody College since 1969. Columbia University has established a planning office for the libraries, headed by Jerome Yavarkovsky, one of the contributors to this volume. The study has key areas of interest: organizational definition, staffing description, operations planning, budgeting, and policy manual development. While the study examined alternative ways in which the Columbia University Libraries might be organized, it was recommended that "a centralized plan of organization for Columbia libraries will continue to meet the institution's total needs more effectively...." Of great importance to academic librarians was the recognition of the importance of the leadership role of the chief administrator and the need for the chief executive officer to work as a peer with the other senior officers of the university's administration, and this recognition is reflected in the recommendation which has been implemented: "that the senior library executive have the title of Vice President and University Librarian." By having the library's chief executive officer at the seat of power in the university, the library's needs, offerings, and responsibilities can be more effectively articulated.[7] The published report of the Columbia study may be used to some degree by other librarians, for the work is valuable both for its results and as a reference tool.

Cornell University, with financial assistance from the Council on Library Resources, has developed a planning program for its library system. Cornell utilized the American Management Association's Center for Planning in the development of what is called a management-by-objectives system that is designed for the Cornell University library system. William E. McGrath raises the question: should all libraries go through the planning process? He responds in the affirmative for the large libraries.

> Large libraries: yes, because the greater com-
> plexity of intercommunication problems can obscure
> principle objectives, and prevent systematic per-
> formance evaluation, and because they may enjoy,
> through their sheer size, a certain degree of au-
> tonomy in the university organization. Small li-
> braries: probably not independently of the univer-
> sity administration. [8]

As we move further into the seventies and closer to
the beginning of the next century, it is my belief that all
academic libraries will have to engage in planning. It is
probably likely that only the large university libraries will
be able to appoint a planning officer for this effort; nevertheless, it is crucial to the survival of academic libraries
that planning of some kind take place. Some librarians may
say that for the smaller libraries this could only take place
during a self-study period for accreditation purposes; however, if the academic library is to obtain its share of its
parent institution's funds to support library services adequately, it must have concrete facts and not assumptions to
justify its growth and development. William E. McGrath
may be correct that smaller academic libraries may not be
able to plan independently, but if the institution has a planning officer who is engaged in institutional planning, it be-
hooves the library to join in the institutional effort.

The Interaction between Students, Faculties, Librarians, and Libraries

Will the library-learning environment be different in
the year 2000? The majority of academic librarians indicate that by and large the academic library as we know it
in 1974 will probably be the prototype in the year 2000.
Those librarians who hold this view concede that the library
as an agency on campus will not be a passive agency, for
its librarians will be interacting with students and faculty to
ensure the availability of resources and services. There is
a small group of librarians and educators who say that the
academic library will be only one of the multiplicity of information agencies that students and faculty members will
use as sources in the information transfer process. Of
course, they cite community organizations, commercial information services that will compete with the library, information retrieval systems, museums, and the information industry in general. While 1 envision change, i.e., users of

academic libraries will utilize information networks and computerized reference retrieval systems, it is my belief that the academic library will be a dynamic, viable component of higher education in the year 2000. In other words, of the alternative expectations Dean Robert S. Taylor suggests in his essay, I contemplate "the academic library will become a true switching center ... in which the dynamic process of negotiating and connecting users to people, materials, and media is the heart of the enterprise." I have reached this conclusion because of the activities that are now taking place in academic libraries.

Since 1969, the Council on Library Resources in cooperation with the National Endowment for the Humanities has provided grants to enable institutions of higher education "to bring the college library into a central position in the educational process." Grants have been given to North Carolina Central University, Howard University, Swarthmore College, Davidson College, Hampden-Sydney College, Jamestown College, Miles College, the University of Colorado, and the University of Richmond. While the major focus is to make the library central in the teaching/learning process, the truth of the matter is that the ultimate goal will provide for a more dynamic library in the information transfer process, thereby bringing about a better interaction between students, faculty, librarians, and the library. The major aspect of this program will lead to the integration of the library program with the instructional program and encourage the utilization of libraries in lifelong learning activities, especially necessary in a world of rapid change.

There are other institutions of higher education that are not the recipients of CLR grants but that are engaged in programs to make the library the core of the educational program. A few of these institutions are experimenting with the library-college idea that has been mentioned earlier; however, most of these institutions have been spurred to action by librarians who are demanding faculty status and a more positive role in the teaching/learning process. In short, the improved status and role of the academic librarian in academia has contributed immensely. This improved status could not have occurred without a change in the attitude of librarians. An illustration of how academic librarians perceive their role is mirrored in a study of the opinions of the head reference librarians or heads of readers services of the 215 academic libraries in New York State. I found that 97 percent of the respondents believed that aca-

demic librarians must be recognized as equal partners in the
academic enterprise, and one of the respondents indicated
that "it is obvious that most graduate students and faculty do
not know how to use libraries effectively. If we were equal
to the teaching faculty, they might be more willing to consult us."[9] It is obvious that these librarians are anxious to
be active agents in the information transfer process in academic libraries.

As an active agent in the information transfer process, the academic librarian in the year 2000 will operate
as though the library is, as Jean L. Connor, director of the
Division of Library Development, New York State Library,
hopes for libraries in the future, part of an "open library
system." Of course, media such as books, journals, audio
tapes, video tapes, films, microfilm, slides, pamphlets,
and computer terminals will be part of the basic resources
of all academic libraries. Some academic libraries will
have access to a multiplicity of data bases through on-line
interactive information retrieval service. Reference departments will provide access to such files as the National Technical Information Service (NTS), Engineering Index, the files
of the Educational Resources Information Center (ERIC),
Psychological Abstracts, Chemical Abstracts, Abstracted
Business Information (ABI), The New York Times Information Bank, MEDLINE, and many others. In addition, the
academic librarian will put his or her students in touch with
resource people and organizations in which there are persons
with expertise and competencies. Library users will be encouraged to use other educational agencies, e.g., museums
and information networks, for information. The library will
no longer be only a place for the acquiring, processing, and
housing of materials, but will also provide for all of its
users physical, intellectual, and bibliographical access to information regardless of whether or not the information is
within the confines of the four walls of the user's academic
library on campus.

The Academic Library and Networks

As we review the growth of library networks and the
role of the academic library in networks, it becomes apparent that although a national library network system does not
exist in 1974, one will have been developed by the year 2000.
The National Commission on Libraries and Information Science, in its preface to the first draft of A New National Pro-

gram of Library and Information Service, supports this view:
"The Commission also believes the time has come to develop a national network of libraries and information centers as a total system rather than as a collection of separate parts." While a total national system is essential, regional systems within states, state systems, and regional systems within the country will play a pivotal role in the national system, and yet these systems do not have to be "a collection of separate parts" but may be an integrated national network.

Library networks, e. g., the 3R's, and other academic library consortia, e. g., Consortium of Universities, Washington, D. C., have been developing throughout the country. Their growth and development is a realization that the academic library cannot survive in isolation as a self-reliant, acquisitive, and independent library. Because of the economics of the times, because of inflation, academic libraries are barely keeping abreast of the available needed information and resources that are being published and produced. William J. Baumol and Matityahu Marcus indicate that from 1950 to 1970 library expenditures per student have risen at a compounded rate of 6. 1 percent per annum.[10] Compare this inflationary spiral to 1. 5 percent for the American economy as a whole during the two decades. At the same time the average annual inflation rate for library materials was 5 percent. Thus, cooperative library networks may be the only solution.

Not only do we find small and medium size academic libraries working closely together in cooperative endeavors, but also the great academic research libraries as well. Identifying cooperation and networking as a means to ensure that resources are available to the scholars at Harvard University, Douglas W. Bryant and Louis E. Martin, in the Harvard University Library Annual Report for the Year 1972-1973, write: "for it seems evident that, unless we succeed in developing much closer ties with other major research libraries, there will be an alarming widening of the gap between needs of the Harvard community and library resources that can be provided. "

The New York Public Library, Columbia University, Harvard University, and Yale University have been studying methods of working closer together in a network. A recent report of this exploration states:

The New York Public Library has joined with the
Columbia, Yale and Harvard libraries in a sweep-
ing and controversial program of combined operations that will entail cutting back purchases of
many publications and systematically exchanging
photocopies of previously published writings.

Details of the project were disclosed by the public
library's president, Richard W. Couper, at a recent luncheon with editors and reporters of The
New York Times. He said the four libraries,
which together house more than 25 million volumes,
would strive for speed in making material from
their collections available to one another's readers.

Accordingly, the libraries are expected to use
everything from Greyhound buses to the latest
electronic equipment to relay original printed material and facsimiles back and forth.

This unified shuttle service is to be orchestrated
by the use of Teletype machines, open telephone
lines and centralized catalogues compiled by computers. It will enable the libraries to save money
by buying only one copy among them, and not four
copies, of expensive sets of volumes, for instance,
or little-used journals.

The venture is 'one of the most important cooperative undertakings in the research library field in
decades, ' a spokesman for the four-library consortium declared here recently, adding that it was
to be expanded 'as soon as practicable' to include
other research libraries--that is, libraries meant
mostly for advanced students and scholars, that do
not regularly lend out their books. Only the non-
circulating divisions of the New York Public Library are involved.

The necessity of joint action was agreed upon by
the libraries' directors last year, and the consortium was formed. The program was elaborated
in a 150-page master plan that is now being studied
by their staffs. It is to be given substance in the
near future, a public library executive said, when
the four libraries set up a corporation, to be

called the Research Libraries Group, to oversee their joint operations. [11]

It should be noted that the Center for Research Libraries is playing a vital role, which in itself may have the embryonic makings of a national network. One of its more recent projects is the "Expanded Journals Project." CRL is purchasing only those journal titles discontinued by member libraries. This program is funded by the Carnegie Corporation, and if the experiment is successful, the research library community is hoping that this will be the beginning of a national lending library of journal resources similar to The National Lending Library for Science and Technology in England.

Each academic library must provide basic resources for instruction and research; however, no single academic library in the year 2000 will be capable of providing from its own resources all of the resources that its users will demand. Hence, I predict that all academic libraries will be members of at least one library network that will provide them with access to a national network. While the Regents of the State of New York were addressing themselves to the problems of library service for one state, it is my belief that their declaration is worth repeating here, for, if one would substitute the words academic libraries for the words New York State and substitute the word Nation for State, in the context of new dimensions for academic library service, the following is quite appropriate:

> we believe the central principle for a library pro-
> gram for [academic libraries] should be the further
> development of an integrated network of libraries,
> with smaller libraries drawing on larger ones,
> and libraries with specialized functions made ac-
> cessible through organized patterns of referral.
> Only through such coordinated services can the
> people of the [Nation] have the benefits which ac-
> crue from adequate, convenient access to sources
> of information, education, and cultural enrich-
> ment. [12]

Only through the development of an integrated network of libraries on a national basis will academic libraries in the country be prepared to meet the goals and purposes of higher education in the year 2000.

The Higher Education Milieu in the Year 2000

　　How should one describe the higher education milieu
of the year 2000? What will be the goals and purposes of
higher education? Will libraries interact in a manner that
will help in the fulfilling of these purposes and goals? The
Carnegie Commission on Higher Education has suggested
five purposes of higher education for the prospective future.
These are:

> 1.　The education of the individual student and the
>   provision of a constructive environment for de-
>   velopmental growth
>
> 2.　Advancing human capability in society at large
>
> 3.　Educational justice for the postsecondary age
>   group
>
> 4.　Pure learning--supporting intellectual and art-
>   istic creativity
>
> 5.　Evaluation in society for self-renewal--through
>   individual thought and persuasion[13]

　　The Carnegie Commission's five purposes of higher
education for the prospective future have serious implications
for library service. It becomes increasingly important that
the library must be a teaching library where students will
receive individual attention by competent librarians, who not
only will have a professional library education background
but subject masters' degrees as well. The academic librarian will be using new approaches in educating users in the
use of libraries, information centers, and library-media
centers so that graduates of institutions of higher education
in the 21st century will be able to determine what source to
use and not be fearful of an information "overload" because
of the sheer volume of information being generated by the
information industry; and thereby, human capability will be
advanced. The library in academe is the one unit on campus
that can invaluably aid its parent institution in implementing
and/or achieving its purposes, primarily because its program is designed to meet the total needs of higher education; its full range of programs constitutes a richly diverse,
heretofore underutilized, resource for postsecondary education.

All of American youth will not be engaged in formal
study. Some of these students will be engaged in independent
study and will be making use of academic libraries at institutions where they have no affiliation. The Advisory Committee on Planning for the Academic Libraries of New York
State indicated that "independent study and external degree
programs bring with them a new phenomenon of great importance to libraries--namely the 'free-standing student' with
at most a tenuous campus relationship."[14] The Carnegie
Commission recognized the educational assistance that public
libraries and museums can offer:

> In our report The Fourth Revolution: Instructional
> Technology in Higher Education, we pointed out
> that the public libraries and museums of the coun-
> try are resources for information, illustrations,
> and other materials that can enrich instruction of-
> fered by institutions of higher education. They are
> particularly valuable as resources for materials
> that can be used with instructional technology--
> audio- and videocassettes, film, slides, and live
> television.
>
> These institutions deserve recognition in their own
> right, however, as agents of instruction. It is
> likely that they constitute the most heavily utilized
> independent learning facilities in the country. In
> some areas--Colorado, New York City, and Cleve-
> land, Ohio, in particular have come to our atten-
> tion--libraries are beginning to assume a more
> formal role in the education offered to adults.
> Some of the programs they provide offer guidance
> and reading programs specifically directed toward
> helping learners master knowledge required to earn
> college credit by examination.[15]

Whether or not the citizen is pursuing his or her education
on campus or is engaged in nontraditional study programs, I
feel that the academic library, the public library, museums,
and other information centers will be in a position to make
delivery of information to the user in person or through interactive terminals in the year 2000.

Conclusions

Several possible alternative academic library delivery

systems may be in existence in the year 2000. There could
be operating the single academic library that is self-sufficient with its entrenched autonomy and which does not co-
operate with its neighbors. There could be the passive academic library in which its librarians serve as handmaidens
to the faculty and no active programs are developed in which
there is interaction between librarians, students, teachers,
and resources. On the other hand, there could be academic
libraries tied to a national information computer system with
a multiplicity of terminals for users and librarians to utilize
in order to manipulate the mass of information products and
services that will be generated.

The academic library in the year 2000 may be difficult to describe with certainty, but the current trends mentioned earlier in this essay and the planning that is now
being fostered seem to predict the following. Academic library buildings will be just as they are today. The use of
technology in the form of a variety of computerized services
through local, state, regional, and national networks will
be occurrent. Even with the computerized services, most
of the small and medium size academic libraries will only
have one or two terminals in their libraries. In spite of
the striking advances in the uses of the computer, the push-
button era will neither alter the contents of libraries nor
change the teaching/learning mode. Books and media in a
variety of formats--print and nonprint--will be housed in libraries. Advances in information retrieval will be evident.
The large university research libraries will regularly make
use of computer output on microfilm. This will be available
also to small libraries through their local library network.
Librarians will play a greater role in the educational process. However, the library-college environment will not be
the dominant mode. The introduction of new educational
methods will leave the student on his or her own, and he or
she will depend upon librarians more in the learning/teach-
ing process. There will be library instruction librarians
who will facilitate user access to libraries with a variety of
programs to educate users in the use of libraries. Libraries will provide SDI services on a regular basis for
their users. All academic libraries will be a member of
at least one library network. Interlibrary loan will be
greatly improved, for a national lending library will facilitate the process, not only because of its economy and efficiency as a national resource, but also because facsimile
transmission and other forms of rapid communication will
be greatly improved. Finally, college and university insti-

tutional structures will be reorganized by their participation in consortia; therefore, some academic libraries will belong to academic library networks as well as general and specialized library networks that will include special, public, and research libraries. In short, there will be cooperation and continuity to avoid duplication of effort. A few institutions will go their own way, then as now; however, if they live in isolation, in the 21st century they will be at the end of the academic procession. Finally, the academic library in the year 2000 will have a visible presence on campus.

References

1. Hostrop, Richard W. Education Inside the Library-Media Center. Hamden, Conn., The Shoestring Press, Inc., 1973, pp. 139-40.

2. Iklé, Fred Charles. "Can Social Predictions Be Evaluated?," Daedalus: Journal of the American Academy of Arts and Sciences, 96:751, Summer 1967.

3. Wiener, Anthony J. "The Future of Economic Activity," The Annals of the American Academy of Political and Social Science, 408:48, July 1973.

4. See Bell, Daniel. "The Year 2000--The Trajectory of an Idea," Daedalus: Journal of the American Academy of Arts and Sciences, 96:639-51; and Bell, Daniel. "A Summary by the Chairman, Some Common--or Loosely Agreed Upon Assumptions," op. cit., pp. 698-704 for an overall point of view regarding the work of the American Academy's Commission on the Year 2000. There are excellent basic assumptions that one should ponder before he or she looks into his or her crystal ball of the future.

5. "Joint SUNY/SED Task Force on Library Data Centers Progress Report, March 15, 1974," The Bookmark, 33:98, March-April 1974.

6. Ibid., p. 101.

7. Booz, Allen & Hamilton, Inc. Organization and Staffing of the Libraries of Columbia University, A Case Study. Westport, Conn., Redgrave Information Resources Corp., 1973, p. 45.

8. McGrath, William E. Development of a Long-Range Strategic Plan for a University Library, The Cornell Experience: Chronicle and Evaluation of the First Year's Effort. Ithaca, N.Y., Cornell University Libraries, 1973, pp. 59-60.

9. Josey, E. J. "Full Faculty Status This Century," Li-

brary Journal, 97:985, March 15, 1972.

10. Baumol, William J., and Marcus, Matityahu. Economics of Academic Libraries. Washington, D.C., American Council on Education, 1973, p. 73.

11. Pace, Eric. "Four Major Libraries Combine Research Operations," The New York Times, March 24, 1974, p. 59, col. 1.

12. Library Service: A Statement of Policy and Proposed Action by the Regents of the University of the State of New York: A Position Paper, No. 8 of a Series. Albany, N.Y., The State Education Department, 1970, p. 7.

13. See chapters 3-7 of the Carnegie Commission on Higher Education. The Purposes and the Performance of Higher Education in the United States: Approaching the Year 2000. New York, McGraw-Hill Book Company, 1973.

14. Report of the Advisory Committee on Planning for the Academic Libraries of New York State. Albany, N.Y., The University of the State of New York, The State Education Department, 1973, p. 4.

15. The Carnegie Commission on Higher Education. Toward a Learning Society: Alternative Channels to Life, Work, and Service. New York, McGraw-Hill Book Company, 1973, pp. 97-8.

NOTES ON THE CONTRIBUTORS

MOHAMMED M. AMAN is Chairman, Department of Library and Information Science, St. John's University. Dr. Aman formerly served on the faculty at Pratt Institute, Graduate School of Library and Information Science, and on the library staffs of Allegany Community College and Duquesne University; was a research assistant at Knowledge Availability System Center, University of Pittsburgh; and worked in several libraries in Cairo, Egypt. He is the author of a number of scholarly articles and two monographs: Analysis of Terminology. Form and Structure of Subject Headings in Arabic Literature and Formulation of Rules for Arabic Subject Headings, University of Pittsburgh, 1968; and Cataloging Notes with Exemplars, New York, 1971.

CHARLES D. CHURCHWELL is Associate Provost for Academic Services, Miami University, Ohio. He was formerly Director of Libraries, Miami University (1969-72), served as Assistant Director of Libraries, University of Houston (1967-69) and Assistant Librarian, University of Illinois (1964-67), and held other positions at The New York Public Library and Prairie View A & M College. Dr. Churchwell served as an American Council on Education Academic Administration Fellow from 1971-72. His book, A History of Education for Librarianship, 1919-1939, will soon be published by the American Library Association.

NINA T. COHEN is Assistant Director of Libraries for Public Services, University of Washington, Seattle. From 1967-73, Mrs. Cohen served as Executive Director of the Western New York Library Resources Council. She has had a variety of professional experiences, including: member of the adjunct faculty, School of Information and Library Studies, SUNY at Buffalo, and library positions at SUNY College at Buffalo, SUNY at Buffalo Libraries, and Grosvenor Library. She served as Consultant for the University of Cincinnati Faculty Task Force on Libraries and the New York State Joint Legislative Committee on Intergovernmental Fiscal Affairs. She is the author of several journal articles and edited Western New York Union List of Serials, 1970.

HILLIS DWIGHT DAVIS has been the Director of the Cooperative College Library Center, Inc., Atlanta, since 1969. From 1965-69 he served as Director of the Library, Hampton Institute, and from 1958-65 he was Assistant Librarian, West Virginia State College. Mr. Davis is Vice Chairman and Chairman-Elect of the College and University Section of the Southeastern Library Association.

JAMES DAVIS is College Librarian, University of California, Los Angeles. From 1961-70 he was Head, Reference Section, College Library, UCLA. From 1969-70 he was on a leave of absence to assist in the planning and preparation for the opening of the Moffitt Undergraduate Library, University of California, Berkeley. Since 1971 he has served on the UCLA School of Library Service staff.

H. VAIL DEALE is Director of Libraries and Chairman of the Department of Library Service, Beloit College. Active in national, regional, and local professional organizations, he is past President of the Wisconsin Library Association. He has been awarded two Fulbright grants to Iran: in 1965-66, he was Acting Director of Libraries, Pahlavi University, Shiraz, Iran, and in 1970-71 he was a member of the faculty of the Library School, University of Tehran, Tehran, Iran. In 1973 Governor Patrick Lucey appointed him to the Wisconsin Council on Library Development. The author of many articles on academic librarianship, Mr. Deale served as editor of the July 1969 issue of Library Trends devoted to "Trends in College Librarianship."

R. DEAN GALLOWAY has been Director of the Library at California State College, Stanislaus, since its beginning in 1960. He has an M.S. in L.S. from the University of Southern California and is currently enrolled in the D.L.S. program at the University of California, Berkeley, on a part-time basis.

LOUISE GILES is Dean of Learning Resources, Macomb County Community College (Michigan). Mrs. Giles formerly served on the staffs of the Detroit Public Library and Oakland Community College. She has served as Chairperson of the Junior College Library Section, Association of College and Research Libraries; President of Michigan Association of Community College Instructional Administrators; member of the Michigan Academy of Sciences, Arts and Letters; and member of the faculty, Graduate School of Library Science, University of Michigan, summer session, 1973. She is the author of numerous articles in professional publications, and her monographs include Aspects of the Junior College Field, a Bibliography, AACJC, 1969, and A Research Project to Determine the Student Acceptability and Learning Effectiveness of Microform Collections in Community Colleges: Phase I, U. S. O. E., 1970.

ROBERT P. HARO since 1971 has been Assistant University Librarian for Reader Services, University of Southern California. He has held positions at California State College, Hayward; SUNY at Buffalo; University of California at Davis; and was Librarian and Lecturer at the School of Library and Information Services, University of Maryland. Mr. Haro served as Consultant to the U. S. Cabinet Committee on Opportunity for the Spanish Speaking. He was Principal Investigator, U. S. Office of Education Grant to study the feasibility for the development of an Optimal Model Concept for the Design of Library and Information Services for Spanish Speaking Americans in the Southwest, 1970-71. Active in national and regional professional associations, he is the author of several research studies.

VIVIAN D. HEWITT is Librarian, Carnegie Endowment for International Peace. Her former positions include work at the Carnegie Library (Pittsburgh); Instructor, School of Library Service, Atlanta University; and Librarian, Rockefeller Foundation. She served as Library Consultant abroad. The recipient of many awards, Mrs. Hewitt was the President of the New York Chapter of the Special Library Association in 1971. Active in international affairs, she represented the Special Library Association at IFLA. She is also the author of numerous articles in professional journals and several books.

ZOIA HORN has served in public, school, and academic libraries in New Jersey and in more recent years as a reference librarian at U. C. L.A. and Head of Public Services at Bucknell University. She has a library degree from Pratt Institute and is a member of A. L. A. Council and the Action Council of the Social Responsibilities Round Table of A. L. A.

MILES M. JACKSON is Associate Professor, School of Library and Information Sciences, SUNY College at Geneseo. Former positions include Branch Librarian, Free Library of

Philadelphia; Librarian, Hampton Institute; Director of Library Services, Government of American Samoa; Chief Librarian and Professor, Atlanta University; and Visiting Professor and Consultant, University of Tehran. Awards include Fulbright Senior Lecturer, 1968-69, and Council on Library Resources Fellow, 1970. Author of many articles and studies, his books include Bibliography of Negro History and Culture for Young Readers, University of Pittsburgh, 1969, and Comparative and International Librarianship: Essays on Themes and Problems, Greenwood Press, 1970. He is completing his Ph. D. dissertation at Newhouse School of Public Communications, Syracuse University.

CASPER LEROY JORDAN is Associate Professor, School of Library Service, Atlanta University. Former positions include Assistant Director, Nioga Library System; Supervisor of Technical Processes, Nioga Library System; and Chief Librarian, Wilberforce University. He is also Director, Library Planning and Development for Atlanta University Center, 1971 to present. Professor Jordan has held many consultantships. He is a member of national, regional, and local professional organizations, and he is the author of many research studies. His monographs include: coeditor, An Institutional Self-study of Wilberforce University, 1959; coeditor, College Preparatory Reading List, 2d ed., New York Library Association, 1968; and A Call to Excellence, a Study of the E. St. Louis (Illinois) Public Library, Illinois State Library, 1970.

E. J. JOSEY is Chief, Bureau of Academic and Research Libraries, Division of Library Development, New York State Education Department; he has been with the New York State Education Department since 1966. Dr. Josey was Librarian and Associate Professor, Savannah State College, 1959-66; Librarian and Assistant Professor, Delaware State College, 1955-59; and Instructor of Social Science, Savannah State College, 1954-55. He has also served on the staff of the Free Library of Philadelphia, 1953-54, and in various positions on the staffs of Columbia University, The New York Public Library, and the New York State Library. Active in national, regional, and local professional organizations, he is the founder of the ALA Black Caucus and is currently Chairman-Elect of the Association of Cooperative Library Organizations (ACLO). He is the recipient of many awards, including the Journal of Library History Award, and has held many consultantships. He is the author of many articles and research studies, and he has edited several directories and monographs including two books: The Black Li-

brarian in America, Scarecrow Press, 1970, and What Black
Librarians Are Saying, Scarecrow Press, 1972.

IVAN L. KALDOR is Dean, School of Library and Information Science, SUNY College at Geneseo. From 1965-68, Dr.
Kaldor was Associate Professor of Library Science, School
of Library Science, Kent State University; from 1950-52, he
was Dean and Professor, State Academy for Army Interpreters, Budapest. Not only is Dr. Kaldor a librarian, he also
holds a Diploma in Law from Pázmány Péter University,
Budapest. He has held numerous positions in special libraries as a technical information officer in Hungary, England, and the United States. He is the author of numerous
research studies. His books include Slavic Paleography and
Early Russian Printing, University of Chicago, 1967, and
Guide to Research Reports in the Fields of Aeronautics, As-
tronautics and Engineering Sciences, Purdue University,
1965; translator of several publications from Russian into
English; and coauthor of Union List of Periodicals on Mathematics and Allied Subjects in London Libraries, University
of London, 1958.

FREDERICK G. KILGOUR is the Director of the Ohio College Library Center. He has had a wide, varied, and productive professional career. From 1935 to 1942 he held
various positions at the Harvard College Library. From
1942 to 1945 he was with the Office of Strategic Services;
1946-48, Deputy Director, Office of Intelligence Collection
and Dissemination, Department of State; 1948-65, Librarian,
Yale Medical Library; and 1965-67, Associate Librarian for
Research and Development, Yale University Library. A
noted editor, he was managing editor of Yale Journal of Bi-
ology and Medicine and editor of Journal of Library Automation. He is active in several national professional organizations, in which he has held many positions of leadership,
and his writing and research are too voluminous to cite.

R. PATRICK MALLORY is an Assistant in Academic and
Research Libraries, Bureau of Academic and Research Libraries, Division of Library Development, New York State
Education Department. From 1967-70, Mr. Mallory was
Acquisitions Librarian, University of Montana. From 1962-
66, he was Assistant Science Librarian and Life Sciences
Librarian, University of Notre Dame. A thespian, he has
been active in the theater and pursued graduate study in
drama at the University of Montana. He is the author of
journal articles and a consultant for many academic library

buildings.

JOAN K. MARSHALL is Chief, Catalog Division, Brooklyn
College Library, The City University of New York.   Ms.
Marshall has been a member of the Brooklyn College Library faculty since 1966.   She is nationally known for her
efforts and views on the need for change in library organization, especially cataloging.   She is the author of journal
articles and is active in national, regional, and local professional organizations.

RONALD F. MILLER has been the Director of the New England Library Information Network (NELINET).   He is the
Principal Investigator for the Northeast Science Information
Center, a project of the New England Board of Higher Education.   Prior to his current position, Mr. Miller was Co-
ordinator of Library Systems for the Five Associated University Libraries, Syracuse, New York.   Active in national
and regional associations, he has served as President of
two ASIS chapters (Upstate New York and New England) and
was former Chairman, Association for Cooperative Library
Organizations; currently, he is Chairman, Council for Computerized Library Networks.   He has taught library automation courses at the School of Library Science, Syracuse University, and is the author of several articles on library cooperation and networks.

RICHARD C. QUICK is Director of Libraries, SUNY College
at Geneseo.   Previous positions include Director of Library
Services, Northern Arizona University, and Assistant to the
Director, University of Delaware Library.   Active in professional organizations, he is presently Chairman of the
ACRL College Libraries Section, a past President of the
Delaware Library Association, and past President of the College and University Library Section, Arizona Library Association.   Mr. Quick has contributed to professional journals,
and has written also in the areas of history and archeology.

ANN KNIGHT RANDALL is Assistant Professor, Education/
Instructional Media/African-American Studies, Brooklyn
College Library, The City University of New York.   Dr.
Randall has held various professional positions on the li-
brary staffs of the Brooklyn Public Library and in the U.S.
Army in Bamberg, Germany, and was Reference Librarian,
Queens College, The City University of New York.   She has
served as a part-time faculty member at the library schools
of Columbia, Pratt, Queens College, and Rutgers.   In addi-

tion, she indexes for ERIC Documents and is a volunteer
abstractor for the Schomburg Center for Research in Black
Culture, The New York Public Library. She is active in
several national and local professional organizations and is
author of several articles and essays.

HARRY ROBINSON, JR., is Dean of Learning Resources
Services and Associate Professor of Instructional Technology
and Library Science, Alabama State University. Dr. Robinson has held positions as Director of Learning Resources,
Prairie View A. & M. College, and on the staffs of the
University of Illinois Library, Southern University Library,
and Kentucky State University. He has been Director of
the Institute for Training Librarians for Special Black Collections and Archives, 1973, and Consultant at Howard University for the installation of the Dial Access Program,
1973. He is active in national, regional, and local professional organizations and is Chairman-Elect of the ALA
Black Caucus. He is the author of several articles and
reviews in professional journals.

DOROTHY BYRON SIMON is Assistant Professor and Library
Instruction Librarian, New York City Community College,
The City University of New York. From 1945-51, Mrs.
Simon served on the staff of The New York Public Library;
from 1952-70, she was Teacher of Library, Boys High
School, Brooklyn, New York. She has served as consultant
to Queens College EPDA Fellowship Program; Rutgers Uni-
versity Library; New York Metropolitan Reference and Re-
search Library Agency, Inc., Public Services Committee;
Columbia University School of Library Service Institute on
Library Leadership; and the Newark State College Library.
She is active in several national and local professional organizations.

ELDRED R. SMITH is Director of Libraries at SUNY at
Buffalo. From 1960-72, he was at the University of California, Berkeley, where he had several positions including
Associate University Librarian, 1970-72, and Acting University Librarian, 1971-72. His other professional experience
was at Long Beach State College Library and San Francisco
State College Library. Mr. Smith has served as lecturer
at the library schools of the University of California, Berkeley, and the University of Washington. He is currently Adjunct Professor, School of Library and Information Studies,
SUNY at Buffalo. Involved in national, regional, and state
professional associations, he has served as President of the

University and Research Libraries Division of the California
Library Association and President of the Librarians' Association of the University of California.   He is the author of
several articles in professional journals.

ROBERT S. TAYLOR is Dean and Professor, School of Information Studies, Syracuse University.   His career has been
wide and varied with experience in publishing and journalism.
From 1950 to 1967, he held several positions at Lehigh University Library; from 1962-67, he was Director of the Center for Information Sciences at Lehigh University; and from
1963-67, Associate Professor and Head, Division of the Information Sciences, Department of Philosophy, Lehigh University.   He is nationally known for his establishment of an
academic library with a new concept in academic librarianship at Hampshire College where he was Director of the Library Center from 1967-72 and Professor of Information Sciences from 1969-72.   Active in many national professional
associations, Dean Taylor has served as principal investigator and director of many research projects.   Among his
numerous publications is his book The Making of a Library:
The Academic Library in Transition, Wiley, 1972.

EVERT VOLKERSZ is Personnel Librarian at SUNY at Stony
Brook Libraries.   Mr. Volkersz began as Special Collections
Librarian in 1969 before he assumed his present position at
SUNY at Stony Brook.   From 1963-69, he held several posi-
tions at the University of California Libraries, Los Angeles.
He has been very active in numerous national, state, and
local professional organizations and has held several elected
and appointed positions, including: President, UCLA Library
Staff Association; Chairman, Committee on Academic Status,
College University and Research Library Division, California
Library Association; and Chairman, Personnel Policies Committee, SUNY Librarians Association.   He is author of several articles in professional journals.

DAVID M. WAX, since 1971, has been Assistant Director of
the Board and Director of External Programs and Development, New England Board of Higher Education.   Dr. Wax
is Director of the Northeast Academic Science Information
Center.   He also served as Special Assistant to the Administrator, Housing and Development Administration, City of
New York from 1968-69.   His work in academia includes an
Instructorship in the Harvard-Yale-Columbia Intensive Summer Studies Program; Tutor in Government and Resident
Tutor, Lowell House, Harvard University; and Instructor in

Political Science, Stillman College, Tuscaloosa, Alabama.

JEROME YAVARKOVSKY is Assistant University Librarian for Planning, Columbia University. From 1969 to 1972 he held various positions at Columbia including Head, Programming Section; Senior Systems Analyst; Chief, The Systems Office; and Assistant to the Director of Libraries. Mr. Yavarkovsky, in addition to being a librarian, is also a trained engineer and a management specialist. Before his venture into librarianship, he held professional positions at Auerbach Corporation as a member of the technical staff; Systems Analyst, J. C. Penney Company; Administrative Specialist, Bell Telephone Laboratories; and worked in the Personnel Department of J. Walter Thompson Company. He has engaged in considerable technical research during his professional career.

INDEX*

---

*Compiled by the noted cataloging specialist, Sanford Berman.

multi-media catalogs; integrated, multi-media collections; learning centers
audio-visual materials processing See processing of audio-visual materials
Audio-visual school library service, 157
audio-visual technicians See media technicians
author entries See descriptive cataloging
authoritarian administration, 77
automation, 36, 43-4, 51, 60, 81, 86-98, 202-3, 232, 248, 281, 298, 309-14
auto-tutorial carrels See study carrels
availability of library materials See accessibility of library materials

bachelor's degree, three-year, x
backlogs, 213
Balliot, Robert L., 104, 106, 110-13
BALLOTS Project, Stanford University, 89, 310-11
Baumol, William J., 319
Bell, Daniel, 309
Berman, Sanford, 139
Bettelheim, Bruno, 157
bias-free subject cataloging See neutrality in subject cataloging
Bibliographic Automation of Large Library Operations using a Time-sharing System, Stanford University See BALLOTS Project, Stanford University
bibliographic guides to library resources, 176-7
bibliographic specialists See subject specialists
Birenbaum, William, 162
Black Americana collections See Afro-Americana collections
Black college libraries See Afro-American college libraries

Black colleges and universities See Afro-American colleges and universities
Blake, Fay, 122-3, 165, 194
blind students, 129
Blume, Edward J., 140
Bodley, Thomas, 64
Boes, Warren N., 312-13
book catalogs, 26, 87-8, 274
book selection See collection development
bookstores, campus See campus bookstores
Bowman, Ben C., 311
Braden, Irene Andrea, 63
Bray, Thomas, 196
Brooklyn College Library, 135
Bryant, Douglas W., 319
budgets, acquisition See acquisition budgets
bulletin boards, 125
bureaucracy, 78, 124, 166
BUSHMEN (LC subject heading), 138-40
business collections, 296
Byrd, Cecil K., 163

CATV See cable television
CCLC See Cooperative College Library Center, Atlanta, Georgia
CIP See Cataloging-in-Publication
CLEP See College-Level Examination Program
COM See computer output microfilm
CUNY See City University of New York
cable television, 60, 255
campus bookstores, 47, 54
card catalogs, 87-8, 132-5, 217, 274, 301
card catalogs, closing-off See closing-off card catalogs
Carnegie Commission on Higher Education, x-xi, 77, 159, 235, 322-3
carrels See study carrels
Cassata, Mary, 125
catalog copy from external

Encyclopaedia Britannica, 139
enrollments, 21-2, 59-60, 161-2, 239
ethnic nomenclature, 139
Ethnic Studies, 181, 288
Evergreen State College Generic Library, 27
exit checks, 299
"Expanded Journals Project," Center for Research Libraries See Center for Research Libraries "Expanded Journals Project"
experimental colleges, 44
experimental library service See library service, innovative and experimental
"extended library" concept, 43
external degree programs, 24-5, 60, 288-9, 323
externally-supplied catalog copy See catalog copy from external sources

FAUL, 96, 106, 109-114
facsimile transmission, 101, 117, 324
faculty/library integration See library/faculty integration
faculty size, 22
faculty status for academic librarians, 39, 165, 190, 301, 317-18
Farmington Plan, 105-6, 247
federal funding, ix, 22-3, 109, 245, 281
filing, 136-8
fines, 299
Fisk University. Negro Collection See Negro Collection, Fisk University
Five Associated University Libraries See FAUL
"floating" librarians, 129
forecasting, educational See educational forecasting
forecasting, library See library forecasting
Foster, Barbara, 129
Fourth revolution: instructional technology in higher education, 235, 323

Fraser, Walter, 134-5
free press See alternative press
Frissel Library, Tuskegee Institute See Hollis Burke Frissel Library, Tuskegee Institute

G. I. Bill of Rights, ix
Gardner, John W., 30
"Gaver Report," 188
Gaylord, Robert, 46-7
"generic book" concept, 46-7
Generic Library, Evergreen State College See Evergreen State College Generic Library
George Foster Peabody Collection on the Negro, Hampton Institute, 150
goals and purposes of academic libraries, 42-8, 50, 169-74, 210-11, 303-4, 308
goals and purposes of higher education, 30-2, 37-9, 192, 322
Gores, Harold B., 45-6
growth of higher education, 22, 34, 78
"Guidelines for Two-Year College Learning Resources Programs," 52, 56-7

Haak, John R., 73
Haas, Warren J., 269-70, 272
Hampton Institute. George Foster Peabody Collection on the Negro See George Foster Peabody Collection on the Negro, Hampton Institute
handicapped students, 124, 129
Haro, Robert P., 129
Harvard University. Lamont Library See Lamont Library, Harvard University
Heartman Collection on Negro Life and Culture, Texas Southern University, 151
Hendricks, Donald D., 104
Henry, William E., 185

341

hierarchical structures, 77, 82
Hollis Burke Frissel Library,
   Tuskegee Institute, 150
Hostrop, Richard W., 307
hot-lines, 26, 125, 129
Houze, Robert A., 104
Howard University. Moorland-
   Spingarn Collection See
   Moorland-Spingarn Collection,
   Howard University
human information sources,
   318
humanistic attitudes, 81
Hutchins, Robert M., 77

I.D. See instructional design
ISLs See information services
   librarians
ISP, Dallas Public Library
   See Dallas Public Library
   Independent Study Project
Ikle, Fred Charles, 308
Illich, Ivan, 299, 302-3
impersonality in library service, 298
independent study See individualized education
Independent Study Project, Dallas Public Library See
   Dallas Public Library Independent Study Project
individualized education, 46, 157,
   162, 192, 230, 290-6, 301,
   307, 322-3
inflation, 102-3, 319
"information brokerage" concept, 261-3
information hot lines See hot-
   lines
information role of librarians,
   79, 254, 258-9, 261-7, 318
information services librarians,
   260-2, 265
inner city tutoring, 288
innovative and experimental library service See library
   service, innovative and experimental
instructional design, 55
instructional resources centers
   See learning centers
integrated, multi-media cata-

logs, 57-8, 214
integrated, multi-media collections, 57-9, 214, 235
interdisciplinary studies, 38,
   103, 180-1, 193, 221
"interest profiles," 311-12
interior design See design
   and location of libraries and
   learning centers
interlibrary cooperation, 36,
   239-86
interlibrary loans, 68, 102,
   126, 240, 242, 253, 259,
   313, 324
intershelving of print and audio-
   visual materials See integrated, multi-media collections
Interuniversity Communications
   Council, 234-5
Inter-University Library Council Reference and Interlibrary Loan Services See
   RAILS

Jackson, Mildred W., 276
Jenks, George, 123
Jobs in instructional media, 56
Johnson, B. Lamar, 51-2, 57
Johnson, James Weldon, 149
Joint SUNY/SED Task Force
   on Library Data Centers in
   New York State, 313-14
Jones, Norah E., 69
Jordan, Casper LeRoy, 272,
   276
Jordan, Robert, 44
Josey, E. J., 129, 165, 194

Kerouac, Jack, 160
KIKES (hypothetical subject
   heading), 140

LACAP See Latin American
   Cooperative Acquisitions
   Program
LC See Library of Congress
LRCs See learning centers
labor collections, 296
labor sharing, 114

Martin, Lowell A., 189
Maryland Academic Libraries
Automated Data Processing
Center See MALCAP
Massman, Virgil, 206
materials selection See collection development
"media browsing" See integrated, multi-media collections
media cataloging See cataloging of audio-visual materials
media centers See audio-visual education and materials; learning centers
media technicians, 56
Medical Literature Analysis and Retrieval System See MEDLARS
MEDLARS, 235
memory, short-term See short-term messages and memory
mending See processing of library materials
messages, short-term See short-term messages and memory
METRO (N.Y.) See New York Metropolitan Reference and Research Library Agency, Inc.
Mexican-American students, 129
Michigan. University. Undergraduate Library, 64
microform technology, 43, 311
middle-class students, 171
"minimized" catalog, 64
minority-group students, ix, 129, 156, 158, 171, 234, 288
Mitchell, P. M., 194-5, 196
Moorland-Spingarn Collection, Howard University, 149-50
Morris, Leslie, 134
multi-disciplinary studies See interdisciplinary studies
multi-media cataloging See cataloging of audio-visual materials; integrated, multi-media catalogs
multi-media education and ma-

terials See audio-visual education and materials
multi-media shelving See integrated, multi-media collections
multi-media technicians See media technicians

NASIC, 256-7, 260-7
NYSILL See New York State Interlibrary Loan System
National Commission on Libraries and Information Science, 110, 248, 318-19
National Endowment for the Humanities, 317
Negro and higher education in the South, 271
Negro Collection, Atlanta University, 150
Negro Collection, Fisk University, 150
"Negroana" collections See Afro-Americana collections
NELINET, 95-6, 256-60, 263, 265-7, 284-5
networks and consortia, 28-30, 95-7, 213, 239-86, 295, 298, 303, 318-21, 324-5
neutrality in subject cataloging, 139
"new breed" librarians, 44-5, 48
"new breed" students, 193-4
New England Board of Higher Education, 256-7
New England Library Information Network See NELINET
"new learners," 155-67
New York Metropolitan Reference and Research Library Agency, Inc., 106-7, 243
New York State Interlibrary Loan System, 242
New York State union list of serials, 242
newspapers See serials
NEZ PERCE INDIANS (LC subject heading), 138-40
nonbook cataloging See cataloging of audio-visual materials

printed book catalogs See book catalogs

processing of audio-visual materials, 58-9, 218

processing of library materials, 218

processing of library materials, shared See shared processing of library materials

programmed instruction See audio-visual education and materials

Project SPIRES (Stanford University) See SPIRES Project (Stanford University)

public libraries and post-secondary education, 290-4, 302

public services, 134, 198-201, 211, 218-19

qualitative evaluation, 40
quantitative evaluation, 78

racism in higher education, 144-6

racism in subject cataloging, 138-9

radio broadcasting, 53
RAILS, 25
Ramseur, Arneize F., 276
rank and tenure quotas, 81
reader guidance, 178
recataloging, 135, 274, 284
reclassification of library materials, 275-6

Reference and Interlibrary Loan Services (Inter-University Library Council) See RAILS

Reference and Research Library Resources Systems (New York State) See 3R's Systems (New York State)

reference services, 68, 80-1, 93-5, 128-30, 175-82, 311-12, 318

Reform on campus, 159

Regents External Degree Program, x, 294

relevance in higher education, 37-9, 192-3, 288

relevance in library service, 160, 172

reserve services, 66, 299

residence hall libraries, 22, 233

retrospective data conversion, 313-14

Rider, A. Fremont, 102

ROCK MUSIC (LC subject heading), 140

Rothstein, Samuel, 181

Rufsvold, Margaret, 157

Rush, Orwin, 108

SDI See selective dissemination of information

SAN (proposed subject heading), 139

scholar-librarians See librarian-scholars

security checks See exit checks

Selden, David, 82-3

selective dissemination of information, 93-4, 128, 254, 266, 324

self-study See individualized education

serials, 67, 89-91, 116, 147, 171, 217, 242, 253, 313, 321

shared acquisitions See coordinated collection building

shared cataloging, 28-9, 202, 213, 242, 251-5, 313-14

shared processing of library materials, 268-86

SHARES Project (N.Y. Metropolitan Reference and Research Library Agency, Inc.), 106-7, 109-10, 243

Sheehan, Helen, 43

Shores, Louis, 42, 45-6, 48

short-term messages and memory, 303

shuttle delivery services, 320

Sillers, Dan J., 47

Simkin, Faye, 104, 107

size of collections See collection size

SLAVERY IN THE U.S. -

CONDITION OF WOMEN (proposed subject heading), 139
Smith, Eldred R., 163
social consciousness, 128-9
social relevance in higher education See relevance in higher education
South Central Research Library Council (N.Y. State), 114-15
special libraries and postsecondary education, 294-6
specialized research and materials, 38
SPIRES Project (Stanford University), 94-5
staff development, 226-7
staffing, 211-15, 272
standardization, 36, 121, 273-5
Stanford University. BALLOTS Project See BALLOTS Project, Stanford University
State University of New York Biomedical Communications Network See SUNY Biomedical Communications Network
statements of purpose, 210-11
Stevenson, Grace, 189
Stuart-Stubbs, Basil, 311-12
student library committees, 123
student-oriented education, 43, 289, 301
student-oriented library service See user-oriented library service
student publications, 125
study carrels, 42, 46, 54, 59, 214
subject cataloging, 67, 137-40
subject headings, 137-40
subject specialists, 39, 147, 163-5, 196-7, 212
suggestion boxes, 123
SUNY Biomedical Communications Network, 93, 97
SUNY/SED Task Force on Library Data Centers in New York State See Joint SUNY/SED Task Force on

Library Data Centers in New York State
superimposition (cataloging), 135-36
support for higher education, 22-3, 34-5
"supportive" services See technical services
Syracuse University Research Corporation Five-County Project, 294

TWX networks See teletype networks
Task Force on Library Data Centers in New York State See Joint SUNY/SED Task Force on Library Data Centers in New York State
Tauber, Maurice, 272
Taylor, Robert S., 42-3, 124
teaching department/library interface See library/teaching department interface
teaching machines See audiovisual education and materials
teaching role of librarians, 78, 164-7, 170-4, 179, 317
technical service centers, cooperative See shared processing of library materials
technical services, 89, 134, 198-9, 201-3, 211, 213, 217-18, 273
technocratic attitudes, 81
technological change and education, 231
technological change and libraries, 309-14
telephone hot-lines See hotlines
teletype networks, 25-6, 101, 320
television broadcasting, 53, 60
television, cable See cable television
television, closed-circuit See closed-circuit television
television in libraries, 72-3
tenure quotas See rank and

tenure quotas
Texas Southern University.
Heartman Collection on Negro Life and Culture See
Heartman Collection on Negro Life and Culture, Texas
Southern University
3R's Systems (New York State),
239-49
three-year bachelor's degree
See bachelor's degree,
three-year
Time (periodical), 295
Tooms, Kenneth, 69
tracking ("ability" grouping),
158
Trager, Ruth, 125
transportation and education,
232
Tuskegee Institute, Hollis
Burke Frissel Library See
Hollis Burke Frissel Library,
Tuskegee Institute
21st Century academic libraries,
307-9, 316-21, 323-5
21st Century higher education,
322-3
two-year colleges See community colleges

UGLs See undergraduate libraries
U.N.E.S.C.O. (abbreviation
cross-reference), 133
U.S. Library of Congress See
Library of Congress
undergraduate libraries, 22,
62-73
underground press See alternative press
Unesco (acronym), 133
union lists and catalogs, 100,
102, 240, 242, 244-5, 251-5,
257, 310, 313, 320
unionization, 82-3, 191
United Negro College Fund,
145, 148
University-Without-Walls program, x, 294, 301
use instruction in libraries
See library use instruction
user/cataloger interface See

cataloger/user interface
user/library interface See
library/user interface
user needs, 121-30, 159-61,
299
user-oriented library service,
81, 124-30, 157-8, 160-61,
175-82, 210, 299-304

Van Doren, Mark, 78
Veihman, Robert A., 58-9
voucher schemes, 301

Washington. University. Undergraduate Library. Contemporary Issues Center
See Contemporary Issues
Center, University of Washington Undergraduate Library
Wasserman, Paul, 50, 56
Weber, David C., 310-11
Welsh, William, 134
White, Carl M., 184-5
Wiener, Anthony J., 308-9,
313
Wilberforce University (Ohio),
143, 150-1
Wilden-Hart, Marion, 110-11,
113-14
Wilkinson, Billy Rayford, 63,
65, 69
Williamson, Charles C., 186
Wilson, Logan, 44, 47
Wilson, Louis R., 192, 196
women students, 160-61, 296
women's information programs,
160-61
word-processing technology,
215-16
work-flow charts (CCLC), 280,
283
work force patterns and education, 232
WOUNDED KNEE CREEK,
BATTLE OF, 1890 (LC subject heading), 138-39
WOUNDED KNEE CREEK, INCIDENT AT, 1890 (Proposed subject heading), 139